PILOT'S SUMMER

PILOT'S SUMMER

A Central Flying School Diary

by

Frank D. Tredrey

TIGER & TYGER
London

Also by Frank D. Tredrey

Pioneer Pilot, The Great Smith Barry Who Taught the World How to Fly.
London: Peter Davies, 1976
The House of Blackwood 1804-1954: The History of a Publishing Firm.
London: William Blackwood, 1954

Edited by Frank D. Tredrey

Baring, Maurice *Flying Corps Headquarters 1914-1918.* London:
Blackwood & Sons, 1968

PUBLISHED IN THE UK BY
TIGER & TYGER

TIGER & TYGER DISTRIBUTION CENTRE
Unit 9 ~ Ormskirk Industrial Park
Old Boundary Way
Burscough Road
Ormskirk
Lancashire L39 2YW
Tel: 01695 575112
Fax: 01695 570120
www.tlyster.co.uk

First Published by Duckworth, 1939 (reprinted 1941)
This new edition © Louise Elliott and the Frank D. Tredrey estate 2000
ISBN 1 902914 12 0
Technical drawings © David Howley 2000
Photographs by kind permission of:
Flight International/Quadrant Picture Library;
RAF Photographs;
Royal Aeronautical Society;
Peter Hearne.

Contents

Photographs and illustrations

Foreword

by Frank Tredrey, May 1973

PUBLISHER'S NOTE: In 1973 David & Charles Ltd proposed to reprint *Pilot's Summer* and asked for a foreword to the book. Frank Tredrey accordingly prepared the following. The firm later reduced its publishing list and the reprint did not take place.

In 1935 a London publisher announced a prize competition for a book about flying, so I wrote this account of a flying instructor's course and sent it in. The typescript was shortlisted by the selection committee, but the publisher later announced that none of the entries had met his requirements, and no awards were made.

I sent the book to a number of other publishers without success, and threw it on top of a cupboard at Netheravon and forgot about it. In 1938 a friend suggested that that I should send it to the literary agent Audrey Heath. I did so, and she promptly placed it with Mervyn Horder of Duckworth. He published it in June 1939, and then joined the RAF himself, to end the war as wing commander (Intelligence) on Mountbatten's staff in Japan.

I had two fan mail letters about the book, one from a young lady who lived at Hendon and watched all the flying displays, the other from an old lady who said, 'I am seventy-five and my sister is seventy-nine. We are spinsters and share a cottage and do the gardening together. I am deaf and she is blind. Neither of us understood what any of it meant, but we enjoyed every word of it.' To my regret I never replied to the letters, being then busy taking over command of my first squadron.

How youthful those days at Wittering in 1935 now seem! I am surprised at my preoccupation with batmen, seeing I had spent three years at Doctor Trenchard's Academy (Halton) and five years in our outposts of Empire, first as a corporal (fitter aero-engine) and then as a sergeant pilot, so I knew all about polishing my own boots and buttons and blancoing web equipment. But I took to batmen with remarkable ease. Bertie Wooster's gentleman's gentleman Jeeves was our yardstick in judging them. Our attitude to the fair sex was conditioned by C. B. Cochran's musical comedies and the novels of Dornford Yates. I see in the writing of

Pilot's Summer more than a trace of Rupert Brooke and *Poems of To-day*. Clouds blowing to a quiet tune in June, that kind of thing. We still had horses ploughing. A good dinner cost three shillings and a hand-tailored suit six guineas. The debunkers, with pens as sharp as stilettos, had not then got busy on T. E. Lawrence. After *Journey's End* and the Jarrow Marchers we had moved again towards an age of innocence.

As to flying, in the 1930s the Treasury's influence was very strong. We had all flown Avros, DH9As, Vimys and Bristol Fighters left over from the Royal Flying Corps, and were still under the ill-judged 1912 War Office ban on monoplanes. None of us appreciated what Pégoud had achieved with his amazing loops and bunts in 1913. Oliver Stewart considers that Pégoud taught the world to fly. Trenchard said that Smith Barry taught the world how to fly. Both statements are true. I am glad that I mentioned Smith Barry in the book.

Try as we could, in the pre-war Air Force we lacked the engine-power and flexibility which Whittle was to give us. The C.F.S. instructors still had the daily 'mad half hour' which Smith Barry started at Gosport in 1917, and diving between the sheds they strove to get a Fairey Fox 'blue note' out of their Jaguars and Jupiters. Our heroes were Dick Wallace demonstrating inverted spins and Reggie Elsmie, Hilary Dale and Jack Stratton floating around upside down, sweating at formation-aerobatics in the little Avro Tutors. They were the forerunners, and today from its world of concrete and electronics up on the Cotswolds in Gloucestershire the C. F. S. puts up its flashing aerobatic team, the Red Arrows.

Wallace, Elsmie, Dale, Stratton—those are the real names. Old-timers will no doubt see through the aliases in the book and recognize Mayor as R. B. Councell, Cowling as Craigie, Trout as Larry Ling, Doe as E. C. Kidd, Hickory as Jackie Hicks, and Garrick as Tom Kean. Reggie Smart was the Commandant. Since the instructors and pupils of No. 45 Course had their group photograph taken nearly forty years of vapour trails have passed and some have joined 'the great majority'. I know that three of the brightest and best went west during the war—Anode (John Gillan), Joule ('Papa' Watts) and Esterhazy (A. W. M. Finney). 'Tell them of us, and say, for your tomorrow we gave our today.'

Frank D. Tredrey
May 1973

Pilot's Summer

EVER since I was a small boy aeroplanes have been my passion. And it must have been during the days of 1916 and 1917 that I fashioned those models of matchbox, cardboard and sticks that were indirectly to determine the course of my whole life. I pass the details of their construction on to you because you may like to know for your own small boy, and I believe that were I to make a model now I could still find it a fascinating toy, even after flying some two thousand hours on real wings. You get an empty matchbox and two strips of cardboard about six inches long. They form the sides of the fuselage—you tuck one end of each into the sides of the matchbox and gum the other two ends together at the tail. From cardboard you cut wings and tailplane and rudder and pin or gum them on; matchsticks stuck in underneath make V struts for the undercarriage, with the cardboard wheels mounted on an axle of pin. A spent match stuck into the front of the box serves for an airscrew shaft, and on this you mount your twisted cardboard airscrew spinning on a pin. Paint the whole thing silver, colour in the rudder and roundels on fuselage and wings, and there you are. It sounds crude. But *make one*. Watch a single-seater fighter—or if you are an American, a one-place pursuit ship—come to life under your hands. If you are still young at heart its imperfections will not matter very much to you. Make several monoplanes, twin screw biplanes, bombers, general purpose craft, training 'planes and scouts. The value of a toy doesn't matter much to a child; he'll cherish an old tin steam-roller in the face of all the blandishments of a Hornby train. And then let him run against the wind with his 'plane held in one hand close to eyes and ear. The world was well lost to me ten minutes after the completion of my first model. And as I rushed round and round the lawn, leaning as I skirted the flower-beds to make the craft bank in my hands, the unfocused grass and plants became wheeling fields and pastures and woods six thousand feet below my tilting wings; the noisy, steady whirr of the little propeller, the roar of a castor-fed rotary Gnome, its tappets battering out their hundred horse-power in front of my helmeted head. A child can alter his size and perspective at will, and become Jack the Giant Killer at one moment, Hop o' my Thumb the next. And if ever you see one with a crudely rigged sailing ship bobbing among the reeds at the water's edge, his head craned down to the deck level to watch, tread softly else you tread on his dreams. For that coiled watchchain on the sharp pointed little plank is a watchchain no more, but a mighty anchor chain lying on the caulked decks waiting to roar down the hawse pipe at his bellowed "Let go the Kedge!" And peering up through the stretched cottons at the skylight between the roughly tacked linen sails, he is gazing at the tarred rigging and storm-battered, sea-darkened canvas of his fifteen-gun command. And the grass spikes? — the mysterious jungle trees bordering his creek anchorage, of course!

And so at the tender age of twelve I projected myself completely into the cockpit of a real aeroplane, and by so much running to make the airscrew spin, began then to strengthen my bellows to blow up that R.A.F. Central Medical Board mercury in the years to come.

Of learning to fly and serving abroad with the Squadrons, this is no place to tell. But in the fullness of time it was my fortune to return to the green pastures of England again — how green only you who have lived on the desert will know. And the smell of aviation petrol and hangar dope and oil had worked deeper still into my blood, the clink of the parachute harness buckles, as one walked towards the craft with her engine warming up, became keener music still. And yet I had not drawn the full sweets from the airborne hours of my daily life. I doubt whether the full poetry of flying will ever be sung. Can be sung at all now, for that matter; because much of the old spirit is even now on the wane. The sense of adventure is lessening. With enclosed cockpits and motor-car controls, no more the rich odour of engine-burnt castor oil, the muddy, dope-smelling workaday bucket seats before the twisting copper pipes and gun cables and quivering dials. I tried to catch the moment and write poetry, but failed. Perhaps my back hair is too cropped, and my jaw that of one with too taciturn a manner for me to throng on Olympus with the rhyming host.

And so the need for self-expression hammered vainly at the gate. I had schooled myself through the years after the training

2

days to fly as well as I knew. But could I fly well? And did I fly as often as I would have liked? Were fairly heavy day-bombers cruising at a hundred all that could be desired? And on them could I get back to aerobatics again? The answer to all the questions was No.

Master the art still more, fly harder and more often for your daily bread. Live all day in the air and carry flying into your dreams. I respectfully asked the Air Ministry through the usual channels that my name be considered for selection when the next roll of pilots to be trained as instructors was being prepared.

28th of April

King's Cross for Stamford. White clouds moving like slow galleons down the empyrean blue between the chimney pots, and the darling buds of May waiting in the hedges along the Great North Road. They only run one train on Sundays to Stamford, and it leaves at 10.15, a respectable after-breakfast hour one would think. But get there a moment after 9.30 and the only chance you will have of a seat will be either in the guard's van, or wedged in with a pack of toffee-sucking infants; although the train itself seems a good hundred yards longer than the station built to accommodate its kind.

Indeed, the whole affair seems to savour of musical comedy. King's Cross receives and despatches famous trains, it serves famous towns. But it has never grown up or severed its connection with the early Victorian days. The place is surprisingly Lilliputian for a terminus. Here are none of the vast, echoing domes that grace Victoria and Waterloo; no immense plains of macadam, dotted with people and toybox bookstalls, intersected by roads running under a roof of glass. You will find no lordly hotel entrances or news-reel cinemas at King's Cross. From the roadway arch you walk across a few yards of wooden flooring into your train.

It has a homely and familiar look; the associations it evokes are those of childhood and the leisurely days when travel was a leisurely thing. The railway stations of youthful holidays, stations immortalized in a thousand cartoons in *Punch*, stations where advertisements newer than those for Eno's Fruit Salts, Pears' Soap (complete with picture of Bubbles), Bond's Crystal Marking Ink

3

(John Hassall) and the *London Charivari* just cannot be found. Regarding King's Cross, one thinks rather of hansom cabs and the London of the old Haymarket, of the days when progress was a jingling procession and there was time to stop to buy a buttonhole from the flower sellers under Eros. Long, low boat trains do not recall one with a jerk to stern modernity. Even the ticket punchers' low wicket gates are of white old wood worn with the service of fifty years. None of your clanging steel grilles and automatic indicators for King's Cross. Nor does it disdain the honest rattle of milk-churns, a noise that is completely lost under loftier roofs.

But we are proffering our pasteboard to a ticket puncher on Sunday morning at ten o'clock, desirous and anxious to board the 10.15, the only train. They even seem to have imported the station staff from some country town. They are brown and apple-wrinkled. Over the tops of their steel-rimmed spectacles one catches a kindly twinkle in their eyes. Beneath their drooping moustaches lurk tolerant smiles. They lack the sterner stuff, the brisk business manner of their Cockney brethren. Their ways are slower, more leisurely and there is still some trace of the hempen homespun in their speech. At King's Cross we are on the edge of the country already.

The mile-long train — or thereabouts — is quite in keeping. The carriages are low, angular, spidery affairs, made of pale varnished wood with sooty roofs. They belong rightly to the 1870 Holmes-and-Baker-Street period. One suspects that on their crawls at night through the country the compartments are lighted with oil lamps; and one knows before the engine moves that one will be sitting uncomfortably near to the wheels, and that the wheels will clank and rattle cheerfully over the iron way. The doors and windows are curiously high and oblong, fitted with queer antiquated sliding devices to preclude or admit the weather. And the people! Hundreds of them. Packed in the compartments, overflowing into the corridors, spilt with their bags and baskets onto the platform. Nearly all country people, all cheerful, each with at least three children, it seems. The flat middle counties must have been almost emptied of folk this weekend. Four obvious chorus girls going on tour and one gentry lady in a fur coat are almost anachronisms in this throng. Somewhere in that mile of packed humanity some more would-be flying instructors are securely ensconced behind their newspapers, waiting for that whistle to blow. A five-minute tour down the station and back again fails to reveal either their presence or any prospect of a seat. At last, however, one contrives to wedge with a market town family into its crowded compartment, father in his best Sunday suit and watchchain, mamma in her straw hat and tailored costume, her pretty homely face quite innocent of powder and salve. Their luggage is ample and curious, stowed in imitation leather suitcases and string bags, and completed with two straw baskets crammed with the necessaries for travel, oranges and sweets, magazines, and two rag dolls. Mother and father are contentedly lapping up the crime scandal in the *News of the World*, young Gertrude is putting her doll to bed, and Alfred is contentedly sucking one of the strongly-smelling oranges. Thank heaven, at any rate, they show no signs of wanting to talk.

Then the doors slam, whistles shrill and officials shout, and with a mighty roar and wheel skidding from the far engine we get slowly under way. One gathers that Bert is attending to his simple needs, and has been doing so for nigh on a quarter of an hour. Those in waiting are a young matron with an infant daughter and, one would imagine, a gardener, a bookie's clerk, a provincial newspaper journalist, and a cement mixer. Earnestly entreated by a large notice neither to loiter nor smoke in the corridor, they loiter and smoke. Odds are freely being placed on the possibilities of Bert having done away with himself. The cement mixer is in favour of thundering on the door and if necessary breaking it down. Until at last all their doubts are happily put to rest by the distressingly loud sound of rending toilet paper from within.

The Observer is the last newspaper one should buy to read in a small and humanity-packed compartment on the Stamford 10.15. To digest successfully the news in this ample broadsheet calls for a large armchair, and the floor of a large empty room on which to crawl about afterwards to reassemble the pages. They became more and more crumpled and twisted as I endeavoured to manipulate them in the two-by-four of carriage space left to me. Gradually the thing began to threaten the comfort of father. I grew more and more desperate, but the paper gradually assumed the proportions of a Frankenstein as I dealt with it. Until at last I gave it up and, screwing the whole thing into a big ball, thrust it under the seat.

Stamford at 12.35. We had to change and chug into it on a little country train. In any case the station could not accommodate more than three carriages at once. This terminus would need a

Dickens to do it justice, for it is definitely to the age of Pickwick that it belongs. The single railway line ends at buffers a few feet from the station entrance doors, and you can step out of the carriage on either side onto the wooden platforms. One tiny little Smith's bookstall boarded up, one advertisement for *Punch*, one for Waterman's Pens, and that was about all. The passengers gradually drifted away, until five only were left grouped around the R.A.F. Morris six-wheeler in the yard outside. They were for Wittering beyond all doubt. One glance at their trench coats, old grey flannels and tweed coats, pipes and heavy shoes proclaimed them as brothers of the cloth. The naval officer has been defined as one who has nine gins on board and then dresses like a tramp to go ashore for the tenth, but we can always guarantee to run him pretty close!

The two railway officials, a hoary old porter and ticket-collecting station master, proceeded to manhandle the pile of baggage into the lorry, shuffled and touched their caps at the tips, and with half-nervous How-d'you-do sort of smiles at each other, we clambered on board and were under way. One can't tell much of people at a first glance. To each other we were just so many different types in different clothes. Twenty-six years on this planet have taught me that the face is the worst index to the character there could be—though some sort of character is usually clearly stamped on a face to make things more difficult still. So one made guesses with a reservation that in all probability later days would prove them to be entirely wrong, and contented oneself, as usual, with trying to guess to what squadron or school the ties belonged.

We watched the country road receding and Stamford drop away into the hollow behind the trees as under the canvas hood we sped along. What associations do these names bring? For me very little. The Great North Road, Stamford and York. Dick Turpin and Black Bess, Kch-Kch. Very famous ride. A roadhouse a few miles away called The Wansford Knight. And a famous old coaching inn called The Haycock in Wansford itself.

Stamford Aerodrome, now given over to the plough again, had a great name during the War. They used to train the Canadian aviators there, and these chaps would loop Rumpetys before the peculiar stresses of the loop were known or allowed for in aircraft design. They buried them with full military honours at the rate of three or four a day.

We left the Great North Road, passed through the guardroom gates, past many beds of spring flowers and shaven lawns, swished round the pebble drive, and drew up at the main doors. Mess like a large and very palatial, spaciously planned two-storey hotel. Wide vistas of countryside all round, walls of already mellowing red brick, white enamelled window-frames, and flower beds on three sides. We were shepherded in by a page-boy in full blue-and-buttons and requested to fill in a form on a table in the long hall. This document, against our names, told us our bat-man's name and our room, and requested us to say:

(a) exactly how much was a half of one day's pay, and

(b) what games did one play.

So soon, so soon. And a brave man or a fool indeed who dared write in answer to (b) "None at all."

We were shown to our rooms, and our luggage brought up by the duty waiter. Well, here at any rate, were no grounds for complaint. With customary guile I had written to the mess secretary a week before asking, if possible, for an upstairs room. At the end of those long corridors, over-looking the gardens, you live in quiet peace. Whereas in the downstairs rooms you can always hear a traffic of busy feet, and when you're in your bath on chilly nights some ass will keep on opening and slamming the doors and blasting in great gusts of arctic air.

The whole mess was built in about 1927, so everything is as solid and fresh and modern as you could wish. Polished brown linoleum on the floor, two carpets, oak writing table, armchair, dressing table and wardrobe. Pale distempered walls, bright green enamelled doors, white window-frames of good heavy iron with cheese-cutter catches opened outwards to the summer air. On that bed with its white counterpane I shall rest my air-weary body and no doubt book-weary mind for three months of nights in the sweet o' the year. And already in the mind's eye too I can see the coloured backs of my books unpacked and ranged in stout rows behind the shining plate glass of that built-in bookcase by the fire.

For efficiency I take off my hat to C.F.S. Already on the table lay a bunch of typed orders. Routine for the next day and then for the whole term. Allocation of pupils to classes and flying instructors, programmes of lectures and syllabus of subjects. Thirteen weeks in all to cover, just a hundred lectures of half an hour to an hour each. Thirty-three on air navigation, eleven on engines, eleven on aircraft, five on airmanship and flight work, seven on instrument flying, and odd ones on theory of flight and meteorology. So that no matter how many wet questions our aspiring pupils may ask us in days to come, we shall have no excuse for not having a profound and learned answer pat.

The duty waiter begins to lay about the man-high bronze gong in the entrance hall with a big drum stick. Lunch. Well, tomorrow events will begin to unfold.

29th of April

Monday always has a character of its own in the R.A.F., for on that day one has to wrench oneself from the outer world and get back to the intense business of workaday things again. Over the weekend you loosen the girths, rest the load, expand and give your leisure-personality full rein. If you stay in mess it's a grey-bagged, newspaper-reading weekend; or if, as is much more usual, you make one hairy dash as soon as you can land, and rush down to the mess to change and get away on Friday, you entangle yourself in heaven alone knows what romances, or enmesh yourself even firmer in such as may already exist. In either case it calls for a distinct effort to launch your resisting personality back into the mainstream of events on Monday morning. And it always seems to be on such a day, too, that one makes one's first appearance in a new mess.

0815 hours found some forty young gentlemen seriously devouring breakfast, all their eyes glazed to the newspapers propped up against the silver trophies and coffee pots in front of them. It was easy to pick out the other fourteen strangers who arrived here sometime yesterday by train or car to commence this course as well. They all wear their best tunics and hard collars. The tables conceal their heavy polished boots and putteed legs. Best Blue is always *de rigueur* for arrival and report. The older hands, instructors and auxiliary staff, are easily picked out. Their tunics are work-worn, their breeches faded with use, and their blue stockings gone pale in the suds of a hundred washes. And they do at least say "Good morning" to each other. But conversation can never be said to be at a premium at breakfast times, particularly after the weekends. In the navy they never pass the time of day.

And there is that story of an R.A.F. officer who joined a cruiser for duty with a catapulting floatplane.

Breezing into the wardroom for breakfast he saw someone reading a newspaper who, judging by the thick rings on his sleeve, was obviously the Commander of the ship.

"Good morning, Sir," he said cheerfully.

No answer. Perhaps he hadn't heard.

"Morning, Sir," in a slightly higher key.

Still no reply.

The Flying Officer sat down and opened his napkin. Must observe the courtesies. He tried all over again.

"Good morning, Sir."

The newspaper was lowered, and a great red face came into view over the top.

"Good morning, good morning, good MORNING. And now may that do for the rest of the damned cruise."

Nine o'clock finds us all in the passage outside the C.O.'s office, ready for the usual preliminary interview. Fourteen sergeant pilots now swell our roll, also booted and putteed and wearing obviously new caps with shining peaks. Outside white clouds drift down the blue of a summer morning, and aircraft, Tutors and old Avros, with an occasional silver-gleaming Fury or Hart, roar overhead as the instructors take off for the daily morning test of all 'planes. Then another newcomer rolls up, a lieutenant from a country of the Middle East, one Abdulla el-Hamêd by name. A young, bulky man with swarthy face, clipped black moustache, and white teeth. We at once size up his khaki, the devices on his buttons, and the oriental inscription on his wings, and can greet him with a salutation in his own tongue. We've served by his rivers and palms. It's nothing strange to see foreign officers at C.F.S. They come from all over the globe; Mexico, Greece, Poland, Ireland, China, Australia, Japan... drift through in ones and twos, learning to become instructors, to fly by instruments, or to be refreshed on ordinary flying after staff duties or ground work.

One by one we knock and go in, and covertly size each other up as we wait. One or two fall into obvious categories. There is the chap who talks too much. Already he is chattering away, and calling people by their Christian or nicknames although he's barely known them a day. Then the very quiet type, who rarely says a word. You wait and wait, thinking he's a dark horse who will soon give forth some pearl of wisdom, only to find suddenly and to

9

your complete surprise that he never has had anything to say. Next is the Bentley type. You can't mistake him. The white inches of (slightly grubby) shirt cuff with monogrammed gold links. The slightly disreputable tunic and breeches, the battered cap at a rakish angle, the carelessly wound and secured puttees, the somewhat down-at-heel boots. C.O.s and Adjutants are constantly at him, but find it a despairing game. A chronic affliction is not amenable to treatment. And while motor-cars are his passion, nothing short of cells will persuade him to spend money on uniform kit. Practically every squadron has one such as he. Unable quite to afford a brand new Bentley or Lagonda or Isotta Fraschini, he must have one of those makes all the same. So he buys a second-hand job and lives in penury to pay away £50 every year in tax and insurance and pour petrol into its capacious maw, a gallon to approximately every ten miles. Being usually of a 1926 vintage, the car literally drinks oil, too, and being a racing car it must have a racy smelling oil, too, at a fabulous number of shillings the gallon. You get the racy smell all right. Any 1926 Bentley which has had the guts flogged out of it by a succession of R.A.F. officer owners is slack enough of piston and big end, and plenty of burnt oil makes plenty of blue exhaust smoke. And so he is a happy bankrupt with his Bentley, whose stern juts out of the garage that is too small to accommodate it.

That tall chap is the riding type. Heir to a family of happy estate, he can afford to talk nothing but ponies and describe even an aeroplane as being so many hands high. You know before you see him in plain clothes that all his tweed jackets will be long and ample of skirt and slit up the back. His mantelshelf will be stacked during the autumn months with invitations to meet and ball, and when the unspeakable is in pursuit of the uneatable, there also will he be in full and muddy cry.

Now that long, nervous, refined-looking chap should be worth knowing. He has a cavalry moustache, and fine hands that play with a fifteen shilling pipe of naturally grained briar. Quality, you see, at a glance. And his blue eyes have got some quiet sense in them. Next to him is a smaller fellow, swarthy of skin, black haired, and with keen, constantly moving dark eyes. A strung-up, vital chap who smokes cigarettes like Ricardo Cortez and can ripple dance stuff divinely out of a piano. He found a baby grand in the ladies' room in the mess last night and really got an hour's rhythm out of it. The Army Co-op type you just can't miss. Trout is his name, six feet three of overgrown boy; his well-worn breeches are stretched tight, and he wears the most execrable cap imaginable. Army Co-operation pilots, for some obscure reason, have to live day in and day out in breeches and puttees. In case, I suppose, once in ten years they may be forced to land near an Army Camp and be ushered into the presence of the G.O.C. forces in the field, when it would be an unspeakable crime not to appear fully booted and spurred as for the C.O.'s memorandum of our own squadron life. A cap, too, would be an essential in such a contingency, so they always have to carry that stuffed somewhere in the aircraft, with muddy ballast weights, or in a locker full of oily spanners and spare sparking plugs. But if the C.O. doesn't roar like a bull behind his glass door when he sees Trout's hat, then I shall be a very surprised man.

That old flying officer (rising twenty-seven) with the brushed up moustaches and fierce military look (assumed with his puttees and cast aside when he removes them) has already been lurked for Senior Pupil, poor stiff. Nacelle is his name. He'll be morally responsible for the whole gang of us. Millions of programme changes will be passed to him for broadcasting during the next few months. Lecture changes, alterations in flying periods in dud weather, particulars of parades and duties and a hundred other things. He fathers the whole bunch of us, not for an extra penny a day but because it's his misfortune to be higher in the Air Force list than the rest.

It's pretty easy to tell what sort of a job a fellow has been doing these days. The Coastal Area pilot off flying boats always has a green eagle in the middle of his cap-badge. When new they're gilt, but sea air and salt water soon coat them with verdigris. His talk, too, in unguarded moments, is web-footed. He talks about going ashore and going aboard, of slipping cables and the like. That long, lean flying officer propped against the wall and telling some anecdote with a twinkle in his eye is one of them. The red and white striped ribbon? A.F.C. — some job or other he did with a flying boat that foundered in a gale in the Irish Sea. The speech of fellows who've been in the Fleet Air Arm, however, is surprisingly free from nautical jargon.

And there is one to my knowledge who delighted in getting under the skin of the N.O.s by announcing his intention of going downstairs to his room to lie on the bed under his window. And when a sailor would naturally go below to his cabin to lie on his bunk under the scuttle, that sort of thing is calculated to annoy him intensely. You may not like the English and their idioms, but never poke fun at them, whatever you do. How to tell an Air Force officer who has served in a carrier? Easy. We landlubbers sip a glass of sherry wine in the ante-room before dinner. He invariably orders gin and onions.

You can easily spot the twin-engine, night-flying, heavy bomber pilots. They have that awful strained sort of married look. When the wind's over 30 m.p.h., they can only fly to aerodromes downwind of their own. And the fighter boys, as they're affectionately, or derisively, known. Well, if anyone ever says to you 'Area', just that, look down, because you will know that the top button of your tunic is undone. I don't know why, but it's a 'line' in Fighting Area to wander about with that button undone. They also let their hair grow a bit longer than usual and curl round the sides of their caps. A line, by the way, is something that is shot. If you shoot a line, in effect you do or say something in order to impress the uninitiated and fail. Hence the saying 'He who shoots a line rarely shoots anything else.'

But this isn't getting us any forrader with the training of flying instructors. Gradually we all pass in front of the Old Man, saluting, feverishly tearing off a glove and shaking hands, telling him where we learned to fly, how many hours we have done, the number of our last squadron, and how pleased we are to be serving under his command.

A roar like that of a bull comes through the muffling glass soon after Trout goes in. He eventually emerges with red ears, and the Senior Pupil persuades us that now the next thing on the agenda is to fill up the adjutant's book and then read and sign orders waiting for us in the school.

We fill up the books. Rank, name, from where, how, pedigree and gender of dog desired to be kept if any, and number, make, vintage, colour and H.P. of motor-car ditto.

Millions and millions of orders in the school. There always are. Mess rules — fifteen pages. Station Standing Orders, about fifty. Orderly Officer's Orders, Orders for Fire Pickets and Guards, Station Flying Orders, Officers' Confidential Orders (Moneylenders, Low Flying, Teetotalism, Cyphers, Relations with the Press, etc., and so on), Unit Aircraft Orders, and about ten other groups one forgets. We read solidly and woodenly for about half an hour. None but a Datas could remember one tenth of anything but the vaguest general drift of them. Relying on common sense and the good offices of our guardian angel, we sign as having 'read and understood' and pass on.

10.15 now. Publication and Books. Books, books, books, we draw and sign for them in stacks. *Manual of Air Navigation, Manual of Rigging, Lynx IV Aero Engine, Jaguar VI Aero Engine, Avro 504N Aeroplane, Atlas Army Co-operation Type Aeroplane, Flying Training Manual Part I,* and the *C.F.S. Syllabus of Instruction.* Six notebooks, and the usual navigational gear—C.D.C., parallel rules, Douglas protractor and dividers. The powers that wear brass hats and sit in high places evidently intend us to work.

11 p.m. 'Opening Address by the Commandant', Lecture Room No. 2. We file in and sit at the desks and goggle at the airmen's Higher Educational stuff scrawled on the blackboard. $\frac{1}{2}f42x.d.$ $\rho\pi4 = K$. And they're the chaps who adjust our tappets and clean the plugs. Well, well.

We all struggle noisily to our feet as the C.O. comes in and sets his gold-braided cap on the table in front, then sit down again.

"Well, gentlemen," he begins, "I hope you'll enjoy your stay here." Then hands out in a few pungent sentences what we'll have to do now, and hereafter as qualified instructors, and on what points he expects good behaviour of us under his command. Quite a usual, good address. His roving hawk eye picks out the good 'uns and the not-quite-so-good 'uns as he talks. We clamber to our feet again and he goes. Observe that the cap is tilted over his eyes as he walks out, for it is a barometer to the mood he is in. Before I came here, a chap said to me, "If you see the Old Man walking along with his cap on the back of his head and he's whistling and looking cheerful too, for heaven's sake give him as wide a berth as you possibly can. For you'll know that he's like a raging volcano inside. Something or someone will have got under his skin, so keep away. But if the cap's over his eyes and he looks pretty grim, all's well. You'll find him in the sunniest of moods!"

Next the Chief Flying Instructor—a Squadron Leader. By deductions probably the best and most accurate pilot in the world. The best pilots in the world belong to the R.A.F. of course. They're trained by instructors, obviously better still. These in turn are trained at C.F.S. by instructors of instructors. And they finally are tested and re-categorised by the C.F.I. himself. Q.E.D.

What he has to say is also brief and to the point.

"You have come here to be trained as instructors. There's a lot to be learned in a short time. Don't go into the air and waste time. Use every minute, because if you don't you'll suddenly find that the final tests are only a week off and you don't know, and most certainly won't have time to learn, patter and how to synchronise it. Practice, practice, and practice. Reckless flying or disregard of flying rules we won't have. Among other things your place will be to set an example to pupils. But we do want polished and dashing flying. And finally one other thing—secure and keep your pupils' respect. Lose that and you lose their confidence. That's all."

We clamber to our feet again and he goes out too.

We consult our printed programmes again. 'Draw parachutes. Report to flights.'

The parachute room becomes a hive of industry. One by one the sergeant adjusts the harnesses and fits the 'chutes to the pilots, while two airmen steadily go on with the packing at the long tables. Hour after hour, day in and day out, they are at it throughout the year. And every month some seventy canopies are opened up and hung for twenty-four hours to air and be inspected.

There is a happy surprise in store here. In the old days— which ended a few months ago—the harnesses had two leg straps that came up underneath and snapped on to hooks on front. And you could walk along in comfort with the parachute bumping loosely behind and these two straps hanging loose. The buckles on the end would clink together and ring and chink with a sweet clear note that was always music to the ear. And to hear it even in the imagination recalls by association a hundred other happy sounds and sight and smells. The wump-wump of great all-metal airscrews idling round as row upon row of lean silver snouts already tilt up to the blue and the drifting white cloud armadas. Or the hurried, glittering propeller flicker-nick-flicker as your bull-nosed and squat-tailed little fighter strains squarely against her chocks, all hurry to be off and rip her seven hundred horse radial through the air with the pilot hidden somewhere behind it. The smells come crowding in too—the faint, doped drift of silvered fabric, the rich exhaust smell of burnt aviation petrol, the satisfying odour of hot engine metal and oil, and mingled with them all that other smell you notice on playing fields and horse gallops on the downs, clean chalky earth and bruised turf. Flying for a living is the very prince of occupations, and I for one wouldn't trade my heritage for all the messes of pottage in Christendom.

14

But those were the old days. For everywhere you go now you'll find a different type of harness, the Single Point Quick Release. All straps come to a metal release-box about as big as your fist, on the chest. The ends snap in and are securely locked by a turn of a round, flat milled plate on front. Then, if you bale out and land in water, one turn of the plate the other way and a smart rap will release the whole lot and you can swim free. No more the music of the clink. Except at C.F.S., that is. For there, an inland unit never given to flying over water or the possibility thereof, they are using up old stock. And I went away harkening as gleefully as a daft poet to the clink of those buckles again.

We wander over to the flights, meet our Flight Commanders, and are allotted flying-gear lockers. Dump the parachutes and then head for the mess and lunch. This afternoon we fly. No time wasted here.

After lunch batmen and motor-cars heaped with unpacked flying kit go down to the flights. In the mess we raided the bar and bought two pairs of blue stockings each, for it is an old tradition that the flying staff of C.F.S., and C.F.S. only, wear breeches and stockings every day. Army Co-op have breeches and puttees, and all other units slacks.

One more formality while the aircraft are being started and warmed up, and then we're off. Each instructor buttonholes his pupils and gives them a run over on the Avro 504N and the Tutor petrol systems. Airscrew swinging and starting up drill. Sign the flight book, and off we go.

It runs one instructor to two pupils. A cheery, red-faced little flight lieutenant who looks as though he could tell a good after-dinner story and be a very useful howling savage in a rugger pack takes a sergeant pilot and myself under his wing. Cowling is the sergeant, of an open, pleasant Scottish countenance and athletic frame. He's from Sidestrands, quickly moving twin-engined bombers that can be chucked about to bring any of their defensive guns to bear.

Neither of us has flown Tutors before, so we crack off in turn with Mayor. He takes off, climbs to three thousand, does a steep turn and a spin or two, then comes in and lands. Having weighed up the speeds, engine revs. and general performance while he's been flying and chatting about it, one takes over, does two or three circuits, turns, spins and landings to his satisfaction, then taxies in to the tarmac. He gets out and lashes up his cockpit straps, one signs the Serviceability Sheet, and then off again for three-quarters of an hour of flying practice on a new type.

Avro Tutors are now the standard R.A.F. *ab initio* training type. Gentlemanly little things from the flying point of view. Nicely balanced controls, light and smooth to handle, beautiful for all manoeuvres, no tricks or vices, sweet glide at seventy, and as easy to land as buttoning up your coat. Neat instrument board, excellent hidden and yet easily accessible arrangement of controls, hand-lever wheel brakes, and the usual slots. 180 H.P. Armstrong-Siddeley seven-cylinder Lynx. And now you know as much as I.

This evening after tea I went on a solitary voyage of discovery round the mess, finding the lie of the land, where the card and billiard and library rooms and squash courts were. Central Flying School started in 1912 at Upavon, sixteen miles above Salisbury on the downs near the Wiltshire Avon. And through the passage of days since then it has collected many relics and trophies of real historic interest to the R.A.F. In the ante-room you will see two bowl match holders of roughened white stone with the inscription round their battered but polished silver rims 'Presented by Major Smith-Barry —1914.' Who was Smith-Barry? The story goes like this. In the early aviation days pupil and instructor clambered together on to the windswept and chilly framework of their Farman or Martinsyde and, perched precariously on wickerwork seats, bumped and howled off the ground together. Then the instructor would bellow above the wind at the top of his voice "Do it like me!" and bank and turn and glide and land, next let his pupil try and try until he could imitate sufficiently well to be sent off to fly on his own. But then mysterious rumours drifted in that one Smith-Barry was applying revolutionary methods of instruction at Gosport with great success. He had burned a lot of midnight oil in analysing what actually happens in turns—how aileron drag, keel surface, and airscrew torque come into play, and the different effects that the controls have for different degrees of bank and rates of turn. And considered the other manoeuvres in flying as well. Then set about instructing by explanation of all factors involved, teaching manoeuvres by stages, and finally co-ordinating the whole. Simple now, it seems. But few people in those days knew much about the theory of flight, particularly its finer points. The odd University don who was up to date with his science perhaps, but not the average young horse-riding subaltern after his 'wings'. Anyway, the Smith-Barry school of thought was adopted, and now forms the basis of the world-famous C.F.S. system of instruction. And we have two match holders he presented when he left the school. Among other things Gosport gave us our speaking tubes as well. They're still called Gosport tubes. Wound from metal strips to make flexible pipes and bound with black cotton, they run from one cockpit to another in all aircraft devoted to dual instruction. The instructor talks into a rubber mouthpiece at one end and the pupil listens with his earphones plugged on at the other. A duplicate tube to his instructor's phones enables him to complain and answer back. You can hear an ordinary talking voice even with two hundred horse-power crashing away in front; foolproof, simple, and with no working parts, they obviate any need for microphones or any other delicate electrical stunts.

There's a very fine clock, too, on one of the ante-room mantelshelves that a Brazilian officer presented after some course of instruction. It is of dark wood carved in the form of an owl, with a silver plate screwed on to the base. The eyes tell you the time — outside are dashes marking the minutes and hours, and as the pupils on the ivory eyeballs slowly revolve, the left eye tells you the hour and the right the minute of the time. On the table in the entrance hall stands a very fine miniature bronze head presented by some Greek officers. And at dinner the table is fairly loaded with the departing gifts of many years — gimbal, antelope-horn mounted cigarette lighters, and silver models of the old D.H.9A, Bristol Fighter, Avro Mono, and Tutor on ebony stands. And, of course, cups and trophies galore.

It's a good way of furnishing a squadron or a school mess. And sooner or later you always come back to dip your pen at the writing table into the silver inkhorn you presented to commemorate all those happy hours of 1922-25, or to bag at the annual sports the magnificent Victor Ludorum trophy that the silversmith had engraved 'Presented by Wing Commander Aileron-Flap 1930-34' for you.

The billiard-room is a young museum in itself, for on the walls hang photographs of all the officers who've ever been taught to instruct at C.F.S., from the first in 1912 to the one before us, the forty-fourth, this year. And underneath the early ones you can read many famous Service names, Trenchard, Barrington-Kennett, Breese... of course you know them all. A more polyglot lot of uniforms though, you never saw. They don't become uniform until about 1924. Royal Navy, Guards, Scotch regiments, Sappers, they're all mixed up. And in each you see about six varieties of R.N.A.S. and R.A.F. outfits as well. Forage caps, stiff caps, soft caps; tunics, double-breasted ('maternity') jackets; puttees, field boots, slacks, walking sticks and swagger canes. But the dogs in the foreground, spaniels, sealyhams, and wire-haired terriers are always quite thoroughbred and the same!

In one of the passages hang some old maps under glass. With all the wartime aerodromes marked in (and Kent and Norfolk just swarmed with them), they are flagged and red-gridded and annotated for Staff H.Q. use. Maurice Baring could no doubt tell you of hours of suspense over them as the hurriedly pencilled, battle-hot reports came filtering through.

And in the music-library room are two oil paintings of which nobody seems to know the tale. A large one of an old B.E. flying along the side of a towering host of dark evening cloud into the great, serene, glowing heart of a six thousand feet sunset. The other of a winged Ganymede pouring wine from an earthen jar into the cupped, outstretched palms of a kneeling man. The colouring is superb, and the sky as prismatically powder blue as any of the *lapis lazuli* that Fra Lippo Lippi ever mixed.

30th of April

There's no nonsense about this flying game. Already we're at it good and proper, as though the course had been under way for a month. At 8.10 a.m. you see the instructors wiping their mouths as they charge out from breakfast, grab their caps from the pegs, and rush off up to the flights. By 8.15 they're in the air doing the daily test, and at 8.25 we're on the tarmac in flying gear reading the Detail Board for our trips.

Another crack with Mayor. I flew this time while he watched my flying, ready to criticise minor faults. On a squadron doing specialised jobs as opposed to pure flying, one can develop habits and idiosyncrasies. The odd pilot is fond of haring round on a low circuit, shutting off down-wind and landing off a right hand 180 degrees turn. This one has formed the habit of gliding in like a bat out of hell and then violently swish-tailing off his speed with great swings of the fuselage from side to side as he's holding off. Another 'stirs the pudding' as he lands, an agitated control column moving all round the cockpit as he 'feels' his ailerons to tell him when the stall is coming near. Another will fly along the ground for a hundred yards after coming unstuck and then ease her nose up and simply sail up in the lift to a thousand or so like a rocket on a stick, until he hangs on his slots before unstalling her again.

All safe, spectacular effects that aren't really useful but just give the squadron pilot a minor kick and take some of the boredom out of his routine jobs. But as habits they won't do. Polished, accurate and consistent flying is what is required and the best pilots are rarely spectacular. They drift over at one and a half thousand feet, do a wide, leisurely circuit and carefully weigh everything up—circuit flags, wind velocity, obstructions, other aircraft, and the exact point on which they wish to put her down. Then shut off and quietly come in on a long, straight glide off a ninety degree gliding turn and sit down gently with no fuss at all. No roaring up the hangars and doing full rolls downwind at five hundred feet as they do in Yankee films. That's merely bad form, and the tarmac critics and duty pilot look very pained.

Flew carefully and drew no comments. Anyone who is keen on flying is his own sternest critic, and although you may never fly with another pilot for perhaps a year on end in a squadron, you're an ass if you don't study flying the whole time. After three hundred, a thousand, or three thousand hours in the air, there's still plenty you can learn. Neat, firm turns. Smooth execution and recovery. Accurate approaching without sideslipping. Consistent gliding and turning speeds. Gentle use of the engine. Elimination of all jerky and violent manoeuvres. Gradually you'll get nearer to the secret, the heart, the rhythm of this flying game. There's rhythm in everything done superlatively well. Cricket strokes, dancing, hurdling, golf, prose, poetry, music, and flying itself.

Then your practice will stand you in good stead on critical occasions.

Mayor takes over to do the final landing. Amazing judgement. We come in on an incredibly split-ass sideslip. He recovers from this and flattens out a foot from the ground to land, chatting away down the speaking tube quite casually all the while about the theory of sideslipping. The corner of the hangar swings past fifteen yards away. We skate over the turf between two stationary aeroplanes only about three spans apart. Then up goes the nose and back comes the stick as she stalls, and we sit down plumb on three points. Towards the end of the run he rudders round, and as she trundles to a stop at the petrol filling point the engine splutters and dies and the airscrew comes to rest. He turned off the petrol cock just before we flattened out. Only the hundred per cent certain can afford to take what would otherwise be risks. But you see, these chaps are A1 at Lloyd's, as it were.

After an hour's solo practice our class, four officers and three airmen pilots, push off to A.R.S. In all, we'll have thirty periods each of an hour and a half in this place, the Aeroplane Repair Shop, a great big lofty hangar with some thirty aircraft in all stages of dismantling, inspection, repair and re-erection. And we've got some work to do. Split up into four classes, each of seven men, going into the hangar at different times we'll rebuild from bits two training aeroplanes, an Atlas and an Avro 504N. A rigger sergeant supervises all our work, and at the end of the term we all fly our handiwork.

As production jobs they will certainly be expensive work. Skilled men would do it in a quarter of the time we'll take. But the great idea is to teach us as we work. If you've built and rigged an aeroplane from a heap of junk, you'll be able to shoot a pretty strong line to any pupil asking awkward questions about the innards of his crate when the time comes along.

Sergeant Stagger, a red-faced, blue-eyed, rotund little Cornishman with that irrepressibly cheery outlook on life of all good N.C.O.s, grins all round and introduces himself. Then he takes us round, shows us where to get tools and odd nuts and bolts and spares, and assigns us off to jobs. Away we go, while he hangs around helping and giving advice. Four of us labour on the Avro, while the other four attack the Atlas with large hammers. Next time we'll swap round.

The Avro, to the unprenticed eye, is a sorry mess. Wings, tailplane and rudder nowhere to be seen. They're in the dope shop nearby. The undercarriage a collapsed heap against the wall. The engine yet to be spirited out of the bowels of the engine shops. Only the fuselage left, a bare wooden framework stripped of all fabric and supported on trestles off the ground. That's what happens after four hundred hours flying, when a complete overhaul always falls due. Sarge has inspected everything with an eagle eye. All parts are serviceable, and erection can begin. We square up the fuselage with spirit levels and packing blocks, stretch our reference cords, and then begin to 'trammel and adjust'. While the other gang wrestle with screw jacks and cock their all-metal Atlas framework (derelict and wingless, too) up at a perilous angle called Rigging Position, to enable them to get on with their trammelling and adjusting, too.

At 12.15, by now seven grimy and horny-handed sons of toil, we dab our superficial wounds—for spanners will slip and hammers miss their mark—and strip off our overalls to make a beeline for lunch. In the afternoon we fly again, another hour each of general solo flying to get these Tutors thoroughly wrapped up before getting down to the serious business of learning how to instruct. There seem to be millions of 'em up in this summer air. Wherever you look you see yellow-painted Tutors haring round on the circuit at a thousand feet, gliding down to land and rising up into wind off the ground again. The aerodrome is in reality a small hill, a big bump of a ridge running along the middle and sloping off sharply to the hangars on one side and towards a wood on the other. So it's no use taking off from the tarmac when another chap may be innocently sitting on the ground ticking over, completely out of sight, on the other side. Hit another aircraft on the ground and the powers that be will never, never forgive you. Their censure will be less severe if you bale out at five thousand and they find your aircraft a tangled ball of metal in the heart of Dead Man's Wood than if you taxy gently into the aeroplane of F.O. Trout. So we charge up and down the ridge like frightened stags looking for hidden strangers, before blinding off again.

1st of May

First hour and a half, Engines. I knew we couldn't escape this for long. We put on our overalls and found the Work-Lecture Room among the hangars. The usual forms round the wall, and blackboard, and wall diagrams of ignition and petrol and oil systems, valve timing diagrams, engine sections and performance graphs. All very complicated. But what was more serious still, two zinc-sheathed benches with vices and bays for engine parts, and four hefty tool kits. And in the middle of the room were mounted on steel stands two engines recently taken out of aeroplanes, a seven cylinder 180 H.P. Armstrong Siddeley Lynx, and another fourteen cylinder affair, its 400 H.P. big brother, the Jaguar, all very oily and dirty. With all this junk, the eight of us, and the tubby, careworn Fitter Aero Sergeant who instructs, the place was pretty full.

He bade us be seated, and at our ease, and to smoke discreetly if we wished. Then he read over the syllabus.

"It's like this, gentlemen. We work on the engines for one period and 'ave lectures and take notes on the next. Engine data, order of dismantling, particulars of crankcase, cylinders, crankshaft and connecting rods, pistons, front and rear covers. Then carburettors, mags, and supercharger. By this time we're cleaning and viewing. Then valve and ignition timing and we slap 'em together again." All this is rather frightening.

"But Sarge, who sets the end of term exam papers?"

"I do."

"Then for heaven's sake be kind."

"You can rely on me, sir. The last course all got over eighty per cent. Just listened when I talked, and read their notes. Believe I've got their papers 'andy. Yes, here we are. Two papers of three hours, one on Jaguar and Lynx, one on General Aero Engineering. Eleven questions, answer ten. *One.* Describe the lubrication system of the Lynx IV. Give sketch. *Two.* Sketch and describe the action of the airscrew thrust. *Three* —"

"All right, that's enough." Holt-fflair feebly moans. "You might as well fail me now. Shall we proceed to the business in hand?"

"Right, sir. Well, our job for a start is to strip down these engines" — he patted the fourteen cylinder brute affectionately — "and clean and overhaul them completely. Fit new parts as and when necessary. Then we reassemble and stick them on the test benches. Give them a two-hour cruising throttle run each. Remove and strip 'em down again to see everything's hunky dory. If it is, then back on to the benches again for a final test run and a short time at full bore: petrol and oil consumption test: then whip 'em out if nothing's run hot and our filters are clean."

Whip them out. I loved that. A three-hour job, if it takes a minute.

"Finally we bolt them in the Avro and Atlas you're putting together in A.R.S., and then each one of you flies each aircraft as a vote of confidence in your own work. And now to dismantling."

He begins to unlock toolboxes. We gingerly climb into overalls. Esterhazy dons a pair of white canvas gloves he mysteriously produces from somewhere. Once of the merchant marine, he learned a trick or two from American sailors when, as an apprentice, he had to chip paint. And if you ever see a deckhand on a Yankee boat working without gloves, then you'll know he's not a real U.S.A. tar. We begin to peel external bits off the fourteen — or was it forty? — cylinder affair.

Afternoon, we fly again. Fairly straining at the leash to get strapped into the cockpits, slam open the throttles, and get away. Must be something in the blood. We're all salted warriors with a thousand odd hours on the books and yet the urge rises afresh, phoenix-like, with the coming of each fine day.

Taxying patter first of all over in a leeward corner of the aerodrome. Oh, there's much more in that than you'd think. You don't just open the throttle a little and trickle along. Upwind, crosswind and downwind you use your ailerons and elevators in different ways. Then there are the brakes. And general rules of airmanship when moving about on *terra firma* (the more *firma* the less *terra*, as *Punch*'s old lady once said) to be committed to heart. For half an hour one listens, watches, repeats, tries, corrects, listens again, repeats, tries and so on. And then off we go to analyse and discuss and learn to talk about and demonstrate the Effect of Controls with Engine On at two thousand over the chequered countryside of Northamptonshire.

2nd of May

I thought we couldn't escape the old Avro 504Ns for long. There are a few stacked in the sheds, but most of the instructional aeroplanes are Avro Tutors. Nice machines.

The other Avros are old crates. Not much different from the 1912 product, the original and one and only. The old one, the 504K, had a French rotary engine that chucked a lot of oil over you, and a 'toothpick' sticking out in front under the airscrew to tip the nose back obligingly if a 'Hun' flew her into the deck. Otherwise the modern one is a replica of its 1912 forerunner. Heavily staggered wings. Nice robust construction. Staring yellow struts, a mighty long tail with a tiny rudder on the end, and a marvellous undercarriage. You can crash her on to the ground from ten feet and she'll stick there. But the refinements are few. None of your palatial instruments and nickel fittings, adjustable seats and pansy windscreens. Good Spartan construction. A long wooden crate braced with piano wire and covered with fabric. And you sit inside on two wooden box seats, with a stick between your knees a cross between a policeman's truncheon and the wooden spoon they use for stirring puddings, just a few bare and necessary dials in front of you, and away you go. They're probably still the best training aircraft that has ever been produced. Sensitive enough on controls to show up faults easily. Fast enough to be called an aeroplane—they cruise at eighty. Absolutely no flying vices, kind to a degree. Spin sweetly for demonstration purposes. Come out exactly and at once. Nice, primitive, open air and draughty flying machines, with two tanks stuck on the centre section above your head to hold thirty-two gallons of juice. That's fed slap to the carburettor. No link feeds and pressure pumps, relief valves and autovacs here. Simplicity's the keynote of the hour. They've taught chaps to fly in them since the year dot. They're teaching them now. Which is the reason why we've got to fly them now.

I rolled down to the sheds and blithely clambered into flying kit and parachute this morning expecting to fly a nice kind Tutor again. You can put down an absolute king of a three-pointer on those every time. Muttering to myself odd bits of patter the while.

"…and when the control column is eased over to the left, the left wing goes down in the direction of the undercarriage. This is known as movement in the Rolling Plane."

But up came my Instructor, all fat and tubby in his sidcot suit, and his red face beaming over lashings of Old Cranwellian scarves round his neck. "We're going to fly a Crab this morning," he said. "Get in."

We clambered in and did up all the straps and things. "Now I expect you've flown one of these before—" the voice came down the earphone pipe. Yes, I had. Etc., etc., etc. "You will remember that these have to be landed without the slightest bit of drift on, or else they drop a wing." I remembered too well. "I want you to taxy out and do three circuits and landings; then we'll do some spins. Then you can go solo and get in some flying practice on her. Try gliding turns and landings in the circle when you do. You've got her."

"I've got her."

We waddled out, turned into wind and roared and lurched off the deck. After the heavy stuff I've been flying lately it was like sitting in an old sugar box on a bumpy day. Thing wobbling all over the place, stick lashing from side to side in the cockpit to keep her straight. Climb at 55-60. Glide at 65. The angle of glide at first is most alarming. Fairly plunging at the green fields and hedgerows to keep up the speed with motor off. On windy days I should think you have to shut off over the circle in the middle of the aerodrome if you want to scrape in over the leeward hedge. Down we went three times, coming down like a feathered brick. My instructor has a bit of a speed complex.

"*Don't* let her drop below seventy," he pleaded once or twice coming in. Now they glide all right at 65 and I happened to mention this to another pupil in the hangar afterwards. "Oh, a pupil put him into the deck last term," he said.

"How do you mean?"

"Stalled on a sideslip doing practice forced landings, and shoved a wing in."

So now he's mighty pleased if you come in like a bat out of hell.

We made two wheely landings before I managed to make the tailskid touch at the same time as the wheels. You have to make 'em sit up and beg like a dog to get a three-pointer. Dropped a wing once, although it was one of those heat-hazy, almost windless days. You have to watch like a hawk for drift. A little rudder on as you glide in, or touch down the slightest bit out of wind, and whoops! down she goes.

The instinctive thing to do is to pull the wing up. Which gives you aileron drag on the tipped wing and swings you more out of wind still. Ergo, down goes the wing still more. The correct thing to do directly you feel a wing going down is to rudder into it, which is a very hard thing to do instinctively. On ordinary squadron aeroplanes one never has to bother frightfully about drift. A few degrees out of wind make no odds at all. But Avros are good for training the young idea, so we've got to polish up our rusty principles and keep an eagle eye open for this bogey, drift. We did a few pleasant spins to right and left just to get the feel of her again, then came down and taxyed in to the tarmac. Mayor hopped out and buckled up the harness in the empty back seat, and away I went to practise landing in the circle.

In the afternoon we had another hour in A.R.S., crawling under and about the Avro fuselage still on trestles, pulling up bolts and split-pinning them and doping on fabric strips here and there and generally being useful by doing the workman's job.

Then the other pupil, the sergeant pilot, and I shared the Avro, doing patter practice on the stuff we learned yesterday, taxying in one corner of the aerodrome and then Effect of Controls with Engine On. One feels a bit of a fool at first doing baby talk to another pilot down the telephones. The feeling very quickly wears off, though. At first, when trying to learn the stuff, one says some strange things without noticing it. Cowling very carefully explained to me how the rudder is connected to the control column, and then got in a hell of a tangle trying to make it work before he realised where he had tripped up.

Even flying instruction is governed by laws of the Medes and Persians. One must never talk about a 'machine'. Always 'aircraft' or 'aeroplane'. Never talk about the 'stick'. Toujours 'control column'. You always 'ease it over to the left', and 'gently apply' rudder. Plenty of phrases like that to impress on the pupil's subconsciousness that he must handle her gently, treat her like a lady. Already one is constantly being told on odd occasions that the flying pupil is the most slavish mimic there is, and that he copies the instructor's flying habits down to the smallest idiosyncrasy.

Coal issue stopped yesterday. It always does on May the first, even if an arctic blizzard is raging. You huddle over an empty, cheerless grate, while the Royal Navy walks the ice-covered poops of the dogwatch wearing the white cap covers that, for them, May the first has also ushered in.

3rd of May

Another grand flying day. Always in an English winter the weather is completely undependable. Sometimes for whole days on end one chafes in the flight office or hangar, watching the drizzle keeping the visibility down to a few yards, or mist blotting out the trees and hedges on the far side of the aerodrome. Non-flying weather in either case. So that the beginning of every summer seems too good to be true. One goes to sleep with the quietness of an early summer night outside, all the stars shining brightly through the still air, and the faint noise of fast cars whirring past on the Great North Road coming in every now and then through the open window. To wake each morning to a cloudless sky, the sun already steeping the country in its golden light, a blue haze that will soon clear hanging over the distant fields. The brown holland windsock hangs almost motionless from its mast on the high hangar, and when one reaches the tarmac the aeroplanes are already lined up on the grass, chocks in front of the wheels and the engines warming up. Each flight's aircraft in separate rows. A Flight's with vertical red bands round the fuselages, B Flight's with blue bands, and the Service type Flight's aircraft as well. A brave sight on a summery morning like this, twenty or so aeroplanes in all, 504Ns, Tutors, Moths, Bulldogs, Harts, Atlases, and Furies. One is falling into the system now. Each morning during the first hour and a half the instructor takes one of his pupils while the other does lectures. During the second half of the morning the other pupil takes the air under instruction while the one who has already flown does lectures. The flying hour and a half is split in two. First the pupil hurtles off with the instructor who checks him on patter already learned. Corrects and makes him repeat where necessary. Then hands over to the pupil and tells him to do some flying manoeuvres or other and checks up on the execution of those with the idea of gradually bringing his flying skill up to a degree of perfection, too. Then they land and for the rest of the period the pupil goes off alone to practise general flying.

In the afternoon the instructor doesn't fly. Gives his two pupils instructions on the tarmac before they leave, sees to whatever ground jobs he has to do while they're away, and then after the hour and a half returns to see them land and chat things over with them.

This morning we cracked off in the old Tutor again. Nice morning, nice machine, and so far we know by heart the two chunks of patter we've already been told. God's in His heaven, etc. and so on. We ran over the taxying and Effect of Controls with Engine to his satisfaction. Good enough.

"Now climb up to two-thousand feet and we'll go over Effect of Controls without Engine."

We throttle back into a glide, and he begins to talk, moving the controls to suit the description of their effects. That's the secret of it all, synchronise demonstration with patter. Easy enough now. But wait till we have to roll an aeroplane over on to its back and then career along at 120, hanging on the straps with blood rushing to the head and eyes fairly popping out, calmly talking about what's happening at the same time!

"Right, have you got all that?"

"I think so."

"All right, climb up to two-thousand again and run through it."

Like the little boy in the fable, we try, try, and try again. They must wear out some aeroplanes here on this instructional racket.

I saw a very curious thing at lunch-time. The Great North Road was shimmering under the heat of an early summer's day. And the labourers were already enjoying a quiet siesta under the trees after their bread and cheese. When past me, coming from the direction of York and heading in the direction of London, there chugged a vintage London taxicab with spinning whitewashed wheels. The windscreen was vertical, and adorned on either side by oil lamps of polished brass. The taxi-driver, huddled over his wheel and quite oblivious of everything but the strip of road just ahead of him, wore many coats and two mufflers. While beside him, head back and mouth wide open, sat a fair-haired young man in white waistcoat and tails, fast asleep. And this in the drowsy, sober light of high noon.

What do you imagine? This is the only construction I can place upon it. Scene: The city of York. Time: 5 a.m. of the same morning.

Dionysus: Charioteer — hurrup — take me home.

Jehu: Where do you live, Sir?

Dionysus: The Athenaeum Club, London, I b'lieve. Yes thashit.

Jehu: Werry good, Sir. 'Ome we go.

And they were still going.

4th of May

Except for the Orderly Officer, the pupils are entirely free over the weekends from 3.30 p.m. on Fridays until after breakfast on Monday mornings. If you stay on the camp on Saturday you

28

breakfast in flannels and a tweed coat and loaf as you please all day. The airmen clean down the aeroplanes and square up the hangars. Perhaps a few instructors practise special flying jobs; but that's all.

This morning was far too lovely to stew in the ante-room over the *Times* crossword. I smelt that as soon as the batman came in at eight o'clock. The full promise of summer seems to have gone to his head, too. Starting with the weather, he gradually drifted on to a discussion of the Wiltshire downs during wartime, and the old C.F.S. at Upavon, and the good times he'd had when he was an R.F.G. servant in 1916. He knew all the little towns in that part of the world. Devizes and Pewsey, Warminster and so on and so forth. All this as I gradually shook off the mists of sleep and sucked down my tea and groped for a pipe. Now a little conversation as a batman lays out the rig for the day is all very well. But the clock hands crept on, and breakfast only went on until 9.15. By the time I had finished shaving he was still fussing and messing absentmindedly about the place, pulling shirts out of drawers, gazing reflectively at them as though he'd never seen them before, and then putting them back again. Rambling on this time about the Passchendaele mud and the exploits of Baron von Richtofen and his ground strafes.

There is a time and a place for all things. Over a can of beer at 11 p.m. I'll sit all ears to listen to this sort of thing. But before breakfast, when no man is a hero to his valet, is not one of these times. I hadn't the crust to tell him to dry up, for there is all too little of the milk of human kindness in this world already. Not until I got into the corridor at 8.30 and headed for a bath did I shake him off. No more battening on me with the earnest look of the perfect talker who has found the perfect listener if I know it!

One would have to belong to a rich county family or go to a hotel of the ten-guineas-a-week order to live in a lordly place like this. The mess gardens are a constant delight. Wide smooth lawns, huge tulip beds, a blaze of colour, and on the far side a big rockery with two old gardeners messing about this morning potting out bits of saxifrage *Apollinaris* and all that. I'm no botanist, but it's all rather lovely. And round them, fantails and big white chaps of pouter pigeons fluttering and pecking for food.

About a mile across the fields lies the little village of Wittering, from which this place takes its name. After breakfast I took the path by the games field on to a country lane with elms on the high banks at the sides. With the sun on the walls and the dogs blinking sleepily in the warmth, a more perfect little village would be hard to find. It is quite unspoilt—no garage, none of the squalor that has sprung up on the outskirts of so many lovely old villages to kill their charm like a malignant growth battening on beauty. I only saw one sign of modernity, a small board painted with white letters nailed to the wall of a three hundred year old cottage with a heavy thatch, announcing that J. Roffe was a Cycle and Motor Engineer. No outward signs of his messy trade were visible however, thank heaven. All the cottages are built of that grey stone, hundreds of thin slabs stacked one on the other with no cementing compound between. The whole covered with straw thatch. Two thatchers were busy on one roof against the blue sky as I went past.

The village Post Office seemed too good to be true. The whole shop was no bigger than the cage of a London Underground lift. The window was fairly stacked out with things, the inside a veritable treasure cavern of delights. Two very small round-eyed and inarticulate boys had come in search of sherbet dabs, holding sweat-blackened pennies in their moist palms. An old labourer had come for two pennuth of caraway seed for the Sunday cake. And when I squeezed in, all the standing room was completely filled. Once the door was moved, a sheepbell attached to the inside by a long arched spring nodded and tinkled for nearly a minute on end.

Stacked all round were all the confectioneries and groceries any child or housewife could desire in a hundred years. Liquorice bootlaces, giant wasp-striped humbugs, love's whispers in all their pastel shades and inscribed with sentimental rhymes; flat slabs of toffee to fly into sticky splinters under the exhilarating rap of a small hammer; everlasting strips of attenuated toffee at a ha'penny the stick. Hundreds and thousands by the million in two big glass bottles. Then tops and toy pistols, Red Indian outfits bravely displayed on cardboard sheets, stacks and stacks of packets and bottles, jellies and herbs, cheeses, dried fruit, playing cards, ink, toothpaste, tobacco, soap, furniture polish. One could expend a whole page and a half on the inventory of stock alone. How the creaking shelves bore it all is a mystery. But greatest mystery of all, behind a tiny counter and iron grill, in the midst of all this stood a young woman, bespectacled and wispy of hair. How she got in I shall never know. That she can ever get out is a supposition too foolish to entertain for a moment. All traffic of merchandise in bulk must be done through the little window. When bedtime comes I suspect that she curls up into a ball and rolls under the counter to sleep the night away.

Incredibly she had a half-crown postal order. One day I shall go in there and ask for a shilling stamp. That should catch her out.

Posted on a wall in the village I noticed a list of cricket teams:

WITTERING SINGLES

v.

WITTERING MARRIEDS

SINGLE	MARRIED
B. JONES	C. ROFFE
C. WALDRON	J. ROFFE (SENIOR)
J. ROFFE	W. SMITH
P. ROFFE	B. MOULD
W. BARNES	T. BARNES
A. WITTLE	W. ROFFE
A. BARNES	W. WITTLE
C. CROFT	J. DUKES
DR. COKE	A. PICKLE
N. BARNES	R. JONES
R. DUKES	VICAR

Five Roffes, two Jones, four Barnes, two Wittles, and two Dukes, you see. As English as the cross of St. George. I found the war memorial in the church, one of the hundreds of little grey places to be seen in the villages of England, embosomed in high elms and by now mellowed down until it has grown into and become a very part of the green country during the passage of so many slow centuries. Three Roffes, a Jones, three Barnes, a Wittle and a Duke had laid down their lives for England and St. George.

These villages have changed very little since the Domesday Book was compiled and their churches built. The fields and copses, manors and labourers all bear much the same names as those you may read in that curious tome. And if you want to get to the living past of a place, read the Church records, and the inscriptions on its brasses and crumbling stones. All its lives, their births and deaths and joys and sorrows, lie behind those written and sculptured words. And let us be sad with Edmund Burke that the innkeepers have not fulfilled their rôles as godsent historians of the people, by cherishing their records.

Batmen are queer birds. I lay in my bath tonight thinking about them, as I so often do. I will not say they constitute my King Charles' Head, but I always have found them to be such a race apart that it affords me alternate amusement and despair to dwell upon their foibles while my epidermis is slowly changing to a hue of salmon pink.

The first personal servant I ever had was a wonder indeed. So short of sight that he would sometimes lay out odd socks, and shirts inside out; but he could on no score be accused of lacking in culture. His speech was always exceedingly precise and adorned with elaborately chosen words. His appearance was that of a conscientious bank clerk greyed by the office of years.

On one fine morning he happened to notice *Jill the Reckless* on the table beside my bed, and I do not think he altogether approved. The young master's tastes had turned the corner on the primrose path to the sound of the wrong kind of flutes.

"Would you be requiring any literature to peruse, sir?"

At 7.15 a.m. this sort of question conveys nothing at all. I always feel very old before 9 a.m. and he might just as well have addressed me in Chinese.

"Er—come again, will you, Watson?"

"Would you be requiring any books, sir, to read?"

"Read? No. I want (1) some tea and (2) a bath, and (3) very little noise."

"I mean, sir, for the evenings and your leisure time."

"Why, I don't think so, thanks very much. The mess library's all right."

"Because, if you do, sir, I have a comprehensive library at home. Some seven hundred volumes, if I may say so, sir. All the World's Classics included. Philosophy, philology"—as true as I hold this pen—"science and travel, literature and the arts. A good book is the precious life-blood of a master spirit, John Milton, sir, once observed. I would be very pleased to lend you any volumes you might care to choose."

This way, perhaps, lay untold complications. I might next find myself sharing his frugal supper board, and discussing the eternal verities over a guttering lamp.

"Well, that's very kind of you, old Watson, but I don't think so, thanks very very much, my life is such a busy one, you see—"

32

"Well, the offer still holds good, sir, if at any time you care to think about it again."

"That's extremely kind of you, and now I really must have this bath."

When I came back he was still dreamily fiddling with shoes and tunic and things, padding about like a gentle old hyena in its cage. He peered at me again over his glasses.

"Are you interested in politics, sir?"

"K.R.s and A.G.I.s aren't frightfully keen on it, you know."

"Because I'm standing for election to the local urban council, sir. Politics interest me very much indeed."

"Yes. Quite. Quite." What else was there to say?

"I also do a good deal of public speaking, sir. I address the populace on topics of the day."

"Really."

"Yes, sir, on all sorts of divers topics of the day."

"Well, Watson, I'm very pleased to hear it. Very pleased indeed. We are all proud of you, I'm sure. I must come along and hear you some day. And now would you pass me that tie? I'm in the most devilish hurry. No breakfast inside Little Mary yet, and parade's at eight-fifteen."

But that same night, going to blue a shilling at the local cinema, I happened to pass a public meeting under the gaslight at a street corner; and someone in a clear ringing voice was haranguing the mob. I lingered on the fringe to listen. Facing the crowd there stood a young Blackshirt, mounted on a dais bearing paintings of the bundled sticks and the protruding axe that form the emblem of his party. But he was not talking, he was listening, hard. So also was his body-guard of two more Blackshirts and two large, blue-coated, ruminative policemen, who chewed their chinstraps and scissor-like eased their legs below the rostrum. It was someone facing them who was delivering the goods, and the speaker had come to listen to his audience and no mistake.

"...What did John Stuart Mill say about the same thing? And Bentley? And, for that matter, every other political philosopher of repute? They were all agreed, sir, that in inverse ratio to the imports factor, the production index must increase. And likewise the cost of living, bearing in mind seasonal unemployment and the townward drift, must fluctuate in a similar manner, particularly if the gold standard is not stable and the national credit has suffered a reverse—"

33

"What abart Mussolini?" a navvy growled.

"Even such an authority as Sir Norman Angell," the ringing voice continued — and somehow it seemed faintly familiar — "even Sir Norman Angell, who has made a deep study of these things, is of the opinion that an increase in shipping tonnage must be met by a stability in the raw products markets and a net increase in manufactured exports for the prosperity to be other than a statistical illusion —"

The young man on the rostrum was hanging over his counter with a curiously wooden expression on his face and a glazed, codfish look in his eyes. I edged forward to see who this golden-tongued orator might be.

There, in the centre of the front row, stood a middle-aged little man in a dark overcoat, with an immaculately white silk scarf crossed over his throat, and a carefully brushed, high-crowned bowler hat in his hand. Only Watson, my batman, of course.

Some batmen refuse to hang coats on coat-hangers. You can buy them in stacks and suspend a whole forest of them from your wardrobe pole. But still they hang jackets loop-wise from hooks. Others simply cannot remember to put trees into shoes. It is as though their brains were brimming with Instructions to be Followed and this last one simply will not penetrate and stick.

Into the Service from time to time drift bodies of unskilled men. After six weeks' drill and knocking into shape at Uxbridge they are posted to units all over England under the name of Aircrafthands. They may be employed on one of many menial duties. Cleaning aircraft, lighting office fires, manning the coal cart, keeping the airmen's dining-hall clean, running errands, or even as servants in an officers' mess. Seven weeks prior to my introduction to him, another of my batmen had been a coal miner, and the blue marks of the pit were still on his hands. It is rather painful to dwell on the memory of him at all. He hadn't the faintest, the remotest idea. He would put coal on the fire with his fingers and then ram links and studs into a clean dress shirt. Stepping into the first bath he mixed for me, I simply peeled the skin off my legs before I could roar and leap into the air. The two other officers on whom he waited eventually took to keeping shotguns permanently trained on their doorways in case he should try to come in to administer to their needs. He left very soon, but his successor wasn't very much better. Four of these aircrafthands divided their wage pennies between the purchase of noisy jazz records for a gramophone in their room at the end of the passage, and the financing of a syndicate to run a 1925 bull-nosed Morris Cowley saloon. This they had acquired by clubbing together £5. Unlicensed, untaxed, uninsured, each off duty weekend they swayed and wobbled in it down to London. Eventually we got the Station Warrant Officer (our name for Regimental Sergeant Major) to take a kindly interest in their careers. No threats of the sack ever daunted them. The sack was the very thing that they desired. Better a thousand coal fatigues than one day's valeting for a gent.

Even abroad, bearers also seem to belong to a race apart. On one's arrival in Baghdad, a gang of mahogany-faced blighters in striped nightshirts and black coiled ropes to hold the kerchieves on their Arab heads used to line up on the verandah outside one's room. Each presented testimonials from previous young officer employers, and a kind of passport in Arabic and English script. Having chosen the most likely looking man of the lot, one sent him to the Station Warrant Officer, who seemed to know every native, pickpocket and honest man, in the great and thriving city. Then, if this worthy passed the candidate's credentials, he was engaged. He looked after one's wardrobe for a couple of pounds a month, while one of his three wives did the laundry (and did for it) for about twelve shillings a month. Wearing fresh linen every day in England would cost a good ten shillings a week. But English laundries prefer the more expensive method of ruining shirts in chemical vats to battering them to pieces at the riverside between two stones.

The first time the coffee-coloured rascal of my choosing laid out my clothes, I returned from perspiring at tennis to discover upon my bed a shirt folded for display as neatly as Austin Reed's might have done it, the cuffs linked and symmetrically crossed on the bosom, the collar fully attached, and a tie properly knotted in position and opened at the end in approved arum-lily style. This was the result of *Punch* being left around the mess, and then engaging an erstwhile mess servant.

My bearer took to being late with the tea at the end of the afternoon siesta, and then one day did not turn up at all. He came in at seven p.m. when it was quite dark, all shy gestures and white, fawn-like smile.

"Where the devil have you been, Achmêd?"

"Sahib — I go to play fotball."

"All right, you're sacked."

"Sahib—Sa-hib!"

"I don't want to hear any more. Eskit. Rur."

He burst into tears. Great fat tears. And plucked piteously at his robe.

"My master—what I do without you? What I do?"

You turn away.

"Oh—well, all right," you growl. "Don't do it again. Now get my shoes."

Later, in another part of the country, I had a Persian youth rejoicing in the name of Ispanha. He wore European clothes and the pillar-box cap with flat peak of his town-bred race. He would have cheerfully worked for threepence a day and his rice so long as he could keep in employment on Arab territory. Once they got their hands on him at Mahommerah, three miles on the other side of the river, he was in Persian clutches and—woosh—he went into the army as a conscript. Always at Christmas the bearers gave their employers Christmas Boxes. Achmêd's gift usually took the form of a big open wickerwork basket holding about twenty oranges and a gallon of walnuts. The head waiter once placed in the centre of our tea-table with evident pride his curranty offering, a gigantic cake messily iced. Four thin candles burning on it illuminated this touching message in pink squiggles of paste: *To my Every Sahib from faithful Ali.* We solemnly ate it, despite its heaviness with cooking lard, and pronounced it fine.

There are batmen who are hearty, and batmen who are mouse-like. The man I have now is so respectful that he never dares to wake me up, despite my overnight entreaties that he will do so. He gently whispers "Seven o'clock, sir", which of course I never hear. Then returns at seven-thirty to see if I am shaving; this time he does wake me.

"What is the time?" I demand. The tea is stone cold. Feeling guilty he says, "Seven-twenty, sir." He always does this. So that if I want especially to be called at 7.30 I have to do a mental calculation. If I tell him to call me at seven, he calls me at seven-thirty and says it's seven-twenty, so that meets the case.

Still, he's preferable to one man I had. One eye looked at you, and the other wandered. And he used to come in at all odd hours and insist that one should hear poems that he had written.

Another high summer's day, with the barometer stuck up at 1030 millibars, and the high clouds drifting down the blue to a quiet tune. Seems quite funny to see the mess crowded with people in uniform again, earnestly devouring breakfast with bulging cheeks, and the news from papers propped against the coffee pot with bulging eyes, after the slack weekend.

We started the day with one and a half hours of crowding along the little zinc-covered bench in the engine lecture-room workshop, each scrubbing the carbon and burnt oil from a piston out of the Jaguar IVc. I suppose one does learn. It's a messy business, rubbing away with a wire brush and then finishing off the polish with emery cloth dripping with dirty paraffin. It takes about a week to scrub the stuff out of one's fingernails afterwards. Second period of the morning we flew again. The instructors had their hands in again after flying with the first period pupils, but we weren't so clever. The subject matter wasn't too easy, either. This difficult stuff is beginning to come. We climbed up to 3000 and then he said from the back, "We're now going on to the further effect of controls." And we went on. He talked for a good ten minutes, then we climbed up again and I had a crack at the patter. One listens with the bent brows and gritted teeth of concentration, but this was far too difficult to absorb in one go.

"Now we apply rudder. And—would you mind just telling me that little bit again? I've quite forgotten just how it goes."

"And the nose swings in the direction of the left wing-tip. Now as the right wing is travelling faster than the left..." comes the voice helpfully.

"Oh, thanks very much—it therefore obtains more lift. So we notice the right wing rises and the left goes down. Then gradually the nose begins to drop... er, why does it drop?"

"Because the rudder is still acting in the yawing plane. Therefore the nose still swings in the direction of the left wingtip..."

"Oh yes, and as the left wingtip is now tilted towards the earth, therefore the nose goes down."

Well, now we've finished with the rudder. Continued action of elevators is easy. No complications with them. She either loops, stalls or dives. I know a chap who once tried to loop round a little cloud. But it was a big little cloud and he couldn't make the grade.

37

She stalled on the zoom and did a horrid tail slide. The stick—as you were, control column—was fairly lashed out of his hands and gave him two big black bruises on the knees. They thought the controls were a bit sloppy afterwards. When the riggers checked them up afterwards they found they'd stretched one and a half inches, and fifteen hundredweight cable at that... Well, we negotiated elevators all right. Now for the last and worst of all, the ailerons again. We're gradually losing height, stalling along at 1500 revs. as we talk, keeping an eye on the aerodrome far below, and the sky for other aircraft too. It's incredibly hard to see them sometimes when they're at a lower level and against a background of fields and things. Until there's a sudden silver gleam and you know it for another aeroplane banking its wings against the sun.

Frankly we make a mess of ailerons. Far too involved to remember at one go. Still, this is the only way to learn.

"Climb up and go through it again."

We climb, reach 3000 and start again. Rudder finished.

"That was all right. A little bit halting in the middle. And you must synchronise the actions with the words. You said the aeroplane starts to bank long after you'd let it begin to do so. Still, that will come in time. Right, elevators."

Elevators all right.

Ailerons we made rather a halting mix-up of again.

"We'll do ailerons once more. Remember in sequence what happens. Wing goes down. Nose rises due to aileron drag. Aeroplane sideslips. Aeroplane begins to turn owing to action of airflow on keel surface, etc. Right, you've got her."

"I've got her."

One goes through ailerons again hopefully. Please heaven he'll be reasonably satisfied with that.

"Well, that's about enough for one morning. How long is it since you did aerobatics?"

"About three years."

"Well, we'll have a run through now."

Thank heaven for that. We begin to climb. Controls aren't so easy as the book of words lead one to believe. Effect of Controls with Engine, without Engine and Continued Effect are all rolled into one to make one patter, and they're only one number on the sequence of instruction. Flying an aeroplane, from the teaching point of view, is divided up into twenty-eight sections.

1.   Passenger flying (initial air experience).
2.   Taxying and handling of engine.
3.   Effect of controls (including aileron drag). I like the story of the A.P.O. who thought aileron drag was another name for the Cranwell Beagles.
4.   Straight and level flying.
5.   Stalling, climbing, gliding.
6.   Taking off into wind.
7.   Landing into wind and judging distance.
8.   Medium turns.
9.   Gliding turns.
10.   Steep turns (with and without engine).
11.   Spinning.
12.   Elementary forced landings.
13.   Low flying.
14.   Solo flying.
15.   Climbing turns.
16.   Sideslipping (and there are three ways of doing this).
17.   Action in the event of fire in the air.
18.   Taking off and landing across wind. (Very clever this.)
19.   Advanced forced landings. (About twenty pages in the book of words on this.)
20.   Aerobatics. (And how. Loop, stall turns, roll of the top, slow rolls both ways, flick rolls, inverted flying, and a bunt if Aircraft Maintenance Orders Part 2 allow it and you're good.)
21.   Front seat flying.
22.   Air navigation. (Damned great volumes have been written about this. patter just isn't in it.)
23.   Forced landing test. (More — much more — about this later on.)
24.   Height tests.
25.   Full warload test.
26.   Passenger-carrying.
27.   Instrument flying — which is a three weeks' course in good flying weather alone. And
28.   Rough-weather flying.

And each number, even the simplest of them, with about three notebook pages of patter apiece. Boy, when we've done this lot, at least we should be able to fly.

We're nearly at 4000 feet. The sky is fairly lousy with aircraft. Half a squadron of green, night-flying Heyfords has just slipped past at 3000. The big chaps with a dustbin underneath where one of the three gunners sits. Dirty great things with two Napiers, and the pilots' cockpits about thirty feet off the ground when they're tail down. Doing some nice cross-country cruise or other. Ahead and to the right a flight of Harts slides across the sky, all silver in the sun and doing their regulation 120 knots. Some local day-bomber squadron taking the air. And everywhere, if you look keenly enough and have sufficient time, you will spot Tutors and Avros and Bulldogs and the like from C.F.S. all doing their peculiar and individual stuff.

"Now we'll begin with the ordinary loop. I'll do each manoeuvre once and then you can have a couple of goes.

"First of all, as with spinning, we have a good look round, below and behind and above, to make sure that we're not going to approach dangerously close to any other aircraft. Now we wind the actuating gear wheel a little forward and gently dive the aircraft to about 120, making sure..." etc., etc., and we execute three neat loops in succession, cutting the horizon with wings level each time, coming out facing the same direction within a degree or two, and still at 4000 feet. Any fool can throw an aeroplane round in a rough circle, but to do it with accuracy and a polish is another thing. And to talk as one does it, describing exactly what is happening *as it happens* makes things a little more difficult too.

When I learned to fly, the patter never intrigued me very much. I thought it was a pretty fair description of what was going on, by a chap who ought to be able to chat about it because he'd been a long time at the game. Most of the time to begin with I was wondering what the hell was going on. But now one takes a peculiar interest in the artless and skilful chatter that comes drifting down the telephones as the aeroplane rolls or dives from one improbable attitude to the next. For it's artless chatter no longer. It's stuff that later on one will have to learn to the point of painful perfection.

I did a couple of quite decent loops. They're easy enough and curiously enough not half as sensational as they look from the ground. Not a frightful lot of skill in them. Just ease back the stick and over she goes. There's far more sensation in a steep turn. And slow rolls, that look so effortless and casual from downstairs— they're brutes all right.

Next we passed on to rolls off the top. Dive her to 130. Ease up in a loop. Look well back and when you see the horizon come swinging up, keep the engine on, ease the stick over and forward so that you're going along upside down, then stick and rudder puddingwise, and round she comes. A nice wartime manoeuvre for single-seater scouts. Gain five or six hundred feet in height and reverse direction at the same time. Instructor chatting away as cheerily and capably as usual. Only never tell him to manipulate the controls puddingwise or he'd have triplets on the spot.

Well, we try a couple. Not bad. Not frightfully good. After three or four years on big, service aircraft, this sort of thing is rather youthful. One is inclined to grit the teeth, apply the controls with desperate determination, and get the right way up again as soon as is decently possible. It would be very trying indeed at the present juncture to be expected to talk as well. However, they can't be too bad, because nothing comes down the 'phones. We pass lightly on to the next. Slow rolls. Ah, they had to come sooner or later. Over we go. There's one terrifying moment when you're flung onto your side and trying hard to fall through the side of the cockpit, and then over, over, and you're floating along upside down in space. All your weight on the shoulder-straps, your bottom about six inches from the seat, the weight of the parachute also under what is now your top end. You are groping blindly up in the air inside the cockpit with your feet, defying the laws of gravity to keep them on the rudder bar. And, with the right arm stretched out straight as far as it will go and the top of the stick only held between the fingertips to keep it further forward, still the stick could be further forward to keep the nose up. Whatever dust and bits of mud and grass there may be floating around in the cockpit at once seems to fall out and get under your goggles and into your eyes. You could swear you did the straps up as tightly as possible, and yet it feels as though you're suspended about a foot out of the cockpit in thin air. In a slow roll you get all those sensations in about three seconds, while the oil-impregnated air is wooshing past at a hundred, and you're feeling with the controls, a little of this and a little of that, to keep her straight.

We did three of those fairly well. "Right, now one to the left."

Ha-aaah. Do you know, everyone hates rolling to the left at first. I don't know why, but they do. You've got to do scores of them and really become a nark at it before you begin to enjoy them. Have to sort of—screw yourself up to do them each time.

41

Chaps wouldn't admit it, but you get to know, by odd things they say, that they do. Well, there's nothing else for it. Dive her a bit. Right, up with the nose. Woosh. Over we go. In the first one you get panic-stricken in a mild sort of way. Not panic-stricken exactly, but your mind seizes up when you get upside down. She tends to dive, too, on her back, and we loop off. Have to use the left arm next time going to the left — get the stick further forward then. The mind refuses to think out what to do, so we bring her back the way we came with nice sweeping lunges of the controls.

"Have another go."

Dive. Woosh. W-oooo-sh. Woosh. We seem to be going in the same direction again right side up, engine coughing and picking up again.

"That was all right."

"Thanks very much. I'll bet you wouldn't say that if I did exactly the same thing in a month or so's time."

"Everyone's bound to be a bit rusty at first. With a bit of practice you'll soon do them all neatly and instinctively, without having to think about which control does what at a given instant and why, as you do now. Then you can begin to analyse and explain. Right, it's 12.20 now. Shut off and go down to the aerodrome and land."

7th of May

Orderly officer today. At nine a.m. we roll into the adjutant, booted and putteed, best tunic, breeches and cap. Hard collar and new leather gloves. Report, receive any special instructions and two typewritten pages of routine orders, and then off to lectures. We fit in the odd duties and carry on the normal working programme. It's a nuisance pulling on oily overalls and getting one's hands filthy decoking the Jaguar, but there it is. Orders is orders.

Mayor, by telephoning the Adjutant, Guardroom, and Exchange, takes over while I clamber painfully into a Crab and rudder her round the sky with my heavy boots for an hour. Still, it's a better life than that of the other two Services. In the Navy the officer of the watch has to spend ghastly hours on end with an ornamental telescope tucked under his arm, picking his way up and down a small steel deck littered with ropes, torpedo tubes and things, while the deck heaves about, the biting howling wind freezes his bones, and the green seas come washing and pounding inboard. Or else wandering up and down a deserted deck, gloomily surveying for hours on end an empty, littered, evening dockyard. In the army they stay subalterns and do orderly officer for donkeys' years, eight, ten, in some regiments even fifteen. Whereas after eighteen months as pilot officers and four years as flying officers, if we're good boys up we go to the giddy rank of flight lieutenant and get 'lightning conductors' down the sides of our mess kit pants. And you don't very often see a captain in the army aged twenty-six.

The orderly officer has to be an earnest young man. By Service writers he has been called the C.O.'s Representative for the Day.

The Fire Picket is his to direct and command if a sudden blaze breaks out. At 1000 hours he inspects and checks the Wireless Section cypher books. At 1100 hours, accompanied by a no less uncomfortably attired orderly sergeant, he does his rounds — barrack rooms, canteen, cookhouse and dining hall, guardroom, sergeants' mess, and gym. At 11.30 he watches the issue of rations to kitchens with a knowing eye. At 12.30 noses around the airmen's cookhouse again, looking for cooks not wearing white clothing, and calling for complaints when the men are served.

Things ease up in the afternoon, but after tea a weary pilgrimage commences. For nearly an hour he tramps on his boot-blistered feet around the camp and along the aerodrome, peering into deserted workshops at masses of stripped engines and tangled machinery-belting, trying doors and goggling up at windows to see they are all closed.

1800 hours finds him pacing the barrack square for Guard Mounting. The ensign is lowered to the trumpet call and the new guard marched off.

Next he checks the guardroom key-book and sets off with a heavy bunch of selected keys. With these he unlocks odd buildings to do a percentage check of main switches, ensuring that they have been pulled out. When he gets back to the guardroom again an awful doubt assails him that perhaps he did not relock that petrol pump-room door. Chance it? Better not. Back he tramps again, a quarter of a mile, to find that he did lock it after all.

Seven o'clock now. Time to bath and change for dinner. Just as he sinks into his bath with a weary sigh the duty waiter rushes up and knocks at the door.

"Sir, you're wanted on the telephone."

"Oh, God bless my soul. Couldn't you take the message?"

"Well, Sir, — I —"

"Did it sound important?"

"Sounded most important, Sir."

"Oh well, I'll come."

He clambers out and dries himself, cursing. Huddled in a bathrobe he flip-flops down the stairs and along the long corridor. Improperly dressed in public rooms. Well, the P.M.C. can say just whatever he likes. He crosses the hall to the telephone box.

"Hello. Orderly officer here."

"Guard commander here, Sir," comes a faint voice over the line. "All keys are now in."

The bath-robed bundle raises his eyes imploringly to the ceiling.

"Ye gods." And dragged from a bath to be told that. Too spent for further words, he slams the receiver on and crashes out into the hall again. To bump into the P.M.C. and an elderly colonel-looking guest. The P.M.C.'s eyebrows go up into the roots of his hair and he exercises liberally his prerogative of free speech.

Nearing 2100 hours he goes out into the evening to visit the two sentries, one at the guardroom gate and the other to be found on a roaming patrol among the hangars. On his way back he looks in at the canteen to see that Good Order is being maintained and cracks his usual feeble joke by asking odd airmen sitting about with pint glasses and pipes if the beer is as weak as usual.

2200 hours finds him at the guardroom again for Staff Parade. The Guard is reported present and correct, the Orderly Corporal reports all airmen present and correct, the Orderly Sergeant reports canteen closed and correct (have you ever heard of an incorrect canteen?). Then back to the ante-room, to while away another couple of hours over a can of beer and the evening papers.

After midnight the orderly officer rises again creakingly to his feet, blinks his cracking eyes, and, struggling into a great-coat, wanders forth again into the night. After signing the Guard Report, he gropes his way fearfully among the shadows along the sides of the hangar walls, tripping over ropes and odd oil tanks and junk left about. Finds the other sentry who reports all hangars present and correct. At 0030 hours he pulls off his thin, dew-drenched Wellington boots and struggles sleepily into bed. Within five short hours the member of the guard doing early calls will be rousing him again. Dismount guard on the parade square at 6.30. See airmen's breakfast at seven. Heigh ho. Well, it only comes once in a fortnight. And we'll soon be Squadron Leaders with no more Orderly Dog to do.

> When you're a Squadron Leader, my lad,
> You can do all the things that you're now told are bad.
> Come into the mess with no muffler on
> After your squash for a glass of lemon;
> At dinner demand Wheat-a-Vite with your fish,
> Eat mash with a fork *and* a knife if you wish;
> And no one will dare to imagine you're — you're gauche
> If you flavour-fla-flavour your soup
> With Anchovy Sauce...

Heigh ho, good-night.

8th of May

This life takes one back in many ways to the days when one first learned to fly. The routine is very similar. Lectures, instructional flying, and then more lectures. Life running very much to a printed programme, with a fair amount of bookwork chucked in. You never finish with books in the R.A.F. The flying training year is one hectic year of books. Cranwell cadets get another year tacked on. A year's breather, then you're at them again for your promotion exam to Flying Officer. Then, after a short spell, short-service officers have to get down to it for their 'specialisation' exam. This is no joke: umpteen subjects, with heat, light, sound, mechanics, electricity, etc., *ad nauseam*. After this comes more swotting for promotion to Flight Lieut. Papers on engines, rigging, stores procedure, army and navy co-operation, flight administration, airmanship and so on to get through.

By this time, if you've a permanent commission, away you go for real solid bookwork, to blossom forth as what K.R.s are pleased to call a specialist officer. If it's navigation you're selected for, a year of logarithms and nautical tables, spherical trig. and astronomical theorising is your misfortune. Engineering means two awful years of toil in workshops mixed with dusty reading. Armament and signals are the other two left. They all give you grey hairs. Next comes Staff College preparation. The best plan seems to be to take three months' leave, pay a crammer about fifty guineas, and go to live with him to get the necessary facts for the entrance exam stuffed into your skull.

Staff College, of course, is *all* bookwork. After this comes the exam for promotion to Squadron Leader. And if you like, you can study a language, too, as you climb the ladder of fame. In fact, if you're 'good on paper', slap to the top of the tree you're bound to go.

Don't think when you see us quaffing the casual, carefree half-can in the local hostelry, that we are carefree at all. Oh no. Even our dreams are hagridden with the thought of the next exam.

But it's not so bad when you're young and fresh from school. And the fairly rigid discipline to which an F.T.S. pupil is subjected doesn't seem to worry you very much. Compulsory P.T. and games, and off to bed by 10.30 all seem to go with a swing somehow, and life's good fun.

I have found tucked in the back of my first flying log-book a list of *Maxims for Pilots* I compiled in my young days. Some of them sound a bit pretentious now, but on the whole they contain much sound sense.

Experientia Docet I prefaced them!

1. Too much speed is better than too little.

2. When in doubt, open out.

3. If you get a stiff neck through looking round in the air, don't worry; it's a guarantee against becoming a stiff corpse.

4. A good pilot when travelling by train or car should subconsciously be seeing the passing country in the light of forced landing-ground.

5. Always take your hat off to your engine as you go by.

6. Always regard the other man as a fool. Then if he turns out to be one, you won't be surprised.

7. A steady, consistent pilot is of far more use than a brilliant, erratic one.

8. 'Honour thy Fitter and thy Rigger, that thy days may be long in the Kite that thy Flight Commander hath given thee' (Old R.A.F. Proverb).

9. 'The perfect pilot, like the lilies of the field, stalls not, neither does he spin' (C.F.S. Dinner Speech, 1931).

10. 'There would be very few accidents if the elementary rules of flying were rigidly observed and stupid risks avoided. The road hog, with whom we are all so familiar nowadays, has his counterpart in the air, so cultivate the sane mind in the sound and healthy body' (*Halton Magazine*, Summer 1931).

11. Never do a climbing turn off the deck unless you've got to.

12. Never hoodwink yourself on forced-landing practice. Would you have got down all right if your prop had been stopped?

13. Always look round, in front, behind and above, before taking off.

14. Never tell the crew to do a job on an aeroplane. Always go to the senior N.C.O.s first.

15. Don't mind the tarmac critics. The best pilots are bum at times. And the people who know the least about it are usually the most critical.

16. *Know thy petrol system.*

17. If you make a wizard landing you may bet your bottom dollar that nobody saw it. If you make a bad one, you may bet your life that the C.O. did.

18. When there's a high wind, come in with engine on, and make a wheel landing.

19. Don't howl along with stiff controls. Cruise.

20. Do everything in the air smoothly—one might almost say with a rhythm. Treat the machine as you would a lady.

21. The stalling speed in a turn goes *up*.

22. Tie the Verey pistol in before you loop; it costs 37s. 8d.

23. If you're carrying ballast, remember that you've got to land some time, and it's better to be tail heavy than nose heavy. If your machine is nose heavy, motor in on a flat glide.

24. If you bounce badly, people think far more highly of you if you go round again instead of continuing to bounce. It's better to break a good record than an aircraft.

25. Waggle your controls heartily before you take off. It isn't pleasant doing a circuit and a landing with a locked rudder. Test each magneto separately before you finally land. You're sure then that they're O.K. for the next trip.

26. When gliding in from an altitude, open up the engine occasionally—even in warm weather, when there is no likelihood of the carburettor freezing. It all helps to form a habit. At least one man has been known to kill himself—to say nothing of his crew—through flying high, coming in to land straight away, and having held off and stalled his aeroplane, suddenly finding that he has done so twenty feet up in the air instead of the customary couple of inches. And, on suddenly trying to give his engine a burst, drawn no response from a frozen carburettor.

Which brings us to the maxim that when descending from high altitudes one should also fly a level circuit of the aerodrome at about 1000 feet to accustom oneself again to proximity to the ground.

27. Always look behind before taking off. Also before doing a turn in the air. The machine you are flying isn't the only one in existence, neither are you the only fool. Make a habit of this, but not the habit that makes you screw your head round mechanically without seeing anything.

9th of May

We're going through this patter like a knife through butter these days. Straight and level flight, and then stalling, climbing, and gliding in a couple of days. The demonstration of straight and level flight is quite easy, just easing on a little gentle rudder as you talk and easing it off again. But stalling is a very different matter. You ease the nose further and further up until she stalls quite quickly, and you have to describe everything exactly as it happens. Had to go through it half a dozen times before I had first the patter right and then the synchronization. I suppose it's like learning anything new—it has to be done with conscious effort before it can be done with unconscious accuracy, grace and ease. One of my vividest memories of being taught to fly is the difficulty with which one learns to 'take off'. One sees the instructor do it with effortless ease perhaps a dozen times before one makes an attempt. One can feel the controls moving quickly a little way here and there as it happens. But the pilot doesn't think consciously of what he's doing. He checks things before they happen. And can talk to you

48

quite casually as he is doing it, the aeroplane hurtling along the ground in a straight line with the engine roaring away, and then soaring smoothly into the air. But wait until you try it! There are three things to manipulate simultaneously—throttle, rudder and control column. At first he only gives you the rudder to look after. "You keep her straight and I'll do the rest." You manage that reasonably well after a few attempts by concentrating furiously. The nose swings a bit to one side or the other before you can check it, and then too much the other way when you overcorrect. But it's not too bad. Then he tells you what to do with the control column.

"This time I'll look after the rudder and throttle, you do the rest. A little forward of central to begin with. Then central when the tail is up. Then back a little to leave the ground. Forward a little again to keep near the ground until we've got full flying speed. Then gently back and assume the Best Climbing Angle I've told you about. Righto, off we go."

Well, that's all right after four or five attempts. Once or twice you feel a gentle pressure when you attempt to stand on your nose or go up off the ground like a rocket, but otherwise you don't have much trouble.

But when you are in complete charge—throttle, stick and rudder—well, you feel you need six hands and two minds! She yaws all over the place. You invariably get the throttle about half open and then forget all about it because all your faculties are required to stop the antics of the aeroplane itself. Concentrate on keeping straight and you suddenly find with a rush of horror that you have forgotten all about the elevators, and the airscrew is trying to bite chunks out of the ground. Concentrate on elevators and ailerons, and you find you turn through about ninety degrees before you leave the ground. For crazy flying it just beats the band. And as for all three at once—of course that's patently ridiculous. It just can't be done.

The instructor is being devilishly unhelpful, too. He knows that as far as possible it's best to let the pupil do things himself. His feet and hands are always half an inch from the controls in case the pupil does do something rash, but on the whole the learner knows that whatever happens he is causing it himself. It's the same with landing. Let the pupil bounce, or glide into the ground. If you save him every time by a little gentle check to help him flatten out, or a burst of engine to soften the bounce, he'll never really know what it is to make a bad landing until he flies solo. The job is to recognise that fine hairline when he bounces so high that if you don't act quickly and take her over at once, she'll hit the ground hard enough to break the undercart. It's all a very absorbing game. But once you have made the aeroplane your servant and can always gently but very firmly coerce it to your will, there's no end to the enjoyment you get out of your mastery.

On the hall table in every R.A.F. mess you will see certain standard manuscript books. There are the Warning In and the Warning Out books. From them your movements, on temporary duty or on leave, are abstracted by the mess clerk to help the chef with his catering, and to compile the book of daily messing charges. But, what is far more interesting, bound in brown leather to match them, you will find the Suggestion Book. Any officer is at liberty to inscribe in it reasonable suggestions in regard to the general conduct or running of the mess. In a mess all ranks are equal, and the junior pilot officer has just the same privileges as the most senior Group Captain. Each can bag the best armchair by the fire, and each has one vote at mess meetings. Each can suggest any improvements he may desire through the medium of the Suggestion Book.
'May carrots be provided at lunchtime?'
'Tonight I had to wait ten minutes before being served. Could the waiters be organised?'
'Suggested that a new set of lights be provided in the squash court. Those in use are very dull.'
'May sausages be occasionally served at breakfast time?'
'May Half Corona cigars and Bootle's Lime Juice be stocked in the Dispense Room?'
'May the tennis net be repaired?'
No officer is allowed to give direct orders or make complaints to mess servants if things are not to his taste. He does it through the Suggestion Book. The mess secretary, usually one or other of the Flying Officers, inspects the book daily and writes his remarks on the opposite page, stating what action will be taken to comply with the suggestion, or giving a reason for not doing so. Then, with the Mess Committee (four other officers) he takes such action as he may think fit. Orders carrots, new electric light bulbs, sausages, cigars and lime juice, gingers up the waiters, and has a man in to mend the tennis net. And everything's happy and bright.

But the Suggestion Book is known in some circles as the Complaint Book instead. And it can make as good reading as anything you'll find in *Punch*. Most of those in use now go back to 1930 or 1931. Seek them out and you'll have one or two quiet chuckles to yourself.

Here are some from 70 Squadron's book:

'Suggested that something be done to improve the waiting at meals. Waiters should learn to anticipate officers' wishes...' T. O. Fairing, Fl.-Lieut.

'I hope this trouble will not occur in future. Actually one of the civilian waiters has been discharged today for slackness, *pour encourager les autres*.' Walter S. Spinner, Fl.-Lieut., Mess Sec.

'Ref. reply to suggestion on 28.8.30, may a French Dictionary be provided for the use of short service officers who have not been to college.' A. Loop, P.O.

'Encyclopaedia Britannica in French is being supplied to meet the requirements of Pilot Officer Loop.' Walter S. Spinner, Fl.-Lieut., Mess Sec.

'In the interests of economy it is suggested that ducks be bought whole instead of by the leg. Tonight at dinner fourteen officers out of sixteen at one table were served with legs.' (Signatures of fourteen officers.)

'Ducks are naturally bought whole with 2 legs, 2 wings and 1 breast. I have worked out that twice as many officers will get wings and legs as breasts. We will try to get some double-breasted ducks.' Walter S. Spinner, Fl.-Lieut., Mess Sec.

'A great night in an officers' mess should be an affair of considerable dignity until the wine has been passed and the royal toast given. Why then were the proceedings last Tuesday degraded by a performance given by a collection of wind and string instruments of the Squadron's Band and consisting entirely of dance tunes, without a single mitigating piece of music? This is not intended to portray a personal disapproval of jazz, but as a vehement protest against its rendering at such an inappropriate time. The question of whether or not the jazz was well played does not enter into the matter. The rendering of any jazz before the King's Health has been drunk is a gross breach of mess etiquette, and it is requested that steps may be taken to ensure that it does not happen again.' A. Bowfort-Scale, F.O.

This time no mere mess secretary's remark meets the case.

'I have seen this Officer,' writes the C.O. And signs himself with grim majesty, Christian names and all.

After which comes this:

'Suggested it would be better if such complaints were conveyed personally to the P.M.C. than placed in a book for all to see.' T. D. C., Squadron Leader.

'This suggestion is most helpful and is much appreciated.' O. Fullbore, W.-Comdr., P.M.C.

Not content with this example of how things should *not* be done, another youth sails in up to his neck.

'On three occasions during the past week food has been served to me containing dead, and presumably cooked, flies. This form of obnoxious uncleanliness is to be strongly deplored in an officers' mess.' W. Bounce, P.O.

'This is a book for suggestions, helpful and constructive if you please. Not a vehicle for ill-placed criticism couched in offensive terms. The mess committee objects very much to the last sentence, especially from one of the most junior members of the mess. Para. 1 is noted.' Walter S. Spinner, Fl.-Lieut.

Fancy coming back four years later as a senior F.O. and seeing this regrettable *faux pas* which you have publicly committed and for which you have been publicly chastised, still in the book for all to read and see!

At one period 51 Squadron struck a very happy note in their mess member - mess secretary relations.

'Suggested that the police be notified that there is no intention of exhibitionism on the part of officers in mess.

'Since the curtains, blinds and whatnot have been removed from our quarters for cleaning, it follows that our hindquarters are visible to the 47,000 cyclists and pedestrians who pass daily from X to Y and return on the main road.

'The resultant Air Force Display is no fault of the actors in the play.' (Signed ten F.O.s)

'This is not a matter for the mess committee, but rather for the officers feeling guilty of exhibitionism.' B. Tankard, Fl.-Lieut., Mess Sec.

'Suggested that every time an officer's dog enters Church during Service, and brings tennis balls to the preacher during the sermon, that officer be invited by the mess to contribute financially to the collection in coin of the realm. (The value of the old tennis balls being nugatory.) If, however, a small metal collecting-box were attached to the dog and he functioned during the collection, it would be a graceful and absorbing gesture on his part.' J. Hassock, Chaplain.

'Although entirely in sympathy with the suggestion, I fear that the question of exclusion of animals from divine service and the imposition of penalties for their non-exclusion is beyond the temporal powers of the mess committee.' B. Tankard, Fl.-Lieut.

'Suggested that a supply of toothpicks be obtained for the Dispense Room. The consumption of onions, olives and cherries with short drinks without these very necessary articles is very difficult.' William J. Throttle, F.O.

'A visit to the Dental Officer would appear to meet the case.' B. Tankard, Fl.-Lieut.

'While I have no objection to using the implements of my trade for removing onions and other foreign bodies from gin, toothpicks would be just as efficacious.' C. Forcep, P.O., Dental Officer.

'It is not customary for toothpicks to be stocked in the bars of officers' messes and I do not intend to create a precedent now.' Arthur W. Thunder, S.-Ldr., P.M.C.

'With a view to making the mess a little more comfortable for bachelors, will the mess committee endeavour to get Mess Rule No. 30 (Dining In Rule) altered? Nobody in his senses who has changed into flannels on Wednesday, Saturday or Sunday afternoon is going to change again into a boiled shirt for the privilege of eating a meal he can buy in the village inn for one shilling.'

'This order,' writes the mess secretary with disarming simplicity, 'happens to have been initiated by the Air Officer Commanding, Air Vice-Marshal Sir Victor Vector-Error, C.M.G., C.B., D.F.C., A.F.C.'

And then the awful voice of authority speaks. 'I strongly object to the wording of this suggestion. This officer will report to me at 0930 hours today.' B. E. Nacelle, Group Captain, Officer Commanding 51 (Pursuit) Squadron.

Nothing daunted, a few weeks later a fresh wit gives his fancy rein:

'In view of the increasing inefficiency of the means of communication between the ante-room and the bar (as the Bureau Vox and electric bell have died the death) could one of the following methods be adopted:

[N.B. — None of these are subject to mechanical breakdown.]

'(a) A large fire bell of the handclapper variety be suspended in the ante-room.

'(b) A noisy Klaxon horn to awaken hibernating pages.

'(c) A voice pipe similar to those used in ships — plus an engine-room telegraph with a tell-tale in the bar. The readings *Full Speed Ahead, Slow Astern* and *Stop* being amended to read *Beer, Whisky,* and *For Heaven's sake put a jerk into it.*' (Signed) B. T. H. Magneto, F.O.

'I disagree. This book is not provided for officers to air their sense of human (*sic*).' B. Tankard, Fl.-Lieut.

And finally this:

'Suggest that elastic bands be kept in the bar to keep one's head in place after guest night.' C. Chock, F.O.

'They are obtainable in the local town. Officers should purchase their own when getting flying speed there prior to dinner.' B. Tankard, Fl.-Lieut.

12th of May

Lord's Day, as old Sam Pepys loved to write. I've always found history full of colour, and it was in this spirit, in search of history, that I set off after breakfast for the village church in which I found that war memorial the other day. A church, as with so many others, that has been the centre of the village life since the Normans built it eight hundred years ago.

Go to the church, and you place your finger on to the very pulse of the country people's life. As small boys, they constitute the choir. In youth they covertly eye their brides-to-be across the pews during the vicar's sermon. Before this altar they are wed. At this ancient Saxon stone font their offspring are baptised in the fullness of time.

Week after week for fifty and sixty years they worship in their simple way under the blackening oak of those graceful roof rafters. Resting from the labours of the week, never questioning the articles of their faith. And so generations carry on the traditions of generations gone by. And by sitting with them today you are in a sense in contact with their sires who heard rumour of Drake's voyagings, who were ploughing the land when the Mermaid crew were slapping the table for another draught of sack and drawing forth crumpled play manuscripts from the folds of their cloaks. You may still hold the bright, guttering torch of human thought and endeavour and dreams in your hand.

Rolling along the road in front of me was a short, broad-beamed old man in a spaciously cut Sunday suit of sober grey worsted. He must have guided the plough over uneven furrows for a good forty years.

I caught up with him on the flagged path leading to the church doorway. We were early, and fell into conversation. And as we talked, faded and rain-smudged notices fluttered on the porchway board. *Election of a Representative for the Wittering, Barnack and Ufford Rural Council. Payment of Tithes. The Adoption of Armorial Bearings. The Firearms Act. Close Season for Blackcock, Partridge and Grouse.* So the titles ran.

He had grey eyes, and a fine and deeply creased cross-work of humour lines on his cheeks. His side whiskers were white, his silvery hair cropped close, his neck bulging in generous folds over the back of his collar. His shining black boots were broad of toe and stout of sole; across his barrel waistcoat lay a heavy cable of dully polished pinchbeck watchchain; and in his buttonhole was stuck a whole bouquet of carnations and dewy fern, the stems wrapped and wired in silver foil.

"No, sir, bain't no village pub," he informed me.

"But this is most extraordinary. I thought every village had its inn."

"No, sir. The lord of the manor don't approve, so no village pub it's got to be."

"Then whatever do you do when you want a drink? Surely Ufford is three miles away."

His rosy-weathered cheeks crinkled into a grin, and he laid a stubby forefinger along his nose.

"Well, as a matter of fack, I 'appens to know the sergeant-major up at the Camp."

No 'Warrant Officer' for him!

"Good friend o' mine, 'un is. And when I wants a pint then up to the canteen 'e invites me, and a pint it is."

By now the villagers were beginning to arrive in their decent Sunday best, and he had to depart to go about his ecclesiastical duties with slow and important dignity. Churchwarden, sidesman and sexton, all three by casual employ was the hale old man. A big single bell in the little tower began to toll, and past my seat against the wall just inside the door the congregation came filing in. Cottage housewives in their coats and skirts of heavy, amorphous black, high-collared blouses and curious dark hats shaped like deep inverted pudding basins and fixed to their twisted buns of hair with long pins. The old labourers, thin and bent, sturdy and stout, or young and upright of bearing, all in rough dark suits and hard white collars, holding in their toil-thickened hands carefully brushed hats, kept during the week wrapped in tissue paper on top of the cupboard. The younger men are perhaps a little more fashionably dressed than they would have been in the past. Here and there you see one making an attempt to copy milord with a fifty-shilling lounge suit, very tastefully cut, and a striped college tie (amber and silver, or red and green) that he bought last market day from a booth in Stamford Square. The girls, too, are colourful in their attire; Marks and Spencer sell frocks of flowered chiffon at three and eleven the time. And even if the sheen of their silk stockings is suspiciously bright, and the gloss of their patent leather shoes too good to be true, are not they more attractively shod than their grandmothers in youth, when for the poor all else but thick woollen hose and coarse leather boots were unknown?

The whispering dies away. The church bell has quickened and, with a final slowing down, ceased its tolling altogether. With a rustling expectancy we are ready. From the vestry comes a short intoned prayer and, in piping chorus, Amen. The small organ softly begins to play a vaguely sacred rambling processional and from behind six small boys file into the aisle, their hands folded in front of their white surplices, their eyes cast down in beatific solemnity. Towering over them follow a bushy-moustached bass and two frail tenors, one with gold-rimmed glasses perched on his hawk nose. And last of all the squat old priest, bent with all his years in the service of God, his Cambridge hood hanging behind his shoulders, his kindly lips pursed in meditation of the worship now begun.

He announces the first hymn, and with a cracking of the little book covers we find our page and, led by the organ, begin to sing. High voices and low, cracked and clear, hoarse and treble sweet.

Outside the same white clouds drift softly down the blue. Those are the same, high rolling woods. The sheep crop quietly still in the same smooth pastures under the leeward wall. And as of old the sun makes his stealing passage across the rounded pillars of the little nave.

The service proceeds. *Venite* is minted clear with the phrases that Sidney and Buckingham used. And slowly you drift back along the paths of your will.

Sunday afternoons in R.A.F. messes can be long, somnolent affairs. After lunch you get your legs up with a book in the long settee and the sunshine warmth under an open window. Until gradually your eyes smart and your senses gently buzz. The pipe goes out and is forgotten, the book drops by imperceptible degrees. And before you know where you are you suddenly hear with a start the chime of the clock striking four. And the duty waiter has come in to tidy up the papers and announce teatime.

Esterhazy and I were determined to resist this manfully, and to get away from the mess, too, which we haven't left all the week, so we set out to walk to The George in Stamford for tea.

Esterhazy, of course, isn't his real name. But it fits very well. He was the tall chap with the pipe and nice hands we met in the passage outside the Old Man's office on the second day. He's the perfect aristocrat, from his signet ring to the brushed ends of his cavalry moustache. A gentle aristocrat, punctilious to the point of amusement where the duties of servants are concerned. I get a lot of quiet fun out of him, and in a curious way I believe he enjoys my sense of humour, too. In mess kit he looks for all the world like a secretary bird; or sometimes, when his long legs are jutting from an armchair, like an attenuated praying mantis — I can never decide which.

I made him curb his impatience and slow down those long legs, and we walked amicably enough down the two miles of Great North Road along the grassy bank, under the chestnuts overhanging the long wall of Lord Burghley's estate, into Stamford town.

A little, grey stone Northern town on the banks of a sedged river, which it spans with an ancient arch. A town for antiquaries. At high noon it is gay and busy enough with shops and people, but after nine at night it mysteriously goes to sleep. Your footfalls echo in the streets off the old walls, there is that drifting, dampish smell you get in old castles and dungeons; and on bleak late autumn nights, when the wind moans round the deserted corners, the ghosts come out. The Normans built it; some of their old walls still stand. And history through the ages is still written large across its palm. The George itself started life as a medieval monastery, and you can still see the walled-in monks' garden behind. Here, through the door in this crumbling wall draped with wistaria, Charles I escaped one night on his last flight from justice.

One sprawling old coaching inn records the fact that bull-baiting in the streets was once the favourite half-holiday sport of the Stamford people. The five churches in the middle of the town, slap on the edge of the winding North Road, are full of tombs of middle-age knights and merchants interred under their blazoned coats-of-arms. The graveyard slabs have weathered Latin inscriptions on them and skull and crossbone devices above. Every house in the place has old worm-eaten timber beams supporting its bulging plaster. And this one records on a tablet just above eye-level that at one time, as a theatre, it had seen the great days of Garrick, Kemble, and Mrs. Siddons, all of whom had acted within. Stamford still lags twenty years behind; for if you go into the courtyard of its old almshouses—in the seventeenth century a hospital for the sick poor—and then turn past its stone-flagged pump, pasted on the wall under the archway you will see a perfectly good notice headed, in large black printing, 'Precautions to be taken during AIR RAIDS' and signed and dated by the Town Clerk in 1915. Sheltered from wind and weather, it is still untorn or smudged after all these years.

But this was no afternoon for ghosts. Golden sunshine lay along the walls, and the blue of the sky moved reflected in the dimpled river. We found a low seat by the window in The George and ordered China tea. Outside in the garden the bees droned from one flower calyx to the next in sudden booming content.

"Why is it," asked Esterhazy, "that I never have a bean?" He began to stuff tobacco from a worn pouch into a pipe the bowl of which looked like a caried tooth, and regarded the dusty shoes on his outstretched feet as though he expected them to answer.

"You have such whacking great mess bills, old boy," I said amiably.

"You're right. Fifteen pounds last month. But how to cut it down? There's not an item of expenditure that isn't necessary."

"The secret of happiness, if I may say so, is either to adapt the environment to yourself or else adapt yourself to the environment. The former process comes more naturally to the male; but if your bank balance won't allow it, then you must adopt the more feminine course and fall into line with things as they are and not as they might be."

"Come again? You talk in riddles, I'm afraid."

"Well, Mr. Micawber put it in a fairly straightforward way. Liabilities nineteen and sixpence, assets one pound. Result, happiness. Liabilities one pound, assets nineteen and six. Result — misery. In other words, you can't live beyond your pay."

"But how to do it? That's what baffles me."

"Well, the last time I went to London with you, you spent roughly a pound that you might quite easily have kept."

"Never."

"We had a taxi to Peterborough. Three of us, five bob each."

"Well, you *can't* go by bus with the *hoi polloi*."

"Next you wouldn't dream of carrying one small leather bag. Porter sixpence."

"I never have carried my luggage."

"You bought the *Strand Magazine* and then left it in the train. Another shilling down the drain. An evening paper with a crossword would have amused you just as well."

"I always buy the *Strand*."

"Porter at King's Cross, sixpence. Oh, and two beers in the restaurant car on the way down. One and fourpence, threepence tip."

"I hate train journeys. I must do something to help pass the time."

"And then a taxi to Waterloo. Another four and sixpence up the spout. It would have cost you threepence by Tube."

"I do not see your point of view, so we cannot argue."

I smiled the good-humoured smile I always reserve for the occasions when Esterhazy is being rich.

"As you like. Let's go back to these mess bills then. What was your wine bill?"

"Just on four quid."

"Mine, old horse, was eight shillings, and I had a half can whenever the fancy moved me. But if you must forever be filled with 'the old familiar juice', then what else would you?"

"I pride myself on being an extremely moderate drinker."

"I heartily agree. And I agree with you also in your taste for a glass of good wine with your evening meal. But you must remember that you can't live like a landed peer on a pound a day. You take, if I remember, a glass of sherry before dinner, another glass of sherry with your soup, a whisky and soda after the fish, and a bumper of number one port in which to toast His Majesty."

"But, my dear fellow, you can't drink the King's health in water."

"In his Regulations and Air Council Instructions he would seem to permit it. And besides, what's that got to do with the two glasses of sherry and the whisky and soda that go before?"

"Nothing. But a little wine aids the digestion considerably, and adds in no small measure to one's enjoyment of the meal."

I passed on placidly to the next item in his monthly bill.

"You smoke Barney's pipe tobacco at one and tuppence-ha'penny the ounce. And Balkan Sobranies at heaven alone knows how much the hundred."

"Call it eight shillings."

"As you wish. Now I never debase my pipe palate with cigarettes. And I can recommend to you an excellent brand of tobacco, a cut cake at elevenpence the ounce tin. Cool, mellow, fragrant—"

"Nothing under one-and-two is worth touching."

"All right. Telephones and telegrams are the next item on which I wish to censure you. You write a letter to your fiancée arranging a date. *Then* you follow it up with a whole battery of telegrams and trunk calls to make sure she's understood. Why? Don't you trust the G.P.O., or is your handwriting too bad to be read?"

"Neither. But I must speak to my darling at least once a day."

Esterhazy pretty well monopolises the telephone booth during off-duty hours. In the middle of dinner the call bell will ring. He drops his knife and fork.

"That sounds like a long-distance call."

His napkin falls to the floor; he rushes up to the President and is excused.

Twenty minutes later when we pass through the hall to the ante-room armchairs Esterhazy can be still dimly seen through the glass plate of the call box. His lips move. Both hands are clasped round the receiver in ecstasy. He comes out eventually nearly on his knees with rapture.

"Whatever *do* you find to say?" I once asked.

"Old boy, you'd be surprised."

And meanwhile the telephone operator is pencilling '6s. F.O. Esterhazy, Bournemouth 0003' in his little account book.

"Well, and what other expenses were there to swell the total up to this magnificent amount?"

"Entertaining, two pounds ten."

"What entertaining? I didn't know you'd given a mess dance."

"I had my fiancée to dinner last week in the Ladies' Room."

"*Dinner*? You must have had a lot to drink."

"One glass of sherry each. And a half bottle of Sauterne."

"Then where the other two pounds?"

What came next was an entirely fresh angle on Esterhazy to me.

"I wouldn't dream of offering a guest the standard mess dinner."

This costs the host three shillings. His own dinner is free, just as though he had it *ad baccalaurium* in mess.

"Why ever not? I may not be critical, but it seems quite passable to me."

"I always order flowers from Covent Garden. I *always* have clear soup. *Always* lobster or whitebait. *Always* bird. *Always* asparagus. And *always* fresh mushrooms for savoury."

"Always?"

"Always."

"In season or out?"

"In season or out."

"And I suppose an eastern potentate to serve it and a damned great cigar to follow. I wonder how you get away with only fifteen pounds. How many lumps. Six?"

I hand him his tea.

For the last two days we've been doing some patter that needs thinking about. Taking off into wind, and landing. You have to describe what's happening exactly as it does happen, not a second sooner or later. So that when there's a strong gusty wind you're already *in* the air while you're still rambling on about easing the control column a little forward to get the tail *into* the air. It all happens in a blinding, wind-blown rush, and you've got to talk about two hundred words.

It looks rather silly, when you're about fifty feet high and climbing so strongly that it's like going up in a lift, to be gabbling "...the aeroplane will leave the ground of its own accord. Then ease the control column forward a little until you have gained full flying speed...!"

Mayor and I went round for nearly an hour yesterday doing it time after time, the bit about leaving the ground and flattening out to gain speed when your airspeed is showing about sixty. Mine showed about eighty each time. And we were going like a single-seater fighter at the trees. One improves gradually with practice! When you get into the air, you have to be very crafty. For the next bit of patter goes "...you ease the control column gently back to assume the best climbing angle. Now the idea of this is to give you as much height as possible so that should your engine fail you will be able to effect a good forced landing. If the engine does fail" — and here you close the throttle, damn nearly stall at once, and ram the stick well forward to get up bags of speed — "ease the control column well forward to prevent the aeroplane from stalling." In which attitude there's a lot of green fields and trees and sheep and things coming up towards you from not very far away, and the wind making a pretty hefty song in the wires. Now all along the idea is to instil confidence into the pupil, and it's not much use doing this sort of thing if, when you've closed the throttle and rammed the nose down, you find that the only place in which you can land is on the top of trees or on a fence, a hedge and six sheep. The dodge is to spin out the first bit of patter as long as possible and climb as hard as you can, and at the same time deciding where you're going to choose for a landing. Then, when you think you can get in nicely, come to the bit about 'if the engine does fail' and throttle back.

Of course, the instructor does it with such artless ease each time that it looks too simple to worry about, and when you do it, five times out of six you find yourself undershooting to hell with nothing for it but a spectacular crash into the trees, or floating over the end of the field you chose, doing about 90 instead of your gliding 70, heading straight for the Squire's house and nowhere safe to turn. You mutter curses down the mouthpiece, thank God for a reliable engine, and slam it on again. Of course, you never land. Just say in a smug, satisfied voice, "*There* we are. Now we'd get down quite nicely in this field," and then open up and begin climbing again. "When you have your C.F.I.'s test at the end of the course," the instructor remarks blandly down the telephone, "he'll keep his hand on the throttle, so that when you go to open it up again, you'll find that you can't and then you'll *have* to land." You wouldn't believe how difficult it is to choose a field when there aren't many of them. Climbing with the nose towering up above you there's a terrific blind spot blotting out everything ahead. And it's surprising how much height you do lose before you regain gliding speed.

Then the landings. It all begins very nicely. "I'm now going to show you how to make a landing on the aerodrome." You float round at a thousand feet and run over the things he should look for as he does his circuit prior to landing. Then you shift your body in the straps to get a better look-out and begin to sweat and concentrate. When you're first teaching landings you don't teach the pupil to do gliding turns at all. He has to be to leeward of the aerodrome flying along into wind and at it. Then, when he thinks he's got near enough to it to do a straight glide in and land, he throttles back. Which is a damned sight harder really than gliding in across wind with a good view and then turning in fairly low.

Well, you manoeuvre in accordance with instructions until you're well to leeward and flying at the aerodrome upwind. You can't see a damned thing. The aerodrome is under the engine somewhere. About fifty aeroplanes under your wing and fuselage blind spots, which are enormous, are doing incalculable things too. You throttle back when you think you'll get in on a glide at a nice steady seventy; and are either still gliding over the far boundary when it's time to start talking about landing—the whole aerodrome having drifted past below while you were still about 200 feet up desperately gliding in—or else you are miserably easing up the nose and trying to 'make it' by snootering over the hedge half a mile ahead of you by hanging on the 'slots'. No sticking on a little discreet engine and doing an imperceptible 'rumble' when there's an A1 instructor in the back! However, after a couple of goes you get a rough idea. You continue to chat away as you're gliding in, about gliding and looking for other aeroplanes, at the windsock and so on and whatever gratuitous advice you can think of while you're losing height. And then the difficult stuff comes. From the time you begin talking until you finish takes about fifteen seconds. And in that time you've to land an aeroplane nicely and tell the pupil what you are doing to effect this miracle. Now landing itself requires concentration. But try synchronising strange patter with it and you'll know. Someone had defined it as 'a tricky business in which you transfer an airplane from one medium to another at a high rate of speed. It's about as easy as taking a girl from a ballroom into the garden and bringing her back without having mussed her hair.' So now you *know*.

It all begins about twenty feet up. "When you're about twenty feet up and the ground begins to rush towards you, begin to flatten your glide by easing the control column slightly back, until the aeroplane is parallel to the ground and about a foot from it." (Deep breath.) "Then keep it at this distance from the ground by continuing to ease the control column back as the speed gradually falls off. Until finally the aeroplane will stall and sink gently to the ground on wheels and tailskid at the same time." Anything happens but what you've said. The wheels bounce on to the ground instead of 'sinking gently', and you balloon into the air again. Or else when you say "the speed gradually falls off" you find that you're still doing about 100 knots and for certain going to run into the far hedge. At which juncture you murmur pained apologies into the back cockpit and roar off again. But usually you land well and truly tail-skid down while you're still talking about "one foot from the ground", and are still explaining how you are busy doing your demonstration landing when the aeroplane's stopped running altogether. One dodge you have to resort to is to stick the nose down a bit and get up excessive speed just before you flatten out to land. That gives you more time to lose speed before she stalls, and so get your patter done.

There's only one place to learn landing. And that's at the R.A.F. Flying School in Egypt. Miles and miles and miles of flat, hard desert. It doesn't matter if you undershoot a mile or overshoot one—you're on the aerodrome just the same. Not good flying practice, I know. But nice for learning. True, you're encouraged to choose a patch of camelthorn and try to touch down a foot from it. But in practice you look round for bits of camelthorn when you touch down, and then kid yourself that it's *just* where you meant to put her down. Yes, Egypt's all right. You do practically all your flying between 0500 and 0800 hours each day, and eat your breakfast when you've done. Some fellows fly with pyjamas under their overalls... but that's another tale.

Air as warm as milk and as smooth as silk. Nice steady breeze not varying 0.1 of a mile an hour. Not a bump if you searched for one down to the Sudan. And a horizon as clear cut as if someone had painted it against the blue with an ochre brush.

England gives you a misty horizon, and vegetation, trees and hills that create all sorts of mad swirls and eddies and soaring currents to give you those damn-nearly-turn-you-turtle bumps. So that when you're holding off to land and swooping along a foot from the ground you are suddenly lifted up to about six feet without a tremor of elevator movement on your own part.

Cowling and I cracked off to share the aeroplane for the usual one and a half hours in the afternoon. We went round time after time, doing the patter for taking off and then circuits and landings each time, rocketing and bumping down the stairways of troubled air and then bawling ourselves hoarse into the mouthpiece as we contrived to land, and remember or frantically invent suitable patter to describe what we did. We overshot and roared off over the hedge again, abandoning all talk of landing as we saw the bushes breezing towards us and we urged open that throttle again; undershot and shamelessly eased on 1000 revs. to help her in. And put her down out of wind twice with a wing tucked down to correct for drift. I tell you, we did some hectic things! And in the end a young blizzard of snow and hail swept in from a low, drifting bank of cloud. Everyone shot in from nowhere. Crabs, Tutors, Bulldogs, Harts, a score or more all going round at different heights on the left-hand circuit and gliding in like a gala day, each anxious to get out of the blinding stuff as quickly as he could. All yammering away as like as not, to get the last bit of practice patter in. We all got down somehow with no one landing on or floating into anyone else. We learn by degrees, we learn!

The snow was too much altogether for Abdulla, the Oriental pilot. In May in his country the mercury has been at 100° for a month past, and they won't see another cloud until the end of October comes.

14th of May

Up today in the old Crab again. Pretty gusty weather, all blue sky and white clouds rolling down it. And April back again for a day, roaring like any sucking dove. Now Crabs, as we have observed before, tip a wing like lightning if you land 'em with more than one degree of drift.

I remarked to an airman as they wheeled her out: "Bit windy for Avros, isn't it?"

He regarded her stretched silver fabric and rakish stagger and flat yellow struts for a moment as he ruminated.

"Well, sir, it is. Usually we don't have 'em out at all when it's blowing like this. But it's like this. These are the last two of the old Avros left in the flight. All the rest's nice new Tutors, as you know. So if any of you could manage to—well, *oblige* us, we'd be very pleased." And he gave us a meaning look.

Well, we strapped ourselves into the old framework again, feet on the two aluminium-covered slats, knees up, policeman's truncheon-pudding spoon in one fist, and the primitive array of dials down by our shoes.

The old Lynx gave her revs. and we rose straight off the ground into the air like a lift with the stiff wind. Then up went the nose to a fantastic angle and we lay on our backs while she plugged up at her best climbing angle.

They really are marvellous training aeroplanes. Modern machines are so often hair-trigger on controls that you can practically loop and roll 'em with imperceptible movements of rudder and stick. The old Avro has plenty of backlash in her joints. If you want to do a slight bank you stick the control column over an amount the pupil can feel and she does a slight bank. You don't have to convince him against his will that you have moved it. For demonstrating aileron drag she's beautiful. Slam the stick over hard and up goes the nose like a lift. No cheating with a little crafty top rudder to make what you say happen, as with so many of them. Then, after a run through what are by now our old friends, stalling, climbing and gliding, and further effect of controls, we passed lightly on to something fresh.

We started the demonstration of and patter for turns. Cockpit full of draughts and icy cold, and hellish bumpy this cloud chasing along the bright blue. Stick and rudder always on the move to wrench a wing up or ease her nose down as we rocketed and jolted and roared through the shifting and dropping fierce, bumping currents of invisible air. Now turns are funny things. When you learn to fly, if you're attentive, you pick up bits of vague theory about them in lectures, take the instructor's word for a lot of stuff in the air and forget it; and gradually, by seeing what she'll do when you do different things, you get turns weighed off.

At first you have to watch the nose and wings and airspeed anxiously to make her turn decently at all. And think out each bit as you do it. But before long you can slam her into a steep turn and go round the clock with the 'slip' needle dead central and rate of turn showing as easily as you please, looking down at a target 6000 feet below for the bomb bursts or for anything in the sky. But what are the things you really do unconsciously? Apply bank and rudder in the same direction; then ease off bank; then put on a little top rudder; then ease on elevators; each in turn, nursing her the whole time to create and perfect and maintain the turn. The more she banks the more rudder changes over to elevators and vice versa. But analyse it. There are three types of turn. In each there are three stages. In each there are innumerable faults. And each has to be gone into, maintained, and come out of. The instructor runs through the whole lot with artless ease. What he describes happens. But you try it; you get foxed; as you're chatting about a medium turn, she gradually goes into a steep one. You give wrong explanations and find yourself looking at the controls and waggling them about like an old spinster trying to untangle her knitting; you've been doing turns for five years, and now can't tell what you do and why you do it unless you sit down in a quiet room with a licked pencil, a pad of notepaper and a furrowed brow. Not in the air bumps and engine roar at 4000 anyway.

The instructor has the grace to laugh cheerily at one's rueful apologies. He'd have been a very surprised man if one had produced any very clear ideas on the subject at all.

A hard day, my masters. We've earned our pay. 0800-0830 hours, Air Navigation Lecture. 0845-1000 doing landing patter in a Crab. Then we clambered up to 2000.

"Now we're going on to elementary forced landings. To do them decently is much harder than to do a so-called advanced forced landing. But you've got to show a pupil the ideal one, and then by the time he's ready for solo at least he'd be able to make a fair attempt at parking safely, if his motor did pack up. Sideslipping is too hard for him before about ten hours' solo, so it can't be used. Right. Now when you're going to demonstrate to him, get somewhere to the leeward of a decent field, and begin like this. 'Cross-country flights are executed normally at a height of two thousand feet, so that should the engine fail you will have plenty of time in which to effect a safe landing. Should the engine fail' " — and here he throttles back and rams down the nose — " 'ease the control column well forward and assume your best gliding angle. Then select a suitable field in which to land and glide to the leeward side of it. I'll choose that field down there with the white cross in it.' "

By arrangement with local farmers, the Air Ministry hires fields in pairs for forced landing practice. The farmer grazes sheep in them alternately, and puts out a white diagonal cross in the corner of the other to show it's all clear for landing.

We glide to the leeward side.

" 'Now lose height by a series of S turns. Never turn your back on the field. Don't do the turns too close to it, or too far away. Finally, at about five hundred feet, do your last turn in and land well up the field in the usual way.' "

By now Mayor has done his S turns, skimmed over the hedge at a hundred feet, and is holding off to land into wind well in the middle of the field. Finally the dual stick comes back into my tummy. The song of the wires dies away to a hush. We ground gently from six inches high and rumble slowly to rest.

" 'Land well up the field, because it's far better to run a risk of trickling gently into the far hedge than it is to undershoot and to stall into the leeward hedge through holding up the nose in an endeavour to get in.' And then, of course, the usual business about his not being allowed to take off again, but to get into touch with the C.O. and wait for his instructor to come and remedy the defect and fly the aircraft out again. Right, you've got her. Taxy round, and then go off and give me what you can remember of it."

We do surprisingly well. One of our brighter days. And S turns are not easy to do well if you've got to talk too. Constant airspeed, even, gently sweeping turns from side to side, and finally no sideslip to rip off any surplus height, but an accurate last turn in and a landing within ten yards up or down the field.

Mayor is doing us proud. The average fellow learning patter concentrates like hell when new stuff is coming down the telephones, and directly he gets down scribbles with a pencil what he can remember of it into a dog-eared notebook he keeps in the knee pocket of his sidcot suit. Means to swot it up the same night, but of course never does: then frantically cons it five minutes before going into the air the next day, mumbling bits of it to himself as he does up the straps. The instructors, of course, remember every single word of it by heart. They probably babble bits of it in their sleep at times. Mayor has taken to typing out each new section in his spare time, and handing Cowling and me a copy each every day. It's in his exact words, just as he tells it to us and expects us to learn it, and already it's in great demand from other chaps along the corridor.

We have a mess garden now of which we are justly proud. In front of the mess, a sweeping pebbly drive. And beyond that a lovely garden now blowing with tulips. In between those are planted rose bushes, and when the tulips fall, the roses, saffron and crimson, pink and white, will bloom; so that we are never without flowers from spring until the late autumn months. The paths are flagged, and arched over with a rambler-twined trellis. In the middle lies a sunken pool stocked with fat goldfish, and a fountain in the middle to amuse them. On sunny weekend afternoons we have deck chairs dragged out there, and slit-eyed against the brightness, smoke and read our library books. Directly you stand on the pool rim the goldfish all swim up to the point in a flotilla, expecting to be fed. A couple of gardeners are always pottering and pruning. I have never seen them do anything else; but they always seem to keep the place in beautiful trim. And in the centre of the garden, at the far end, stands an old stone garden table at the top of a flight of steps cut into the bank. The table bears on its top the school crest, an heraldic swan standing with arched neck and wings half-unfurled on a turret; and below it a brass plate saying that one of our Wing Commander doctors planned and laid out this lovely plot. I came here once before some years ago, and then it was nothing but a grassy field.

From my upstairs window I can now see the dovecotes over by the far rockeries, a blending of colours like daubs on a painter's palette. The doves gurgle and coo and sweep among the bushes for insects and grass-scattered grain. Beyond lies a brown ploughed field, a sturdy horse and labourer following a fresh-turned furrow in the warm glow of the late afternoon sun. And behind, all the red, ancient roofs of the cottages and farm and rectory of Wittering. Below, the tulips, above a flawless blue sky.

This part of the world is famous for its tulips. The fields near Spalding are called Little Holland, and nearly everyone in the mess has been over by car to see them during the last couple of weeks. Even in the market place of Stamford they advertise evening charabanc trips to see their loveliness. We flew over to see them from the air the other day, but you miss most of the beauty from a height and at speed. You must linger, as you must also among the golden autumn woods here.

I met Tucker in the ante-room after tea. He was over from 37 Squadron on some job or other, staying until the morning. I haven't seen him for upwards of a year, but we were in the same flight in Iraq for two years, and besides doing some jobs of work together, played a lot of tennis and many games of squash.

Indeed, his first remark before we bought each other a half-can was, "How's the tennis now?" Queer people, Englishmen. First one buys the other a drink and feels fine — virtuous glow running all over him — bonhomous, spendthrift, carefree — in fact the soul of convivial hospitality. Mentally slaps himself on the back and drinks his own down. Then the other fellow buys him one and has all the same feelings himself. And then they go their separate ways, both feeling fine. And all they've done is to buy themselves a pint of draught beer each in two halves. It's a queer world. But if we have at least discovered — can a moral glow be accounted anything? — how to get something for nothing, perhaps it isn't such an inconsiderable achievement after all.

But that's got nothing to do with the tale. We rambled about tennis a bit. Then he said did I remember Brookie, and Shanks, and John, and half a dozen more. Some I did and some I didn't — and he rambled again... where he'd met them last — mostly in a place

70

called the 'Brasserie' in London, it seemed. And then he suddenly switched over to a new show he'd seen in town, and we talked about shows for the rest of the half-hour until he finally announced, "Well, must write some letters now; cheerio! see you again soon." And he departed for his room.

But as he went the strip of white and green ribbon that he also had worn sent my thoughts idly spinning back; and it struck me how inconceivable it seemed that he had ever done two years abroad. True, his skin still had a little sunburn that now it will never lose, and perhaps his eyes were somewhat bluer by contrast. But he wasn't more than twenty-three at the most and didn't even look that. And of all the other things we had shared and known, he hadn't even mentioned a word. Not from any special reason. It was just of no importance to him. Those two years were common, ordinary stuff, part of the forgotten days' round to us both — an episode that was closed, dimmed in the light of new and later impressions from the English scene on the resilience of a youthful mind.

16th of May

Another icy cold day with a lot of low, rolling cloud coming across the fields and woods on a strong north wind. Have flown nothing but Tutors and the 504N here yet, and we have to fly every type in the Service flight — Bulldogs, Harts and Atlases. One just has a little dual on landings and general flying characteristics of each type with the instructor. Then goes solo, and flies odd hours on them throughout the course. At each flying training school the *ab initio* pupil learns to fly and does his first term on training-type aeroplanes. In the second term he passes to advanced training on Service types — heavier and faster things of the sort he will ordinarily meet in squadrons, capable of carrying bombs and guns, and so on. So the embryo instructor has to get his hand in on them in case he should have to instruct on them in future.

Cowling and I had been looking forward to that. He's been flying twin-engined bombers for the past two years, and I've been on flying boats, seaplanes, and heavyish land-planes, too; so neither of us have flown anything with a decent turn of speed since we can remember. But we were doomed to disappointment. They got as far as starting up the dual Bulldog and then the word came round, 'Wheel all Service types in. Too windy.' They shut off and we wandered off to look for a Tutor again. I suppose they don't want to chance damaging wings, but we growled a good deal into our beards about fair weather flying and couldn't we be trusted and so on, all the same. I went off first with Mayor.

Last week we were teedling round the air in overalls and shoes. Today we'd resurrected our winter kit, sidcots with teddy-bear linings and heavy knee flying boots, rubber-soled and wool-lined. We were soon rocking and bumping our way up to 3000, hardly covering a mile of ground in getting there. Medium turns are difficult. I'd gone through and through and through it on the ground until I thought I had it wrapped up. But no, in the air it's a totally different thing. Here and there one does a bad demonstration, forgets bits, and even has to stop and reason out what to do. Nose too high—ease stick back. Top rudder to keep nose up, or bottom to increase rate of turn? Eventually one comes to a lame ending.

"That wasn't very good, I'm afraid."

"No," comes the quite unperturbed voice. "But you'll get it soon. One little mistake you made—" he explains and corrects. "Now run through it again."

One runs through it again. And again. And again. And so the lesson is gradually learned. Teaching an instructor can't be much fun. The mistakes one makes must seem criminal to the man who's doing the teaching. Then he has to go up again during his second half of the morning and do it all again with his other pupil. I often feel after about four repetitions an absolute dread of having to stumble through the patter again. It's a common feeling. But they seem to know instinctively when you've had enough, and go on to something else. We climbed up into still colder air, went on to aerobatics. Not patter, just doing them. You've got to reach a good degree of polish and then keep in practice to be able to aerobat well. I'm getting more at home with them now; it's becoming more natural to get into queer attitudes and recover from them again. But we're still far from perfection!

"You're letting the nose drop too much as you roll off." Or: "You're flattening her on to her back too soon. Now do this one with me."

We rolled and rolled and rolled, then rolled off the tops of about fifty loops, to the right and to the left. As we were gliding in I said: "I still can't cope with rolls to the left. Get half-way round and then don't know what the hell's happening."

"Oh, it'll come. By the way, hold the stick in your left hand. That helps a lot. You can get it much further over and forward than with the right."

The other pupils, too, scratch their heads at times over this aerobatic game. All fail to see at the moment how on earth they're going to teach people to do things in a few months' time when at the moment they can't do them decently themselves. The root of the trouble is that one gets an inferiority complex flying with a pilot who's A.I., C.F.S.

After tea Nacelle and I walked into Stamford for a haircut and a companionable half-can at The George before dinner. And for amusement we counted the cars passing us from the south. In the two and a half miles of Great North Road just sixty flashed or rumbled by; twenty-five were lorries, six were saloon cars full up, five were driven by girls, and three were speed hogs. That makes thirty-nine. Now you could not expect any of those to stop and offer us a lift. The girls? Well, they didn't, anyhow, well-dressed as we may have looked from behind. But that leaves twenty-one private cars driven by solitary men, young and old. We didn't want a lift, as it happened, walking as we were to blow out the cobwebs and stretch our desk- and fuselage-cramped limbs. But we wouldn't have got one had we desired one, all the same. And the jest of it was that all sixty automobiles were flying one or more patriotic, hail-my-countryman, Union Jacks in honour of the Jubilee. We reflected sadly upon the decay of chivalry during these latter years.

So many women, in our eyes, have become complete cads these days. The young ones as well as the powdered middle-aged, dressed-by-Peter Robinson ones who are so inclined to dignified *embonpoint*. They fight like wildcats to board buses. From Uxbridge it was a good thing to take a Green Line bus up to Oxford Circus. It took an hour and cost a half-crown return. We saw our plays and Academy films, and were spared the strain and time and cost of driving and parking cars. But twice, seeking to get back to the mess, we lost even standing room on what a minute before had been an empty bus. Trading on our innate politeness to give them precedence, the lady passengers just shoved and crowded and squirmed. And so, by playing the little gent, standing room only for us, or none at all. We changed our tactics after that, gave up wearing our old school ties, and then piled into the scrum and gave them dig for dig, set our jaws and barged through. It was distinctly rich to see them look pained and surprised. Bitches is the only word.

Nacelle's philosophy ran thus:

'I used to proffer my seat to women and gels [sic] in Tubes. But by degree I gave some study to the situation. The average girl is amazingly well-dressed. She spends most of her salary on self-adornment, and then, cock-a-hoop at her own elegant reflection in the windows, looks down her nose at your old grey bags. I find a summary of use.

'(1) During the War women crowded into the jobs left vacant by men, in factories, offices and stores.

'(2) After the War they refused to get out. They liked the luxuries that good wages buy. So far, so good. All very logical and, by nature, right.

'(3) But now thousands of jobs are closed to men.

'Elementary schoolgirls study shorthand-typing and bookkeeping free at Evening Classes after they leave school. I know. An old friend of mine, a retired Mr. Chips, is the principal of an Evening School. And some time ago I helped him get out his class lists for the autumn schools. Only two girls out of forty wanted to study cooking, and three dressmaking. The rest went flat for the secretarial work. After qualifying, they pour into offices to earn twenty-five bob a week instead of helping Mum with the washing-up. They like it. Mum likes it. The boss likes it. It gives him pleasure to see their pretty faces about the place. And, what is more, it would cost him just twice as much to employ a family man as a clerk to do the same work. That is the lowest wage with which he could decently buy bread. Now, you see, two girls can be employed for his pay. Where was I? (4) Result — girls have got most of the black-coated jobs. And not those alone. Look at biscuit factories, machine shops, mills... With the wages they get they beautify themselves to attract the male. Oh no, not consciously. But any psychologist knows they do, all the same. As the girls have the males' jobs, the males in their own class are therefore unemployed. And so cannot possibly woo and marry the girls and maintain wives and families.

'Comic, ain't it? You can't get a good domestic for love or money. They're hard to find, please, and keep. Well, they asked for equality. And the haughty, well-dressed girls who have got many a good fellow's job stand now, while I survey them amusedly from the vantage point of a comfortable seat. That is if they haven't got in on the ground floor and grabbed it first.'

We rounded the corner, came upon The George and decided that we were dry enough to have the half-cans first, haircuts being available any hour of the day. Wondering with Omar what things the vintners can buy one half so precious as the stuff they sell, we stepped in through the open door.

17th of May

After supper tonight a Squadron Leader, who has many war ribbons on his tunic, brought in a book of great interest. It was the snapshot album of a young German aviator; in 1917 he was put in charge of a trainload of aeroplane spares that had been captured. And he found it in one of the trucks. We breathed down his neck and gazed in fascination as he turned over the pages and commented on the types of aircraft that were in vogue when we were still youngsters at school, getting margarine instead of butter, and saccharine tablets in our tea to build our growing frames.

Under each snapshot was a short description or humorous remark in beautiful white pen printing. The curious thing about it was that it so closely resembled the albums we ourselves made up during the first couple of years of our own flying life. A general view of his squadron sheds with the aircraft lined up on the grass. Low, dark wooden buildings so like our old aeroplane sheds that still stand at Netheravon on Salisbury Plain, put up by the first military aviators in 1914. Then a couple of pictures of black, heavy-looking fighters taking off over grass patched with snow. One of a bomber standing on its nose in summer corn, with the usual grimy and grinning mechanics standing round, pausing from their dismantling toil to be snapshotted.

Most of us, too, have a similar picture in our albums of some greenhorn who undershot the aerodrome and hadn't the sense to put his motor on.

Then two or three flight groups—the usual flying officers with pipes and mufflers and flying boots, the overalled riggers and fitters with oil smudges on their cheeks. But whereas our dogs in these unconventional pictures are always Sealyhams or rough-haired terriers, they had two Dachshunds, of course! Next came some leave—odd snapshots of a country house and gardens, Black Forest country and a trout stream or two. A heavy Prussian-looking old gentleman with cropped head and Hindenburg moustache figured in some of them; and with him a dignified and kindly-looking lady. No doubt the young Oberlieutenant's parents. He himself was a fresh-faced, pleasant-looking kid aged about twenty. Grim haircut, of course, but then they all had. We saw him playing croquet and seated astride a fine horse. Back to the Squadron again. Several pictures of a new job with which they appeared to be delighted—a small twin-engined kite with three rudders, three cockpits, and machine-guns mounted on swivels bristling out from it in all directions. One picture, taken from in front and above, showed her on the ground with the crew aboard—two pilots and three gunners packed like sardines and all grinning up into the camera. Four snapshots of Richtofen's funeral, with fellow pilots lowering the coffin and heaping white wreaths on to the grave. Then several close-ups of air machine-guns and bomb gear in which the album owner was evidently interested. They had captured a French Caudron, and we saw them standing round it examining and admiring it, peering and poking and prodding just the same as we do now when something fresh lands on our own aerodrome. Next they added an English BE2F to their bag. But that, alas, soon came to a sticky end—one of their pilots obviously took her up to show the boys how she should be flown and wiped off the undercart landing. It sat on the aerodrome with battered mainplanes, a group of officers wandering round it grinning, and a rueful pilot holding his helmet in one hand and scratching his bullet head with the other as he surveyed what he had done. Finally, there were several pictures of the Squadron mess, an old Gothic country house, furnished rather heavily in the Victorian style and with severely ornamental gardens. One or two unconventional pictures of the ante-room were good enough, and except for the high-collared rough tunics and the inevitable close-cropped hair, the youngsters weren't any different from our own in wartime, with their gramophones and whiskies-and-sodas, and their pictures from La Vie Parisienne pinned on the walls. In the last picture of all the whole mess was standing to a table decorated for a Christmas feast, with crackers on the table and champagne in buckets below. The air services always do come off well on active service; while the wretched infantry subaltern is huddled in a muddy dugout making merry over a noggin from an enamelled cup and pretending that bully beef tastes like the choicest Michaelmas goose.

And there we left them. Their aircraft were dark and curiously-shaped while ours were nearly always silver-doped and graceful to look upon. Their officers always seemed to look Prussian and military. But they were just as boyish and easily amused. Many of them are now dead, some still living in Germany, staid and middle-aged men. Young von Schaltz, who made the album, may have paddled over the Styx with a broken airscrew blade for an oar. Or he may have married one of those demure young *Fräuleins* in the pictures he took during his leave. Anyway, we wished him luck wherever he is, and punched the bell for a drink to his good name.

18th of May

The reason for the existence of C.F.S. is threefold. First of all it teaches pilots to become instructors. Secondly it holds instrument flying courses for squadron pilots who left their training schools before this comparatively new technique came into vogue. And lastly it gives refresher courses to chaps who have been off flying for some time, sick or doing language study abroad, things like that. So one is constantly meeting new types — foreign officers from technical schools in every European country, Poles, Chinese, Japanese, Brazilians, all doing the potential staff officer's grand tour of the air forces of every country besides their own. Our own people back from two years in Tokyo, Riga, or Baghdad. And old cronies from squadrons on the instrument game. Nowadays you're not reckoned to be a pilot unless you can fly by day, by night, and by instruments alone. The ability to fly by instruments enables you to keep a steady course in the thickest of cloud, and as the bombers reckon in the 'next war' to go through cloud as cheerily as they go above or below it, then it's a new and very useful trick that's got to be acquired. Nor is it as easy as it seems. You'll hear some more about it later on if you haven't already heaved this book into the fire.

C.F.S. is also very proud of putting up a yearly show that's quite unique – the inverted flight for the Hendon Display. First of all, they get three Tutors and modify the petrol systems so that the engines will run equally well in inverted flight. Then they paint the wing tops with radial red and white stripes so that the crowd will know when the Roman holiday has begun. And lastly they pick any three staff instructors and tell them to get cracking on practice when they can wedge it in. At first they go off separately, foregoing their breaktime tea and cigarette at 10.15 to push off to 3000 and then roll over on to their backs and stay put. When they're used to hanging on their shoulder straps and floating round the sky with their eyes bulging out, they start on turns. It's all very queer upside down. Stick and rudder over to opposite sides. The turn-indicator is of no further use, and you have to rely entirely on your inverted senses to tell you whether you're slipping in, skidding out, or doing a correct turn. Next, you practise turning through ninety, one-twenty, three-sixty degrees, picking ground objects above your heads for guides. That, too, is very queer for a start. And then you begin edging in and floating round in a formation of three. Until finally you can all take off bunched up (right side up) and then do all manner of pretty things. No. 1 is the leader, of course. By now all three have gradually come down with their practices to about 1500 feet. He gives the signal and numbers 2 and 3 roll over on to their backs and he leads them leisurely round the aerodrome, one out on either wing. Try rolling yourself for the first time. The nose describes an arc of about fifty degrees. You swing out maybe fifty yards and lose a couple of hundred feet. In this game you've got to keep level with the leader to a foot, and keep him just one span away. Not as easy and artless as it may look from your enclosure at Hendon on Display Day.

Next, the leader signals them to roll right side up again. This accomplished, he puts his own aeroplane on to her back and continues to lead them round in Flight Vic. And finally they string out and play 'Tail End Charlie', flying round upside down in line astern.

I was talking to one of the fellows in the team at lunch-time today. Never having stayed on my back for more than two minutes at a time, I wanted to know how one felt after a quarter of an hour.

"Not bad. Your upper leg muscles get a bit cramped. The sensations that your eyes are popping out and the blood all settling down in your head disappears after the first few practices."

"What's it like keeping in formation?"

"Well, you haven't got a very wide throttle range. Pretty small adjustment. The funniest bit is the way the nose seems to stick right up above the horizon. You have to have it there to give the wings a decent angle of attack. And curiously enough they're all a little bit faster upside down than right side up. Do about a hundred at cruising revs. as opposed to ninety-five with the wheels underneath."

"But you've got the convex side of the aerofoil meeting the air instead of the scooped out underneath. How does she get good lift?"

"Damned if I know. Chasing X never has been my strong suit."

I pondered over this conversation. Formation flying right way up takes some practice at first. You don't just get alongside the leader and keep there. It calls for a ready hand on the throttle, and in the mildest of bumps you've got to be constantly changing your revs., throttling back a bit one minute and opening up over normal the next to keep station. On turns the inside chap has to throttle back and the outside one open up if you all want to go round together. And on the outside of a squadron formation in rough weather the error of each pilot is magnified more and more with each successive aircraft, so that the outside two are often throttled back to about 1000 one second and roaring full out at 2200 the next to stay put. And next time you hear the steady drone of a Squadron Vic. and notice how nicely each keeps his one span from the next, think of the two chaps on the outside sitting there with glazed eyes and frenzied throttle levers. Now think of it upside down and with almost no throttle adjustment. I just couldn't. They do do it, so I suppose it's possible. I suppose with sufficient practice one could cruise along tail first.

Shopping in Stamford this afternoon we saw some perfectly good Norfolk tweed jackets in the window of a yeoman tailor for two guineas cash, made to measure. If only we could resist the blandishments of the representatives of the London tailors who come round to the messes once a month! Every now and then a card, which reads thus, goes up on the mess notice board:

> *Messrs. Bodkin of Savile Row respectfully present their Compliments to the Officers of... and beg to inform them that their Representative hopes to wait upon Officers on... from... when he trusts he will be favoured with their esteemed orders.*

You forget all about this, and then you roll in for lunch one midday, dusty and oily and hungry, to discover a murmuring knot of people grouped closely around somebody or something near the hall table. You edge curiously into the crowd and catch sight of an enticing array laid out for inspection. Silk shirts, club ties, honeymoon pyjamas (although one school of thought maintains their existence to be hypothetical), hogskin gloves, crested jewellery, blue leather handbags for the best beloved, stud-boxes, scarves—a choice collection of West End attractions calculated to appeal to the heart of the most berserk and roughshod male. Two or three young flying officers are goggling in rapt fascination at the latest things in foulard ties. Flight-Lieutenant Supercharger has removed his tunic and is standing with elbows up while Mr. Musk, the representative, encircles his canary-coloured pullover with a tape measure and jots down figures in a large book.

"Three buttons? Flap pockets? One button on each cuff? Very good, sir. First fitting Wednesday next. Right, sir. I'll put it down to your account."

And in those last few words you have the secret. Your account. Pay them £1 a month and you can trade up to £10. For thirty shillings a month you can owe them £15. And so on up to £30. It's so easy. Banker's order; you don't feel the wrench. And so you pay four guineas for a tweed jacket that a yeoman tailor will sell you for half the price in hard cash. And twelve guineas for a suit that he'd make for seven. It's a vicious circle, and you've got to pay through the nose for tick. And when you want a new suit and at the same time have got to blue a fiver on your car, what easier than getting Mr. Musk to jot your sizes down, show you a book of pattern cloths, all in your own home, and then pay him one pound a month? The merchant tailor studies human nature as well as dyes and woofs and warps.

There is a nice story that when small schoolboys go up for their navy entrance exam, Mr. Musk or one of his colleagues is waiting in the exam room when they appear. And he shows them a lovely book of pictures in which they can see how they will look when they become cadets. Reefer jackets, badged and peaked caps all complete. This never fails to thoroughly stir the youthful imagination. And while they are peering over each other's shoulders into the Book of Cadets standing on quaysides with gigantic battleships looming dimly in the background, all their bunting flying, Mr. Musk is snooping round quietly with the ubiquitous tape measure. That is never far from his person, and it suddenly appears from thin air like the rabbit from the conjurer's hat.

Then, as the invigilating officer appears, Musk bows and smiles and quietly fades out. They are old friends. Musk showed the Lieutenant-Commander a very similar picture book twenty years ago.

But a few weeks afterwards several of the aspiring youngsters get a letter something like this on the notepaper of the Bodkin House:

'R. N. Maintop, Esq.
'DEAR SIR,
[Dear Sir! Obviously Bodkin has spotted already the sterling worth of the embryo Beatty, and the embryo's cheeks flush with justifiable pride.]
'It has come to our notice that you are one of the candidates who has successfully passed the examination held last June at Trafalgar House. We respectfully beg to tender our sincere congratulations to you upon this achievement, and trust that we may be honoured with the commission of proceeding with your outfit.
'We are, dear Sir,
'Your obedient servants,
'BODKIN, BODKIN & PALM.'

Mr. Maintop is already theirs.

And — this is the curious part of the story — some days later Mr. Maintop receives a buff envelope from My Lords of the Admiralty informing him that he has successfully passed their frightful exam and been provisionally selected for the Navy List. Stale news, of course. Bodkin told him that a week ago.

20th of May

A grand blue and silver day, great cloud countries rolling down the sky at 4000 feet and a stiff, gusty, changing wind over the aerodrome. The usual bustle of activity on the tarmac and around the hangars at eight o'clock, rows of Tutors lined up, brave in the sunshine with their blue or red belly-bands, pressing back against the wheel chocks and rocking fitfully in the headwind, waiting to be started up. A silver Fury with a single cockpit half-way down the fuselage and a long polished nose gleaming like quicksilver in the brightness. Three green and silver Bulldogs, old single-seater fighters, roaring overhead at 800 feet doing close formation drill for Empire Air Day. Then higher up, at 3000 from the other direction, five Tutors stream down in line ahead. The leader rolls over on to his back, half loops off and heading on a reciprocal course, nose down, roars at the aerodrome. Each 'plane follows suit, and they do a power dive over the sheds at 300 feet.

This is the instructors' half-hour. We watch the three Bulldogs, hugging together like one man, turn into wind to leeward at a thousand feet, glide in at a fast tickover and sit down on the aerodrome still in formation and only a few feet apart.

Then we dive for the engine lecture-room. Thank heaven we've finished with that messy cleaning, at any rate. We take notes for half an hour on setting up and viewing engine parts. Then spend an hour being shown how the tools are used.

After every 120 hours' running they do top overhauls on the engines. Take off the cylinders and pistons, check up for wear and fracture, grind in valves and so on, and assemble again. After 240 hours the engine goes into workshops and comes down to the last nut and bolt. The complete overhaul is a very lengthy business. Everything tested, with 'go' and 'not-go' gauges, micrometers, verniers, dial test indicators, and any other precision instruments they can think of for checking sizes to 0.0005 inch. The flight-sergeant makes us scrub and scour the aluminium and steel until everything's as bright as a new cooking pot. This, he informs us, is to enable him to detect any hairline cracks. He pores over everything for nearly an hour with a powerful magnifying-glass and seems quite disappointed not to find any. We spend fifteen minutes carefully setting up the crankshaft for viewing, and then Holt-fflair, who has been asking a lot of ridiculous questions, catches the end in the sleeve of his overalls and pulls it off the bench. The flight sergeant swears long and softly under his breath and is still truing it up again when we leave.

Funny business, this flying. On Friday, after a full week of it, something like three hours' hard work in the air each day, you hate having to pack up for the weekend. And yet on Monday you feel a vague reluctance to begin again. You suddenly seem to have become weary of the continual patter, striving after a perfection that seems so impossible to attain. There is a well-worn saying that the more flying you do, the more you want to do. If you're getting in a regular thirty hours a month on a squadron you champ impatiently in the office and hangars if a wet day confines you to the ground. And yet after about a week on leave most of the desire to fly, curiously, seems to leave you; and if you get an office job, an adjutancy or something like that, it needs quite an effort to get in the four hours a month in the air that the regulations insist every qualified pilot shall do when he is employed on non-flying duties. However, the weekend's over now. We tasted the air for three hours yesterday, and storm over to the sheds after the engine lecture to rout parachutes and flying gear out of the lockers. Where's that aeroplane! Cowling walks in unwinding a scarf from his neck. "We're flying an Atlas this morning. I wasn't very brilliant. Stalled three times on my back rolling off the top of loops and kept making 'wheely' landings. You'll find you'll undershoot to hell, too."

I roll round to the Service flight and read up the Atlas petrol system and sign the book. She's running up on the tarmac with Mayor's red, moonlike face peering out of the back cockpit. I clamber in and do up the parachute buckles and lash up the fighting harness. Heavens, this is different from a Tutor! In a heavy sidcot, tight parachute harness and tighter cockpit straps, you feel like an imprisoned giant. The cockpit seems oppressively small and high, with levers and knobs and things sticking into you from all quarters. It's suddenly got warmer, too, and with big leather gloves and a scarf on, and your goggles down, you feel like a cocoon in a steam-heated incubator. And how the dickens are you going to land with this view? You jack the seat up to its full extent. A little better, but not much. Ah well.

We were trained and flew thirty hours on these, so there's no excuse for a bum show.

Mayor begins to chat down the phones the usual preliminary stuff. "As you probably remember, the fuel cock is situated in the centre of the dashboard at the bottom. As you can see, it's always turned to *Both Tanks On*. The gauge under the centre section reads half the total contents. Safe endurance is three hours at 1600 revs. Oil pressure is correct now. The tail-actuating gear etc., etc., etc."

We taxy out and take off. Beautifully smooth-running engine after the little things. Plenty of power, too. Very sensitive on controls. You notice all these differences as the engine opens up to a smooth song and you purr off the deck like a sewing machine. Two or three cars are stopped on the Great North Road and the occupants look up as we roar fifty feet above their heads. We rock and bump up at seventy-five in the strong gusts and are at 2000 before the aerodrome's barely a mile behind. Then we go through the usual sequence on a new type. All the flying peculiarities are explained by the instructor. Type of stall and spin demonstrated. Then you take over and fly her straight and level and do medium and steep turns with engine and on the glide to his satisfaction. They're all as easy as pie to a reasonably salted pilot. "Very good. I've got her. Now you'll have to instruct on these quite possibly, so I want you to learn aerobatics on them and do some back seat landings as well. I'll run through the aerobatics first."

He does the usual things, loop, roll both ways, roll off the top. You have to start rolling off before the horizon comes up on the loop or else you nearly complete two rolls before you know where you are. Otherwise there's not much to it. You take over and have a crack. Loops easy. They always are. Slow rolls pretty ragged. Hang upside down for about twenty seconds—straps too loose as usual, and chunks of mud dropping down from the cockpit around your face. Then with a swish and a rush and a roar you flick her round on to a normal keel again.

Second and third ones a little better. Well, well, we'll improve. Rolls off the top *not* bad.

"All right, go in and land."

It's four years since I flew these, but it all comes back. A nice smooth creditable glide in, a turn into wind, and then a landing just over the hedge. Bit wheely, but Mayor is pleasurably surprised. We go round and do two more landings, one more wheely one and then a good, skid-grinding three-pointer.

You wouldn't believe the satisfaction an exact three-pointer can give. You hold off and hold off about a foot from the ground, gradually feeling and easing the control column back as the speed falls off to keep her the same height up. Unconsciously keeping her level with ailerons and rudder and elevators all moving slightly at the same time as the gusts and eddies try to make you balloon or swing or tilt a wing. Until finally the speed drops to fifty or so. You never look at the airspeed indicator — you're far too busy looking at the grass as it wooshes past. Until your instinct tells you by the feel of the stick and the speed-feeling and the look of the ground and everything that the split second has come. You rap the stick back that last six inches into your tummy and wait perhaps one second. Then the nose comes up, down goes the tail and you feel her lightly hit wheels and skid exactly together. No drop, no bounce, and you run smoothly along the grass; co-ordination of hand and eye exact to the judgement of a second and a foot of height at 70 m.p.h. All that flashes through your mind as the skid touches and you grin the old faint ghost of a grin of pleasure to yourself. One more good landing out of the dozen a day in the hat.

We taxy in and out gets Mayor. The fitter and rigger do up the rear cockpit straps and fit ballast weights under the fuselage, and off we go to do half an hour's solo training flying, mostly landings and take-offs into wind.

This business of batmen again. They are born, not made. I often lie in my bath and brood about them. Another of those baths which I can never enter at the first attempt, but either leap from it with a yell like a scalded crayfish or else emerge after a casual sudden immersion, shuddering with icy shock and blaspheming silently and carefully under my breath. I can't even train this man to prepare a bath properly for me. He puts his horny hand in and stirs the water round, but can't gauge to the faintest degree what the temperature really should be.

I can't train him to do anything. There is a belief which has much to commend it, which maintains that it isn't worth training a batman to your needs when you only have three months with him, or that if you could train him within a few weeks, what is the point when you are merely training him for someone else to enjoy the fruits of your labour? But I couldn't train mine, even if I chose to disregard this counsel. To me he seems to be the purest ivory from the neck up. He just has a happy knack of always doing a thing in the most roundabout way and always doing it wrong.

This evening, after tea, Hickory and I put on our Sunday best, dug out some visiting cards, and went paying calls. We came in again at seven o'clock.

"Broom," I said, "I'd like a bath."

He gave me that wet smile he always reserves for this occasion. I knew what the answer would be before it came.

"I'm very sorry, sir, but both baths are full up."

If I'm in my room reading or writing after tea, he always comes in at the most fantastic hour and tries to urge me to take a bath. Six-fifteen or thereabouts, and dinner isn't until eight.

"But there will be a rush on baths, sir, after seven o'clock." But I firmly refuse to bathe before seven, even if they rush like the Gadarene swine. I won't bathe while the heat of the day is still in, and get into the ante-room in a nice stiff shirt and skin-tight mess kit at 7.15. So I wait until gone seven and then call for a bath, at which he invariably trots out his smile and formula about them being full up.

Tonight was obviously to be as other nights.

"All right," I said, refusing to be shaken. "I'll have one when it's empty. And please, I'd like a clean shirt put out."

I pick up a book and fill a pipe and begin reading. He fiddles and fumbles around for a quarter of an hour and goes out. 7.15. 7.30. 7.45. I begin to wonder a trifle anxiously about the bath. Change into a dressing-gown and give him a hail.

"One ready in five minutes, sir."

And as a result I charge back at 7.55. And so it always is. Having to dress and be in the ante-room at eight. Scramble into Wellingtons and overalls already strapped up, a boot in each leg, and waiting on a chair. And then stop. The damn fool has left the boot trees in. Last time he had the wrong boots in the right legs, left in right, and vice versa. I swear an awful oath and fumble and tug them out. Clean shirt. Hell! She has been at her sewing tricks again. My dress shirts have peculiarities. Different laundries have battered and shrunk them until it is only possible to wear them in one way, and that is with the studholes elongated by cutting them with scissors until the neckbands just meet in front, and with the bottom of the stiff part ripped away altogether from the rest of the shirt to prevent the front bulging out like buckled armour plate, and nearly sawing my neck off and pushing a dent in my stomach. And each time they go to the laundry I carefully write on the fronts with blacklead pencil: 'Please do not sew this—and THIS—up,' pointing to them with big arrows.

His good wife sews them all up each time, of course, with the strongest packthread she can find. And, as I suddenly discover from a sharp pricking sensation in my ribs, doesn't finish her handiwork either. I gingerly burst open the front and peer inside. Then draw out a couple of feet of cotton with a needle hanging on the end. No time to curse him now, 7.58. And all point will be lost tomorrow, when my ardour has cooled. I rip open the sewing and cram in studs, twist on a tie, and leap into the passage, putting on jacket and vest as I go.

"Broom!" I bawl, passing his door. "Light my fire before you go, will you?"

"Very good, sir."

Two hours later I return in serene and happy mood once more from the mess. Well, a comfortable hour by the fire with slippers on, doing a little work, and then bed. The room will be as warm as toast, anyhow. But will it? Sudden misgivings assail me. For as I round the corner of the stairs and enter our passage I see a light streaming from the silent, wide open door of my room. So. So. Thus much for my hopes of a warm room. Once more he's forgotten to shut that door. I go in. It's as cold as an ice pit. One window is wide open to the night. The curtain is billowing and flapping in the wind. And in the grate are the blackened and charred remains of a collapsed fire in which only the paper has smouldered and the wood charred. In a sudden frenzy I seize the poker and scatter the lot, coals and all, over the room. Ah, that's better. And then slowly and deliberately roll up newspaper and carefully build a fire again. And light it. And by the time I've removed my smudged and blackened shirt, washed my hands, pencilled on the shirt-front, 'Please do not sew up this—and THIS—' and thrown it into the laundry basket, the fire is a red and blazing glow.

We learn apace. First spinning. Going in is all right—you have plenty of time to talk. But Tutors come out so devilishly easy that you just can't keep up with them. According to the patter you've got to apply full opposite rudder to stop the spin, at the same time easing the control column forward slightly. When she stops spinning, centralise the rudder and ease gently out of the ensuing dive. I write from memory—all of this chatter is bitten acid deep now into the tablets of my mind. You've no time to think when the nose is pointing vertically downwards, the wings are whizzing round with you and your instruments in the middle, and the earth is just a green rotating whorl. All the talk must come mechanically. And the timing has to be fanatically right. For directly you get the rudder even central the spin stops; long before you can get it over to the opposite side. However, we repeat and repeat and learn how to cheat time, and Mayor's satisfied for the present. Now we go on to landings again.

One unconsciously says some ridiculous things. I constantly announce in triumph, "And she sinks gently to the ground *tails and wheelskid* together"; and when demonstrating faults in turns, talk about a draught on the left wing cheek, when I mean the left cheek. It's an almost irresistible temptation at times, too, not to say 'stick' instead of 'control column'. It slips out so easily in the mad rush of a spin. But Mayor always spots it and pounces like a hawk.

Another difficulty that has to be overcome, too, is the 'stirring the pudding' landing. Lots of us have got into the habit of gently feeling the aileron control as we ease back the elevators to land. It gives you a pretty good idea of how near you are to the stall when you know your aeroplane. So that besides going gently back, the control column is also waggling an inch or so from side to side. And you don't realise you're doing it. Anyhow, the pupil, we are told, is the most slavish copyist there is. And before you've come to landings, he'll hold his hand lightly on the top of the control column as you land and think the waggling business is a normal part of the procedure. And then get into frightful difficulties trying to imitate you. So Mayor won't have it. A gentle backward movement, and that's all.

If you play team games in the R.A.F. you can be rather lucky. Because they have a happy knack of combining business with pleasure. All pilots have to do a certain amount of cross-country and navigational training, so the C.O. of a twin-engined squadron will look at his training chart, and say, "Now let's see how the new pilots are getting along. Young Jones. He's done three good cross-countries and twelve unassisted landings at night. Three more hours' second pilot and one more satisfying cross-country, and he's qualified for first pilot." He picks up the telephone.

"B Flight, Exchange. That you, Jury-Strut? The C.O. here. I want you to do a cross-country to Wittering this afternoon. Take Jones as second pilot. Make him work out his log checked over by you and handed in to me in the morning. As we are playing C.F.S. at cricket this afternoon, you will take the team. I will give them orders to emplane at 1240 hours. Have the engines warmed up by then, and treat this as a practice operational order—emergency movement of troops. Weight sheet summaries and fuel consumption sheets to be rendered."

Which explains why a big silver, fat-bellied Valencia came and sat on our aerodrome just after two o'clock today and twelve men with cricket bags swarmed out, having covered a hundred miles in a little over an hour when by train it would have taken them the best part of a day to reach here from the tawny wilds of the Wiltshire Downs.

This hair does grow. Once a week we ride or trek into Stamford to seek out the barber chirurgeon to our aid. But today I boobed as never before. The same shop as of old, but a different executant. And ah—how different. A heavy-handed, ginger-haired, ham-fisted son of the soil, he got at me with a pair of Number One clippers and all but shaved me bald before I realised what he was about. I didn't know whether to leap at him with a gleaming razor and sever his ivory head from his neck, or burst into salt and bitter tears as my rage mounted in a red tide when I saw in the mirror what he had done. Have you ever seen a wheat-field half shorn of its grain? It looked like that. And I had to sit down again and let him do the other half to match. I noticed for the first time in my life that there were freckles not only on my cheeks, but also here and there on my scalp. I shan't need another haircut for weeks and weeks.

"You from the aerodrome?" he asked.

"Yes."

89

"Oh, that's all right then. You'll see plenty of chaps up there with their hair cut like this," he cheerfully replied.

23rd of May

Went down to the sheds hazily trying to remember the patter for spinning, the last thing we did, expecting to charge off in the Tutor as usual with Mayor for an hour's practice. Life is real and life is earnest where this learning to be an instructor is concerned. There is no time to stand and stare, no 'sliding down the well-oiled slopes of space' with the wires humming a carefree tune, and only the massed clouds sailing along and their shadows dappling the chequered pastures and woodland with their slow drift. One sees little of this. Absently curses the bumps instead for rocking and snatching at the controls and making the airspeed needle flicker in what is meant to be a demonstrated Correct Turn, where 'the bank remains constant, the rate of turn uniform, and the nose neither rising above the horizon nor falling below it'. And one only takes in vaguely the fact that a lovely day is blowing all around, concentrating on the real business in hand, flying and talking accurately for the benefit of the hawk-eyed critic in the back cockpit who can smell a drop of a couple of miles an hour in gliding speed before it even begins.

A pleasant surprise was waiting, however. On the Detail Board was scribbled 'Hart'. And our names. This is something like! Three-quarters of an hour general flying, and then solo, my boys. I've always wanted to fly a Hart and never yet had the chance. Stood on the tarmac many times on a hot summer day and watched them shut off a mile away and come sailing in gracefully on their flat glide, to skim over the grass as the pilot gently nurses back the stick to lose speed, gradually offering up her long silver snout higher and higher until she sits down, wheels and tailskid together. When some day-bomber squadrons first got them a few years back, the unfortunates of us who still had to carry on with our old cruise-at-105 Faireys went fairly green with envy. Here was something a cross between a racing aeroplane and a two-seater fighter to carry your bombs, something that would cruise at 130 and do aerobatics as nicely as a club teaching machine. We lusted after them, and grumbled over our evening tankards of beer that at least it would be a good thing if the Air Ministry were to give each squadron like us one fast aeroplane with which to practise and play, something which in turn we could chuck about the sky once a week to keep our hands in and our young blood coursing free. Anyhow, now the moment had come. I read up the petrol system and general orders about the thing, polished my goggles, clambered into my parachute, and got in. Mayor explained things as before from the back cockpit as the airscrew glittered round while the engine warmed up.

"The queer thing like an umbrella handle on the right is the doping cock. There is a neat device also on the right of the cockpit. If you push it down it loosens the back straps of your Sutton harness, and enables you to lean forward to adjust the bias gear or radiator or anything like that. Push it up and you're tight again." And so on. Eventually we wound out the radiator when the temperature needle had gone up to 65, ran up the engine, and taxyed out for one hour of general flying before I took her solo. What did I discover in that hour? My logbook states barely under the heading 'Remarks': 'Wittering Local; 6, 7, 8, 11, 20.' And then 'Solo, 6 and 7'.

The numbers are headings from the instruction table — taking off and landing into wind; medium, steep and gliding turns, spinning, and aerobatics. She has a tendency to swing to the left as you take off, which has to be firmly counteracted with right rudder; and you can see a frightful lot of the ground ahead over the tapered nose when you're in flying position. Airscrew? That's going round at 2,200 so except for the noise you don't know it's there. Climb seems rather steep after Tutors because she's much more powerful, and you tend to fly at 85 instead of 70 or 80. Straight and level flight, once more you can see a lot of ground ahead, and until you've watched the altimeter for a time and noticed that it doesn't register a change, could swear that you're diving her. Speed, of course, makes no sense-difference. Except that you can turn much more quickly and feel the steeper loading through the pressure in the seat. Turns very nice — many aircraft have their own peculiarities, need little rudder or else you skid out, are very sensitive on ailerons, or something like that. Not vices, but just things to know and watch if you're going to fly the aeroplane instead of just slashing it round the sky. But with the Hart you can rip into a turn and out again as smoothly as slipping down a water-shoot. Spinning, nice and slow. Needs full opposite rudder to make her come out. Aerobatics? Far easier than Avro 504 Tutor or Atlas. Plenty of loading in rolls off a loop. If you try to lift your feet as you pull her over on to her back they feel so heavy that you can barely move them, and just a vestige of that curious thing blacking out happens for a moment if you do a tight half loop. The blood centrifuges away from the brain centres and just as the horizon swings up to meet your craned-back head, you suddenly have a faint, numb feeling in the head behind the eyes, as though a quiet finger were lightly pressing on a vital pulse. A shade of redness goes over everything and the fields and hedges do not so much go out of focus as that for a second or so you can still see them but 'focus' has lost its meaning. Then you roll off and are normal again. Real blacking out, due to blood centrifuging under gravity in the high loading of tight speed turns, momentarily produces complete freezing up of the eye nerves. Everything goes dark red and there is a solid, numbing pressure in your head, which passes off completely after you round the pylon and flatten out again.

Landings a little bit tricky. On a windy day you have to get the stick back that last little bit in double quick time or else she drops on to a nice springy undercarriage and goes up like a lift to about five feet, half bouncing and half ballooning with the wind under the wings. It happened on my first solo landing; got the tail practically down but not quite, and after a masterly hold-off she dropped those few inches on to the wheels and instead of staying 'put' was about five feet high again in a second, with my astonished face looking over the side at the practically stationary ground below. Which is a thing you never see from a landing aeroplane except in a piping wind. Usually it's streaking past like a backcloth on rollers. However, any pilot with over a year at the game has bounced a few times. And discovered that as long as you keep the stick back and give her a touch of throttle as she sinks she'll stay down all right the second time. I gave her a good fat burst and she sat down like a two-year-old.

We finished flying early because they wanted to get the aircraft all teed up for Empire Air Day tomorrow. Directly we landed, the crews filled them up and then pounced on them with buckets of paraffin and cleaning brushes, scrubbers and buckets of hot soapy water, rags and metal polish.

A cloudless hot afternoon with a mighty, gusty wind, so one Charles and I decided to stretch our limbs and walk into Stamford to do some shopping, take tea at The George and then walk back again sevenish. A chap who I know had been an R.F.C. flying instructor at the old Stamford Aerodrome nearby, where they taught 'doughboys' to become pilots during the War, said he always associates The George with breakfasts. After weekends in London they'd skate up on the milk-train, hire an old car to rush them out to the aerodrome, then jump straight into flying kit, lumber off the deck with their pupils in the Old Rumpetys and then lob down in a field near The George for a leisurely breakfast, five or six at a time. Charles knew him, too, in Malta, where they shared 'the joys of sweet Valette, the heat, sirocco, sun and sweat' for two years.

"Those were the days!" he sighed enviously. "They were. And yet the Prof. told me that after he'd done a few months instructing he started to champ at the bit and want to get back to France again. He bunged in an application but they wouldn't wear it. And do you know, he kept worrying them with applications, one a month, until the end of the War. And except for a move to Oxford where they trained Canadians, got no nearer to the fray. For once, those who sat in high places and wore Brass Hats knew a good man when they saw one, and kept him put."

"I never could understand *why* he wanted to go," I put in. "In every other respect he has always seemed to me to be an eminently sane man. His billet was one that thousands would have envied him. In no sense was he wearing the white feather, for it was a job—in those days—definitely not lacking in the spice of danger. No parachutes, aeroplanes built largely in blissful ignorance of stress and strain mathematics. Engines that did pack up occasionally. And pupils who always worked on the assumption that a pilot's life was a short and a merry one, so weren't above roaring straight at the sheds and then climbing up the hangar walls, or looping until they pulled off the wings. Also he was doing more valuable work than he could ever have done over Cambrai and Somme. And he could get the music he loved, string quartet and symphony stuff in London at weekends... his was just the job I'd like. No mock heroism about me!"

Charles laughed. "I'll lay a level bet you'd be volunteering yourself before a month was out."

"No fear."

"You would, when every other chap you knew was out there putting up a show."

I thought hard… and slowly it dawned upon me that he was right. What a discovery to make!

On the dusty road back, gold with late sunshine, we saw the three Tutors up practising their inverted stuff for tomorrow's show for the public. After tea is the only time that the instructors get to do individual things, and for a week now they've been taking off at 5.30 to run through their piece. Up at 3000 tonight to find smooth air and keep out of the bumps, trailing along three together in close formation upside down. It's incredibly hard to do decently. Roughly they spend fifteen minutes each trip on their backs. Curiously enough the standing on the head business doesn't worry them much. It's the weight of the legs and feet that trouble them, apparently it becomes harder and harder to keep your feet on the rudder bar. They tend to fall off all the time, and you get cramp in the muscles. Then there is that difficulty that even few people in the Service realise. The carburettor has to function upside down, so as they turn over they not only have to turn an oil cock to keep a small engine sump system going, but switch over the petrol, too, to feed another jet. And this jet gives them practically no throttle control. With only a very small adjustment they only have two speeds, full out and stop.

It's easily the cleverest show of the lot, and I tip my hat to them. And yet from the public's point of view it isn't frightfully spectacular. They can only goggle up and think, 'Well, there are three chaps upside down in good formation. That's very clever. Well, there they are, upside down.' And that's all there is to it.

And yet a ham-fisted son of a gun with only a handful of flying hours up his sleeve can thrill them to the core with damn fool tricks that are bad flying from the safety point of view and the easiest thing in the world. Take off at the crowd and hold her down until he's about fifty yards from them, with the needle off the clock. Then pull her up in a dirty great climbing turn and go up like a lift till he's hanging on his slots at a thousand or so feet. Engine roaring like a mad traction engine got loose in a tunnel.

Or else he can get a mile away and 3000 up and then stick the nose down, slam the throttle through the gate, and not pull out until he's about twenty feet over their heads, wires and airscrew and everything screaming, exhaust making a racket like six express

94

trains going through Crewe, and his airspeed needle going round on the third circuit, its spring wound up into a neat little ball. The crowd loves it.

25th of May

Our big day. This station lends itself admirably to showmanship. Easy to get at, slap on the Great North Road in the middle of country, so that you can't miss its low, yellow hangars. Everything beautifully laid out, unlike so many R.A.F. stations that are still the husks of their old wartime selves, with derelict buildings here and there making departments even more difficult to find. The whole place is so compact, too. The aerodrome, a row of hangars, and then all the buildings, quarters, offices, lecture rooms, repair and engine shops and so on, on either side of a straight asphalt road beginning and ending in grass, with neat shaven lawns and footpaths between them. The buildings are new and neat, of cheerful reddish brick already mellowing with the weather, with the trim flower-beds about them, and whitewashed posts and fresh painted doors, each named in neat white lettering. The C.O. or some organiser had arranged it all very decently for our gallery today. The necessarily *verboten* places where flying work was going on were roped off, an aeroplane of each type we have ranged up in A.R.S. with big trestle ladders on either side so that visitors could look in the cockpits, each spinner having a big card hanging on it giving all the engine and aeroplane performance and weight figures and so on.

The sergeant pilots who are on the course with us were detailed in shifts to stand by these aircraft and explain anything that visitors might want to know. The exhibits were very popular with the lovelies as we run a very dashing line in airmen pilots; who in turn didn't mind in the least grabbing a neat silk-clad ankle to give a hoist into the cockpit, or putting a brawny arm round a neat waist, to help the damsel down again. Sergeant Stagger, who instructs us in rigging, was perspiring freely and walking around with a face like a great red anxious moon. He had turned round a few minutes before to investigate an unusual and persistent noise. Watched by a host of amused and admiring parents, a three-year-old was gripping the elevator of a Crab between his podgy fists and resolutely slamming it up and down. The noise was made by the control columns in the cockpits moving to and fro in unison and bashing out the glass dials on the instrument panels.

All the other departments were thrown open, too, and everywhere big printed cards nailed to posts and doors directing people to this and that, and telling them what it was, in large black letters when they got there. A regular flying programme was drawn up—the normal stuff we do during the day, but run to scheduled times, and with a parachute-dropping Vimy from Henlow and a monster of a green night-flying Heyford from Mildenhall to help us out. After lunch the crowds began to descend on us, and from the air at 4 p.m. the tarmac looked like Hampstead Heath on Bank Holiday, with upwards of a hundred cars parked on a corner of the aerodrome. The red and white striped Tutors did their inverted stuff, three green and silver Bulldogs with their fat snub snouts of Jupiter engines took off in formation and still in Vic or line astern did loops, rolls, and landings. A Fury and a Hart did some very spectacular upward rolls and zooms, getting up from one to four thousand in a vertical climb in bare seconds. The engines make a cracking good noise in a flattish, full throttle power dive. I still feel my flesh tingle, and grin like a silly girl or a hero-struck schoolboy whenever I hear that soul-shattering, satisfying row. A good thirty mile an hour wind was howling in the sunshine over the country, too. So the pilots only had to hold the Fury down for a hundred yards or so after they'd got off the ground. Then they could just ease back the stick and go up like a lift to two thousand in a mere handful of ticked wrist-watch seconds. In between the events the pupils, two by two in Tutors, checked up their station-time, synchronised watches with typed programmes and came in to do landings. The showmanship was rightly reserved for the Kingpins, and when we weren't loafing around doing patter we did our best to make landings near the tarmac and at any rate pretend that it was worth watching.

We had tea in the card-room while the G.P. wandered about the ante-room and gardens and heard the history of the mess silver from the head waiter. Our soup tureen was used on the train in which the Armistice was signed, and is inscribed to that effect. No one knows how it came here.

One amusing thing happened this afternoon, which perhaps ought not to be reported. However, smile and keep it dark. Holt-fflair and Cork went off together in a Tutor to practise patter. Their only part of the show was to take off. Then the Bulldogs came along to do their stuff, while the Cork-Holt-fflair combine had instructions to keep well out of sight and practise patter for aerobatics. Now Cork is an Irishman. When his turn came, he put her over on to her back at 4000. Both fell on to their shoulder straps, and with the engine throttled back and the wheels sticking up in the air, they began to glide down.

"Going to practise inverted turns," croaked Cork down the telephones.

"Ay ay," Holt-fflair replied throatily, gazing round with bulging eyes.

They glided down. Until the altimeters showed 3000 feet. Now *no* aerobatics should be continued below this height. Holt-fflair watched his needle slowly fall to 1500.

"Hi! What about coming out?"

"To hell wid ye. I'm telling ye 'tis Empire Air Day."

And Cork came out well under a thousand feet over the trees and roofs of the old Haycock near Wansford. Not a soul in sight for miles away. Just his own little private show.

Sitting in the card-room at tea over second large cupfuls and pipes, we gazed out through the large open windows. Somewhere in the aching blue the Bulldogs were still roaring, first crescendo and then dying away as they came down from a formation loop. Girls in gay afternoon frocks passed and re-passed with their gallant escorts along the drive. We pulled at our pipes and made the usual derisive comments to each other about poodle-faking.

It is amazing how safe flying is these days. Part of the old wartime halo still hangs, but the risks have almost entirely gone. In 1914 England had a hundred and fifty aircraft, all uncertain hazardous crates with engines running half on petrol and half on faith, none of them hitting up more than ninety miles an hour true airspeed. In 1916 a war pilot's life was reckoned in flying hours. Was it fifty they gave you as a maximum span? Read Faulkner's *A Soldier's Pay*, and *Winged Victory*, and Elliott White Springs' books on those days. "Silver handles and hello Saint Peter," Springs called the average man's chance.

And now! I've passed the thousand hour mark, five years' flying for my pay without so much — touch wood — as bursting a wheel. And I'm quite a babe among a hoary old staff of Flight-Lieuts. under twenty-eight with a couple of thousand hours each on the books.

Look at us! Married maybe, insured, living in comfortable, settled homes, motoring to and fro each day with all the long security of any business man. Flying's safer than motoring every time. And even poets are learning to fly. Sober, grey-haired, stooping pedants, young and dreamy, gentlemen. And wearing lounge suits and suède shoes to sit behind Triplex in cabin monoplanes to learn. Ashtrays on the dashboard in front.

A Service pilot has a multitude of jobs, gunnery, high or diving bombing, and the like. He's rather inclined to regard a chap who flies a light aeroplane about as tolerantly as a chap who pushes a Bugatti around Brooklands would watch a small boy intently pedalling away on his fairy cycle. But the poets have one up on us every time. They can express what we only feel, speak where we are dumb.

"...the hellishness of low turns in a wind of forty miles an hour and the machine bucketing about in patches of thin air like a crazy horse," says David Garnett. If you only knew how acute and *true* that is! Get *A Rabbit in the Air*, if only for the last page and a half alone. He's seized there on an immutable something about fine weather flying that is for ever crowding into the pilot's memory and yet about which he is wholly articulate. He talks of "the mornings when there are big white clouds and the spring air is soft." Mornings on which, were he blind he would "still go to the aerodrome for the sound of a machine landing... That bucketing hollow noise that dies into a rumble, as though an empty barrel were bouncing down three stairs and tittuping to rest. Gosh, it is the most exciting sound I know."

A chap who has been visiting R.A.F. aerodromes today by air with Grierson gave us quite a poetic account of it all on the ten o'clock B.B.C. news. 'Planes swooping and banking, Harts roaring by, mechanics in blue overalls with hair streaming in the wind, men, in his words, wearing what must be the smartest of all Service uniforms, taking and giving salutes. He got one profound truth over, at any rate. "If you really want to realise the evils of ribbon development, see it from two thousand feet."

Wittering came in for quite a write-up, for during the afternoon he was in our midst and most of us knew it not.

"...Wittering, where instructors are instructed, is famous for tulips also, that blow in the lovely garden outside the officers' mess, where the goldfish wax fat in the pond, despite the fact that the top of the water has to have an oil film scraped off it every two days." And he, too, ended up with a quotation from *A Rabbit in the Air*.

This oil film business puzzled me, and later Loop, the mess secretary, wandered in and I tackled him about it.

"Yes, it's perfectly true. Very curious. Every two days an oil film forms on the surface of the pond and the gardener has to scrape it off, or else the fish die. There was a theory that it came from the soil. You know they often dump old engine oil on the ground where aeroplanes are or have been. But that's quite impossible, because the actual pond is entirely concrete lined. And the mess clerk tells me that during the break when there's no flying no film forms. So it must come from the air!"

27th of May

Low clouds and high winds continue. We had congratulated ourselves on having the best months of the year for flying. The weather can help you so materially if it likes; sunshine to cheer you up; clear horizons to help with turns, aerobatics, every manoeuvre, and light steady winds that help with an approach, are kind to undershooting, and conducive to sweet landings. Instead we have to battle with bumps and occasional drizzle. Search for gaps in the ragged clouds in which to do our aerobatics; keep a more wary eye than ever open for other aeroplanes; work with poor horizons and lowered visibility; contend also with high wind that drifts you miles to leeward if you haven't a constant eye on your position and don't do most of your manoeuvres upwind. Which is harder still when three-quarters of your mind is grappling with patter and synchronised demonstration; and very often after a few turns and spins and rolls you haven't the faintest idea from which direction the wind is coming. Three thousand feet is too high to detect drift with the naked eye; the aerodrome is hidden somewhere behind a bank of mist that reduces horizontal visibility to about two miles and stretches all around. The land below is unfamiliar; just a patchwork of fields and hedges with no kindly cottage or bonfire smoke to tell you in which direction the wind does lie. If you're cunning you set the wind direction of your compass before you take off. When no navigation is being carried out, no courses have to be set on the card to interfere with such a scheme. And sometimes when you do that and then turn to the compass wind it seems incredibly wrong, and the vague idea of the wind direction that you have maintained in your mind is at total variance to the grid lines and red-tipped needle. But the magnetic north pole always stays 'put', so believe it you must. And sure enough it always is right. Lastly, foul weather makes ordinary aerodrome landings and forced landings much harder to do nicely. You bump and rocket about, drift considerably if you're more than a point out of wind, and balloon like old Harry when you're holding off unless you nurse her gently on to the ground. The Tutors aren't too bad, and rarely tip a wing, but land a Crab with an inch of drift and down goes that wing into the grass. Try to lift it up and you only give the wing aileron drag, which sends it down further still. All you can do is to heel helplessly over, rudder into it, and hope that you haven't snapped a camber rib. If you're fool enough to land very much out of wind, then you simply rip off the tyres and bend a wing good and proper. So much for our winter weather. There's one blessing, however, we haven't to contend with the bitter, numbing cold that the winter courses get as well. And I suppose it's all good training. What can be done well in indifferent weather should carry a distinct polish when the weather's fine.

Spinning patter yesterday. Fairly long and explanatory, but not frightfully hard. You explain the cause and nature of a spin, demonstrate that with no yawing couple applied the aeroplane won't spin after a stall at all. Then demonstrate a real spin from a straight stall, and next spins off badly executed turns—medium turn with too much rudder, slow gliding turns, and so on. "Remembering never to commence or continue a spin below three thousand feet and always looking round and underneath for other aeroplanes before you start." The best spin of all is that off a steep turn with engine on. An aeroplane stays in the air because of lift it obtains from the wing area, this lift counteracting the pull of gravity. Now incline your wings to the vertical and you've practically no wing area parallel to the ground. Therefore none of your 'lift' opposes gravity and you stall, although you may be travelling at ninety miles an hour. Which is precisely what happens in a very steep turn. You ease the control column hard back into your tummy. The loading goes up and up until you feel as though you're going to burst through the bottom of the cockpit. The engine's roaring away at 2000 revs. and the airspeed needle showing a healthy ninety. The horizon fairly tears round. And then suddenly, although you've full engine on and bags of speed, you feel a faint shudder and she stalls. You gleefully watch the nose begin to drop and then wheel out your next bit of patter in an unctuous voice. It's really one of the grandest and most effective demonstrations there are.

"We endeavour to keep the nose up by applying top rudder. This is our yawing couple and—she spins." And as you say it she suddenly woofs over the top without any warning and goes slap into a really tight and beautiful spin with engine on. "Recover in the usual way."

The patter for recovering from a spin is one of the few things, like taking off and landing, that you have to learn by heart. A spin is a damned quick thing, and in all these demonstrations you've constantly got to be gaining and keeping height, so you want to do as few turns as possible and therefore spend no time thinking of what to say.

"To recover, ease the control column forward slightly and apply full opposite rudder. When you stop spinning, centralise rudder and ease gently out of ensuing dive."

An inverted spin is a most uncomfortable manoeuvre. A pupil is never called upon to practise it, but is shown it, and the recovery, as a matter of interest. You turn over on to your back and then ease the stick hard forward on to the dashboard until you stall. By this time you're hanging on the shoulder straps, dangling helplessly about a foot out of the cockpit in the air rush, with a feeling in your legs as though they're filleted. Then you jam on rudder and away you go spinning on the *outside* of the manoeuvre, which not only tends to break the straps and hurl you out of the cockpit like a conker off a whirling string, but hurl the insides out of you as well. Your eyes feel as though they're going to leave their sockets altogether. It's difficult to talk, too. Your vocal chords go squeaky and muffled, and it's only a small, woolly voice that manages to say "to recover, opposite rudder and stick forward. Centralise when the spin stops. Now half loop or roll off."

We went up to 4000 and did slow rolls and rolls off the top again for a quarter of an hour. I practise patiently and not very keenly. Aerobatics are hard to do with a polish and fairly uncomfortable at the best of times. One improves so slowly, too. Not until ease and perfection comes will I begin to relish this business of hurling a ton or so of intricate machinery in a spiral about its own axis in thin air with my own uncomfortable body in the middle. The aeroplane never seems to want to do it either. You have to manhandle it round firmly and disregard the pit of your stomach and the howl of wires not in streamline. Whereas in turns and glides and landings gentle handling of controls seems to encourage the thing to help you and coax it round. I'll bet some of those war-time fighter pilots were ham-fisted stiffs. And had to be. Shake the man off — ram down the nose till she's screaming at 200. Stick hard back and whine up in a tight loop with the loading nearly snapping your brain. Lightning roll off the top — full and positive application of controls — and you're streaking along five hundred feet higher the opposite way.

29th of May

Still cramming away as hard as we can go, filling up our logbooks at the rate of a page every three days. Low flying and climbing turns patter first half of today. Then elementary forced landings. Much harder than advanced ones, because they're taught before a pupil goes solo, and so sideslipping won't be in his programme yet a while. The sideslip is a most useful manoeuvre. You glide in with S turns and purposely overshoot your field. Drift in quite high over the hedge; then rip off all your surplus height with a side-slip and put her down neatly well up the field. But if you've got to get into a small field with gliding turns alone, you have to judge your height to ten feet or so, no mean feat in these days.

I despair of Broom, the Slave of the Lamp. He has a genius for swiping up stuff for the laundry. Leave a handkerchief on the table for an hour, and it's gone. I wear clean shirts and socks every day. My laundry bill was nigh on two pounds last month. I might as well try to cure the Sphinx of its melancholia as cure him of this.

102

Frank Darker Tredrey
1908-1988

Plate 1

45th FLYING INSTRUCTORS' COURSE, CENTRAL FLYING SCHOOL, APRIL–JULY, 1935

F/Ofr SER Shepard	F/Ofr AJ Hicks	Sgt. WAJ Kirkham	Sgt. H Lazelle	Sgt. LF Humphrey	Sgt. LJ Dixon	Sgt. HAC Stratton	Sgt. RW Jarred	Sgt. WS Lake	Sgt. WD Evans	Sgt. C Holdway	Sgt. RS Serase	F/Ofr CWM Ling	F/Ofr J Ramsden
F/Ofr JC Sisson	F/Ofr LV Andrews	F/Ofr APS Wills	F/Ofr JBT Whitehead	F/Ofr AW Finny	F/Ofr JA McAuley	F/Ofr GH Stuart	F/Ofr HR Dale	F/Ofr JG Glen	F/Ofr LWC Bower	F/Ofr RL Wallace	F/Ofr GRA Elsmie	F/Ofr EC Kidd	F/Ofr S Keane	F/Ofr FD Tredrey	F/Ofr AA Adams
F/Lieut. RB Councell	F/Lieut. J Cox	F/Lieut. DJ Waghorn	F/Lieut. WMC Kennedy	F/Lieut. FH Wooliams	S/Ldr. C Turner AFC	Lieut. MA Rahman (Iraq)	W/Cmdr. HG Smart OBE, DFC, AFC	W/Cmdr. PH Young	S/Ldr. SH Down AFC	S/Ldr. AR Thomas	F/Lieut. GD Harvey DFC	F/Lieut. PR Barwell	F/Lieut. JW Gillan	F/Lieut. RC Jonas
Sgt. CE Sims		Sgt. TRW Owens		Sgt. F Holt		Sgt. JN Craigie		Sgt. CL Gould		Sgt. GF Oliver		Sgt. WJ Johnson		Sgt. GE Webb

Plate 2

© RAF Photographs

DRAMATIS PERSONAE

Frank
Tredrey

'Mayor'
F/Lieut. R. B. Councell

'Cowling'
Sgt. J. N. Craigie

'Esterhazy'
F/Ofr. A. W. Finny

Commandant:
W/Cmdr. H. G. Smart,
OBE, DFC, AFC.

'Trout'
F/Ofr. C. W. M. Ling

'Cork'
F/Ofr. J. A. McAuley

CFI:
S/Ldr. S. H. Down, AFC

'Hickory'
F/Ofr. A. J. Hicks

'Garrick'
F/Ofr. S. Keane

'Ahmed'
Lieut. M. A. Rahman

'Doe'
F/Ofr. E. C. Kidd

Plate 3

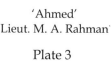

Plate 4
AVRO TUTOR

"Avro Tutors, gentlemanly little things…"

Plate 5

Above: Officers Mess, RAF Wittering, 1999;
"gardeners messing about this morning potting out. . ."
w: 'The George' at Stamford; "a companionable half-can at The George before dinner. . ."

Plate 6
"EVERY TYPE IN THE SERVICE FLIGHT"

Left to right: Gamecock, Atlas, Moth, Fairey III F, Avro 504N, Siskin, Bulldog (Note RAF Wittering, visible bottom left, and to its right the Great North Road.)

Wittering village church

Plate 7

Wittering Mess Garden pool, 1999

"the centre of village life since the Normans built it"

"a sunken pool stocked with fat goldfish"

Plate 8

ARMSTRONG WHITWORTH
ATLAS

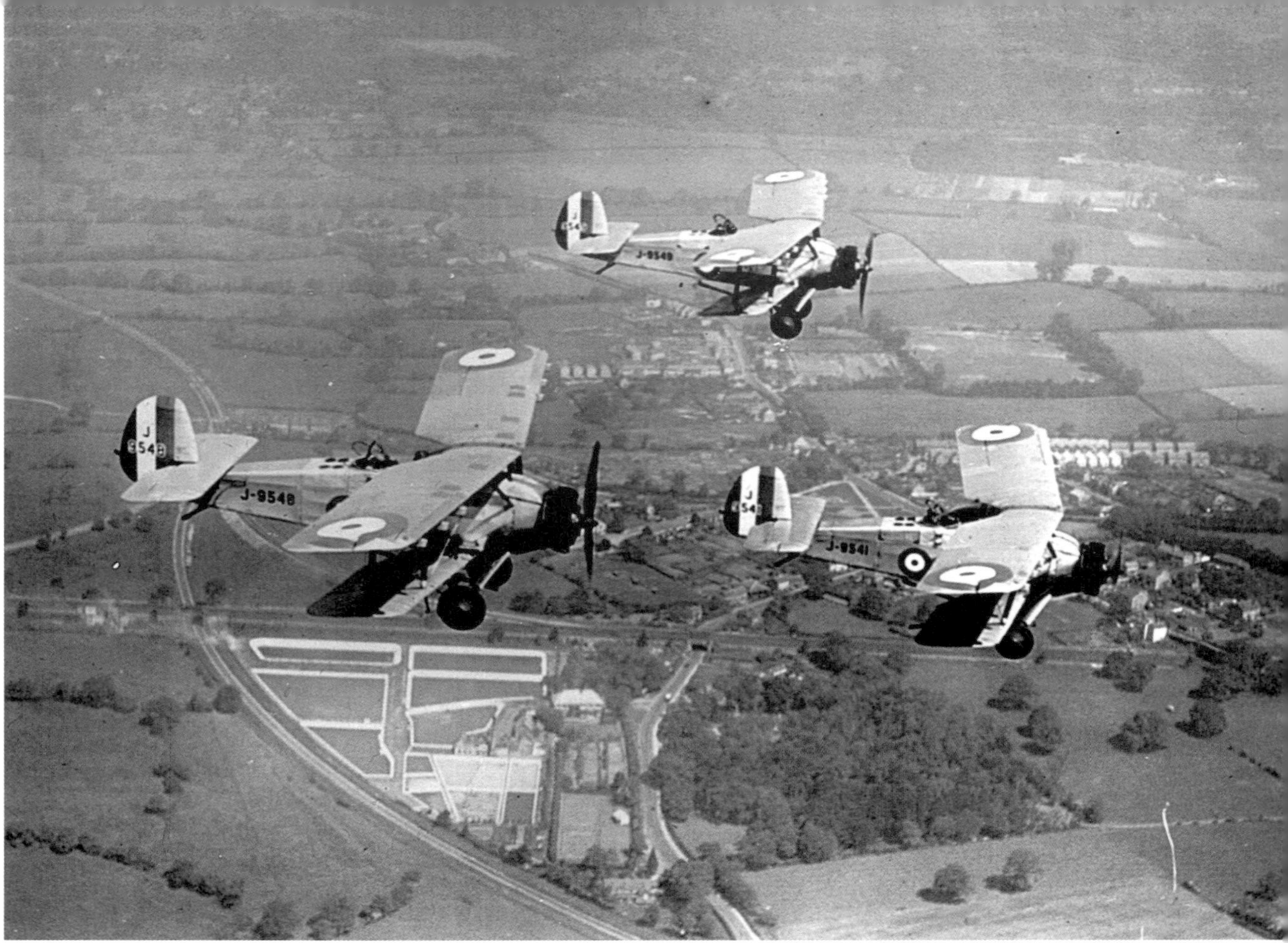

"It's four years since I flew these, but it all comes back."

© RAeS

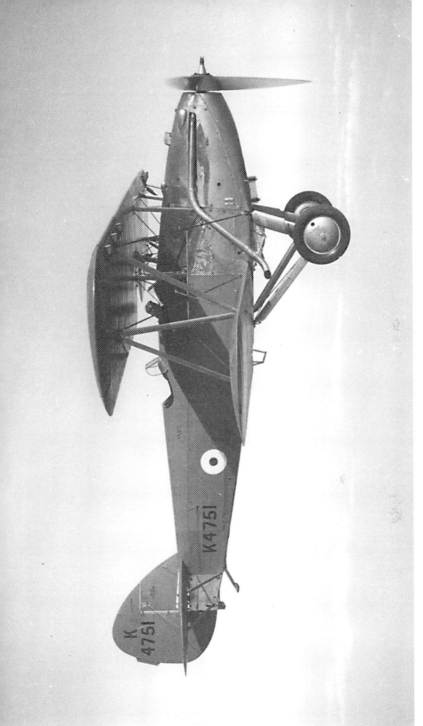

Plate 9
HAWKER HART

"A cross between a racing aeroplane and a two-seater fighter."

© *Flight International*/Quadrant Picture Library

Plate 10
AVRO TUTORS

"Not as easy as it looks from your enclosure at Hendon…"

"A Fury did some very spectacular upward rolls and zooms"

Plate 11
HAWKER FURY

"...somewhere among the still banks of white cumulus clouds."

Plate 12
BRISTOL BULLDOG

Plate 13
AVRO 504N

"The queer, cooped, drumming, flapping world under the hood..."
(W. E. P. Johnson in a solo blind take-off.)

Plate 14

THE HAYCOCK INN
Above: ". . .a famous old coaching inn"
Below: ". . .swim from the riverbank" (River Nene)

Plate 15

CHANGING TIMES
Above: Avro Tutor with the new Grob 115 Tutor, ab-initio trainer for the RAF.
Below: Harriers GR7 and GR10 at RAF Wittering.

Plate 16

CFS Formation Aerobatic Team, 1999: The Red Arrows
"Airmanship in its highest form"

Curious, and annoying, how one occasionally gets an off-day. Got into the Tutor for the usual whack of dual this morning with Mayor.

"Won't do anything fresh this morning," came down the voice pipe as we taxyed out, "run over some old stuff. Give me the take-off patter. You've got her."

Taxyed out, talking the usual preliminaries with an anxious eye cocked out for other aircraft coming into land, as ever when moving on the ground in this place.

Well, nice soft summery day for flying. Gentle wind and broken clouds fairly still and over two thousand feet; with plenty of sunshine to keep the sheep warm, too. Leaned on a wall last night down a country lane and watched a farm-hand, brick-red about the arms and neck, expertly snipping the wool off one, with its head locked between his knees and its feebly protesting forelegs grasped firmly in a horny left hand. Until presently he tossed a complete fleece on to a pile of others and with a dab of tar on a couple of flesh grazes let his naked victim go and dragged another one from the trembling, bleating pen.

We sat heading into wind with the airscrew nickering round.

"Before you take off have a good look round the cockpit. See that the petrol's on, those switches that should be on are on, that the instruments—oil pressure and so forth—are reading correctly, and if necessary set the altimeter to zero."

Early on I was caught well and truly at that.

"Is the petrol on?" came a bland voice from the back. Then I knew the worst, before I looked. The instructor has a duplicate set of instruments and controls in the back. He'd turned the petrol off, sure enough. Ticking over, she'll run on the carburettor reserve for a minute, and I'd gone gaily talking on.

All was well, this time. Explained exactly how to take off, and then headed finally into wind.

"Now lightly hold the controls and see how it's done when I take off. Pick some point on the far hedge or the horizon on which to keep the nose, and with the control column slightly forward of central to help raise the tail in the air, gradually open the throttle to the full extent." (Here one begins to roar to make oneself heard over the engine noise.)

"The aeroplane moves forward and the tail rises in the air." No frantic gabbling now. By George, I've got this weighed off. Synchronised to a T. "Then ease the control column back to central to prevent the tail rising too high, and the aeroplane leaves the ground of its own accord." It does. "Gently ease the control column forward to gain full flying speed. Then ease it back and assume your best climbing angle."

Grand. I shift in the straps and stick out my chest with pleased vanity. We roar up at seventy and the road and trees gradually recede beneath. Now for the engine failure bit. I talk very slowly to gain time and turn slightly to the left. Now comes the time. Yes, I think I can make that bit of park.

"*Should* the engine fail" — and here to the pupil's horror and alarm, you suddenly ram the throttle back and slam the control column forward so that the aeroplane changes from a forty-five degree climb to a forty-five degree dive — "put the nose *well* down to prevent a stall and make some sort of landing straight ahead. Turns up to thirty or forty degrees may be made either way to avoid obstacles, but never attempt to turn back to the aerodrome." Doubt is now beginning to creep into your voice. We're now about two hundred feet over the trees, and too low down to make the grass beyond. However, you keep on hopefully in a bright voice. All this gives the pupil unbounded confidence.

"There, you see, we could land —" but Mayor slams the throttle on and up we go again.

"Do you think so?"

"No. But I wouldn't let the pupil know."

"You *must* exercise ingenuity in choosing your spot to go down."

But already my morning has started to go to bits, although three minutes before on the aerodrome I felt as though I could give the C.F.I. himself points on how to fly. I feel Bolshie, and to short-circuit any more reproaches, which are lashes to my self-esteem, turn on my conversational vein.

"It's practically impossible to guarantee a landing down here with the wind in this quarter, don't you think? It's all wooded stuff with hardly a clearing at all."

But I get no change.

"Yes, but you must exercise ingenuity. Talk slowly, turn a bit, anything to jockey for a good place."

I did all those before I shut off. All right, have it your own way. I dry up and peering moodily out through my goggles climb on and wait for the next bit.

"Now give me a landing."

Oh Gawd, this flying at the aerodrome at a thousand feet and then shutting off and gliding in. Well, I shut off and get in all right. But hold off too near to the ground and spin my wheels in the middle of the patter. Which knocks off the speed, and I bounce six inches or so and sit down stalled before I've finished talking.

"That wasn't very good for this stage of the proceedings. Try again."

Off and round we go. I made a mental note of the place where I shut off before, just over a triangular wood. This time I shut off in exactly the same spot and am still at two hundred feet gliding over the boundary fence. I swear, glide on, and do another not frightfully good demonstration.

"Try another one."

Round we go. That damned wind must have dropped last time. All right, shut off early. I do so, and have to 'rumble' at a thousand revs. for half a minute to get in over the boundary. That's criminal. I try two more. Landing patter all right, but approaches getting steadily worse. Sideslipping like hell the last two times. And it's no use telling a pupil to land on the aerodrome off a straight glide when you can't do it yourself.

"All right, we'll go and do some elementary forced landings. I've got her. Funny thing that experienced pilots can't do that. If you told a chap with a thousand hours in that he couldn't shut off and do a straight glide to land reasonably near the boundary on a place the size of this he'd laugh at you. But they can't, none of 'em."

This, however, is poor balm to my incompetent soul. I no longer notice the sunshine. *Il n'y a plus de printemps dans mon coeur.*

1st of June

It's amazing how the boys just melt away when weekends come. At lunchtime on Friday the place is crowded out; but when you wander in for tea at four o'clock after flying they've just vanished into thin air. From four-thirty until six there are only about four people in the ante-room, listening to dance music, looking at the lovelies in the *Bystander,* or wearily writing letters that can no longer be put off. And those four are usually the Duty Flute, the Orderly Officer and two poor wights who hail from Portperran or whose hearts are in the Hielands. Friday night is a supper night, at any rate, which is a blessing, although the four (or five) of us have to put on dinner jackets to eat it. Still, my dinner jacket is comfortable, which is more than can be said for mess kit.

A favourite conversational gambit in the ante-room before dinner is "Where did you get your mess kit?"

Which in turn naturally leads to the revilement of Service tailors, and then there is no further need to search for anything else of which to talk. Rich are the tales and many you will hear of these forty latter-day thieves.

The day on which you commission one or the other of them to build your Outfit is a day for them indeed. You are invited, on an imposing card, to call at their West End branch where they will be delighted to wait upon you and receive the honour of your commands. Even the pavements are rumoured to be of gold in that part of the world. And you know directly you gaze upon the unticketed pair of string gloves, and the bit of a bolt of cloth (for want of better words) draped over a pedestal that are the sole exhibits in their two vast plate-glassed windows, that you'll be separated from seventy or eighty pounds – sorry, guineas – before you get out of that door again. An enormous commissionaire resplendent in blue and gold braid, and with the medal ribbons of at least ten African and Chinese campaigns across his broad chest, twirls his moustache with a white-gloved hand and opens the swing door for you, with a flourish and a salute. He must have been a Sergeant-Major. No other man could polish a pair of boots like that. You pass in and a vastly superior young man in grey striped trousers, black coat, dazzling white collar and pearly grey tie comes forward to meet you. But already the richness of your surroundings are beginning to have their effect. Your gloves and shoes and hat, hitherto old and well-cared-for, tried and trusted friends, are none of those things any longer. They are merely cheap and shabby togs, fit for naught else but prompt relegation to a distant and discreet dustbin. You stifle this incoming tide of inferiority complex by endeavouring to answer in your one remaining asset, a clear ringing, well-bred and pleasantly modulated voice. By which token the young man will know your clothes to be merely eccentric, but your stock All Right. It being only the rich, in fact, who can afford to be badly dressed. But to your surprise this voice has a sort of strangled, strained-through-butter muslin sound when it comes.

"The manager, sir? Certainly, sir. At the moment he is in consultation, but I know he will be delighted to see you the minute he is free. If you would care to take a seat, I will let him know you are here, sir."

He draws a leather saddlebag chair up to a table on which *The Times, Punch, The R.A.F. Quarterly,* and the Army, Navy and Air Force lists are scattered. Smilingly beckons you to it with an inclination of his neatly brushed head, and then goes into an inner room. He calls you 'sir', but that doesn't fool you. You reflect that he undoubtedly went to a much more expensive school than your own. He implies that the manager has been all the afternoon eagerly awaiting your coming. And that in a moment he will be impatiently trying to dismiss the client in his office so that he can charge out and perspiringly bow and smile and accede to your every wish. Huh.

You look around. Rear-Admirals and Brigadier-Generals and Cabinet Ministers come here for uniform and clothes. It is a famous shop in a famous street of shops. Forty Years On, perhaps, when time has brought its chaplets of fame and garlands of reward, you will find these surroundings to your taste. But at the moment they are overpowering. The carpet is too soft, the lighting in the glass jewellery cabinets too discreet, the appointments in general far too luxurious to make you feel at your ease. This is not yet quite your milieu...

Your reflections come to an abrupt stop as one who can be nobody else but the Tailor-Manager comes bearing down upon you from the *sanctum sanctorum* with pleasant smile and outstretched hand. If there were a more exclusive tie than that of Eton, then for sure it would be curving out above his immaculate vest.

"Ah, sir, we have been expecting you. Mr. Musk! Please take Mr. Aileron-fflap to the fitting rooms. You have all his particulars. He will be requiring a complete outfit. This way, sir, if you please."

By now a young escort has formed up. The head cutter, two junior tailors, and a small boy with four large manifold books. Like

107

accused and escort you step out over another hundred yards of noiseless carpet to the fitting rooms.

Inside there are fifteen mirrors and as many batteries of cleverly concealed lights. It is a blaze brighter than day, and the heavy door closes with a thud on all five of you and completely blanks off the busy outside world. Now you are for it. Off trousers and coat. The three craftsmen produce tape measures and the small boy flicks open his books, adjusts the carbons, and gives his pencil a ruminative lick. From sheer force of habit the head cutter fills his mouth with pins. Could you dictate figures with about fifteen pins held between your lips? No, of course not. But he can. Thirty years in the trade, sir, man and boy. Then he stands five yards away, inclines his body backwards, and views you through half-closed eyes. A horse-breeder sizing up a filly, or a sheik checking over the latest acquisition for his harem, couldn't do it with more studied artistry. Meanwhile you are furtively glancing in the mirrors at the reflections of yourself from fifty different sides. The battery of arc-lights blazes down, and a thousand reflections of your curious self in your still more curious undress dwindle down the corridors of mirrors. The head cutter, two junior cutters and small boy eye you sadly but are sufficiently well bred to keep their thoughts to themselves.

Kings have stood in this fitting room. And here, too, the head cutter tells you, he once stuck a pin into a Prince. We regard with detachment again our puce socks darned with grey wool as he measures on.

The small boy breathes heavily and, with protruding tongue, writes as a man possessed. At any rate he has shifted his fascinated gaze from the hole in the seat of your pants.

Until, eventually, after a very long *mauvais quart d'heure*, you are allowed to huddle into your ill-fitting clothes again and creep out through the swing doors into the street.

Before you left, the head cutter glanced at the label inside the inner breast pocket of your suit. You could not swear to it, but you were almost certain that he sniffed.

Now, before you went up to London, an old hand who had had some, gave you much good advice.

"Ever hear the story of the chap who got a really rude letter from his tailor? No? Well, he wrote back to them and said: 'Now look here, at the moment I'm paying off my bills. And the manner in which I do it is this. Each month I put all the bills into a hat, and with averted eyes grope for and select one. Which I then proceed to pay. If you're not damned careful, your bill won't go into the hat at all.' Not bad, eh?

"There's also another story about the same chap which I think is perfectly rich. Quite true, of course. He was hauled up before the beaks for a motoring offence, or something. Anyway, there he was, branded with the felon's mark, chained to the dock and anchored down with iron balls and several more feet of chain. And a beefy bull-necked copper on each side to keep him under restraint.

"Well, the tailor's representative gave his evidence and the villain of the piece gave his, prompted by sharp digs in the ribs from the bobbies when he was tempted to get facetious and fresh. And then the Head Beak did the summing up. And do you know who he was? One of the members of the Board of Directors of the firm which was preferring the charge! With no shade of bias he soaked the defendant ten guineas in fine and costs. Not a bit abashed, accused just grinned up and said, 'Thank you, sir. Will you stick it on to my account?' And then the old boy came to life. He promptly smacked on another fiver for contempt of court.

"And of course," he went on, "I've made no mention of zinc-lined uniform cases or things like that. I credit you with sufficient common sense not to need any advice at all to keep off them. Oh, you'll see 'em there all right. Mottled red and black tin outsides; stacks of 'em. About four quid a time, I should say, and they'll paint on your rank and name and so forth, in white at sixpence a letter and it'll be no trouble at all, sir, oh no. We once had an ass who really was green. More money than sense, I'm sure.

"He was as a new-born babe in their hands. The potters held in him a fistful of really un — I beg your pardon — of virgin clay. He went along as innocent as you like and spent about four hours doing a grand tour of the whole place. In fact he was the King of All Suckers, and it is credibly reported that gradually the members of the staff got wind of it and began to tail behind the Manager and the Dupe, gazing with an incredulous gaze. First of all they measured him up for the usual greatcoat, caps, tunics, mess kit, breeches and so forth and so on.

"Then he gave them an inquiring smile and asked them what else would he need? The manager winked over the infant's shoulder at the head cutter, and they gently led him upstairs. It's a ducal mansion flight of stairs. Stags' heads and pictures of Nelson all over the place. Carpets an extra half-inch thick. On its way up the procession halted while the infant read a notice about Houses For Sale and to Let that might interest Officer Clients; and remarked how kind and thoughtful it was of the firm to provide a notice-board and such gratuitous information for customers. I expect the bounders get a rake-off — anything from ten to a hundred pounds on every house they let or sell.

"Well, up they went, and he was led round Shirts and Socks. They easily persuaded him to spend about twenty quid in Shirts and Socks. Six of this essential, sir, eight of that. Twelve of these. Oh, indubitably. No officer, with the slightest pretensions to being well-dressed, nay even adequately dressed, would dream of having less than twelve. He had commissioned them downstairs to build him three lounge suits when they were running the tape measure over him for tunic and slacks. Just a happy thought that entered his head, I suppose. Only twelve guineas each suit, that's all. Of course the lad with the manifold book was having the time of his life. Fairly whistling down the columns and over the page.

"Then the cortège trickled round to Ties. The Infant fairly goggled then and became all wreathed in silly smiles. Ties to match all over the place. I believe they sent twenty away to be wrapped up before they could drag him off to Dressing Gowns, Hats, and Shoes. (It was getting near closing time.)

"After another half-hour three or four junior assistants had tacked on to the end of what was now a squadron formation in line astern. And they were freely laying bets. But the manager — all other business now quite forgotten — did manage to pull off his grand slam.

"'Would you be thinking of going abroad, sir?' he gently asked.

"The infant thought for a moment.

"'Well, do you know, I expect I shall. I'm going to an Army Co-op Squadron, and of course they're always being bunged off abroad. Usually for five long years in India too.'

"The Manager had great difficulty not to fairly shriek with delight. Into the Tropical Section they fairly pounded, and you should have seen the junk they loaded on him there. The usual drill outfit of course. Tunics three quid each, slacks, breeches, khaki puttees, ditto shirts, topee and all the rest of the stuff they keep. Remind me in a minute to tell you something else about tropical kit. Well, then they sold the bum: (1) a mosquito net. They're issued free of charge wherever you go; (2) a camp kit—

bed, blankets, copper washbowl, canvas bath, ground-sheet, etc., also issued free to every serving officer during his career; (3) a cholera belt. What a cholera belt is I don't know, but he bought one. I always thought it was a sort of zone overprinted on maps to show you where the incidence of the disease is greatest, but apparently it's not. And (4) mosquito boots. Mosquito *boots*! Might as well have bought snowshoes for all the use he'll ever find for them East of Suez. The only thing there that ever concerned me was to discover a therapy for an unslakable thirst. Of course he'd ordered a full dress uniform before he finally left. Any sane man hires his for the odd wedding and levée that he may be called upon to attend. But not the Infant. Oh no. That came along to the squadron a few weeks afterwards in the pantechnicon with the rest of his gear. I expect he'll use it about six times in the course of a long life. Unless he takes to going to bed with it on. What does full dress cost? No idea. Thirty pounds if a penny, I should say. You *can* keep it in cold storage when you're not using it, I've heard tell, for about three shillings a week.

"In all, I think our young friend spent the best part of two hundred and fifty quid. Flying helmet, overalls, binoculars, prismatic compass, first-aid outfit—he bought 'em all. And each and every one of those items is lent to you free of charge whenever you need them during your Service career. All shareholders got a bumper dividend in that season of the year. Oh, and of course I forgot to tell you about the Jewellery going down. On the second floor they passed through Trunks and Bags. He only stopped there a few minutes to buy a pigskin suitcase or two and some cow-hide trunks, in which the firm kindly arranged to despatch his gear. Can't have spent much more than twenty cracklers in there. But just as he was being ushered out by whole rows of bowing attendants and the manager was holding the door—he'd shooed the S.M. off to whistle for a taxicab—Young Innocent spotted the Jewellery Cabinets. Back he went. Held up the whole of the farewell show, which I thought was pretty inconsiderate of him. Of course, anyone with cash has great scope there. And he was completely captivated with the idea of being able to give presents now on which were engraved or mounted real R.A.F. pairs of wings. Cigarette case and sleeve links for himself, ten pounds. Powder flapjack thing for Sissie. Oh, very cute. Blue, azure, and claret, sort of enamelled moirée ribbon effect. Three pounds that. Leather handbag for Mum, also crested, five pounds. Then they couldn't bear to skin him any more. The manager gently took him by the arm and led him out to his waiting cab.

"The moral behind all this? I don't know. Just that it takes all sorts to make a world."

But did you profit by this good advice? Not you. When the fitting was done with, you weakly accepted the printed list of 'Essential Items of an R.A.F. Officer's Outfit' that the head cutter pushed into your hands.

"Shall we proceed with the remainder of the outfit, sir?" he had asked.

"Yes, yes please," you had gaggled. "By all means, yes, please. Whatever you think I might need."

"Good day to you. Good day," you said, and made hurriedly for swing doors and safety with a quick and nervous tread. And so one more sucker received the hallmark of the trade.

3rd of June

Back to the serious business of earning our bread and butter after the fleshpots of the weekend. Cowling was Duty Pilot (the airmen pilots' chores. We do Orderly Officer) so flew for practice patter with Holt-fflair, who loves the sound of his own aristocratic voice, and burbles away in the purest of Oxford accents, rolling his rrr's and dotting his i's. When he first starts it is really most impressive. But then, half-way through the patter he just packs up—can't remember any more. He does it with the most airy confidence and self-satisfaction, too! His flying is all slash and dash. He'll have to buck up if he's to get pretty marks. Doesn't listen at all to your own patter, and can't criticise it if he does, because his own ideas are of the vaguest; he makes up most of his own explanation as he goes along. Cowling is good. He jumps on me like a pouncing tiger if I make the smallest slip, and by agreement I do the same to him. You just waste your time in the air if you don't. Holt-fflair can't even roll to the left in the sketchiest fashion. Gets nearly over and then roars off in a sort of spiral dive. This comforts me exceedingly. I may roll left badly, but I do get round.

Abdulla is something of a poet. He talks very good English; it is quaint, but you can understand. This morning, sitting in the crew room jotting down our trips on grubby scraps of paper and smoking after our labours in the air, he waxed very enthusiastic over the mediaeval cultural influences of his countrymen. Mathematics, astronomy, medicine, architecture, literature. Look! he said. Regard! They lead the field. He loves the poetical tag. He told me the last words of the Queen to her Master, the man who built the Alhambra, before he went into his death-battle against the infidels. And he told me, too, the oriental comment on the camel's superior, nose-twisting grimace inside its rope muzzle: "Man knows ninety-nine names for God, but the camel knows the hundredth."

Abdulla is very funny in the air. He gets quite excited and jubilant when he puts across patter and then makes the aeroplane do what he says.

"Look—see! I push de chontrrol column forward de nose he go down. Look—de nose he now go down!" Trained by English instructors lent to his own country, he had only flown a couple of hundred hours on comparatively light aeroplanes before he came over to England. In view of this it is amazing how well he flies the Hart and Bulldog with the best of us. He attends all our lectures and practical work in the engines and rigging shops, too. He won't be expected to take the end of term exams, with us, but the gist of everything is soaking into him amazingly well, and to have to learn strange things in the technical names of a strange tongue must be very hard indeed. Of a rich merchant family, he is the first of his line, since it began, not to trade in silks and carpets with Bokhara, Teheran and Samarkand. And now, in our country, he carefully absorbs the high mysteries of theory of flight, meteorology, and air navigation. Anticyclones, centre of pressure, $P = \frac{1}{2}av^2$, rhumb lines and mercatorial bearings, down they all go into his notebooks and at night he masters them in his room and then translates them into rough equivalents of his own tongue. Control Column becomes 'the long stick', Rhumb Line 'the curved map line', Anticyclone 'a wind against the sun', and so on. And to help our clerky staff he has even abandoned filling in his logbook from the back, and going from right to left across the pages.

Those of us who have any rusty schoolbook French left find that a common tongue, for the schools of Beirut in French Syria saw him for three years during his youth.

113

When he goes back to his own country to instruct he plans to motor across Europe and the Middle Eastern deserts in a new car. Last week he wrote a tentative letter to the manufacturers of his choice to start a deal. The reply, half in business and half in automobile jargon, was a bit beyond him here and there. So he consulted Garrick.

"Why certainly, old Abdul. It's a pleasure. I'll answer it for you. Just leave it to me. And if you get stuck again, bowl along at any time."

With the result now that Garrick is carrying on an intensive course of bargaining with the motor firm on Abdulla's behalf! To go into a shop and pay the price that is asked for an article is quite beyond all Orientals. The bartering to them is three parts of the game; and the merchants love it just as much as their customers do. Indeed, they are apt to despise a man who does not haggle for the space of at least half an hour before parting with his cash. They always start by naming treble the value as their rock-bottom price, and not until that has been halved and then had another ten per cent knocked off does the real business begin. And of course Society's sons, paying the starting price without a murmur in the arcades of Cairo and Tangiers, are the delighted talk of all their coffee house hours of sandalled, hookah-puffing ease.

Abdulla carried his bazaar tactics into his dealings with the English motor firms. After much haggling they knocked off three per cent. But this was not nearly enough.

"I drrive to Constantinople. I drrive to Damas. I cross de desert. Verry fine avertisment for your car," he wrote. "I verry good drivver. I command great respects in my country. Many listen to me. Yours will be the first little car in my country of its special kind. Never before they see your little car. Then across the big deserts I come. Paris, Wien, Istanbul, all the big cities I cross. I make for you the big name. Please Ten Per Cent."

"Four Per Cent," came back the exhausted reply. "We ruin ourselves as it is."

"Ten Per Cent, I beg. I tell all the big agents of my own country what a brave big car is your little car. Never before he come. I write of my voyage in the newspaper of our big city. Many read. You do plenty of businesses. Sirs, Ten Per Cent."

In the end, when Garrick was a pen-enfeebled wreck, they sold a £200 car for £182. Now Garrick is girding up his tottering loins to begin on the really difficult stuff. Tax, insurance, routes, visas, foreign customs, permits, and a thousand other formalities that must be seen to if one is to motor three thousand miles across a score of the different countries of the world.

4th of June

At last the wind has come out of the northern quarter and gone round to the sou'-west. But the weather still remains capricious. We seem to be living in a permanent 'warm front' as the Met chap calls it, where the warm air of your depression is sliding up over the cold air in the southern part of the anticyclone and giving us towering cumulus cloud, with alternate brilliant sunshine and heavy showers. However, we managed to fly this afternoon. In the morning the tarmac was littered with Gold Braid so we couldn't fly. Must have been the whole of the Display Committee — an Air Vice-Marshal, two Group Captains, two Wing Commanders, and Squadron Leaders two-a-penny. They were watching part of a try-out for the Hendon Display, all looking very official with shooting sticks and binoculars on straps; more rows of medal ribbon than you'll see in the windows of West End outfitters, and what with the roar of the engines and the pointing and talking and referring to sheaves of papers, as nice and official and technical and efficient a show as any layman could wish to see. An Army Co-operation Squadron had come down to give a display of message picking-up. They had nine Audaxes, or Audaces or whatever the plural is. Real pursuit squadron ships with long silver snouts and a wicked great propeller whacking round that would take your head off like a razor going through cheese. Sort of refined looking Hart. I never know what these things are; I suppose it's a second cousin. The small air-minded boy knows much more about types and statistics than I do. At my last squadron we used to sit in the seaplane cockpits on the top of the slipway waiting for a man below to get away before the hawsers could slide us down, and I learned quite a lot of useful facts about the aircraft I was flying, from the conversation of shrilly enthusiastic small boys who had gathered on the promenade to try to wish-fulfil themselves into the cockpits and away and up and out to sea under the April clouds.

Anyhow, these Audaces seemed to have it frightfully well buttoned up. A team of their crews, who had done a six-hour road journey in a Morris six-wheeler for the occasion, dashed out on to the aerodrome and did mysterious things. Then they dashed back to leave five-foot posts sticking up in pairs with messages dangling on cords stretched between them. The pursuit ships came rocking and streaming into wind, all nine of them doing about a hundred and twenty and only landing height up, V formation. Judging your height to a foot at that speed isn't easy. There's a big ridge on the aerodrome too — I thought someone would bash his undercart on it, but he didn't.

They roared through the poles a few yards from us, and when they zoomed up, all but two had the red, yellow and blue bags streaming from their M.P.U. poles. And as they zoomed, a big white puff of smoke shot up from each pair of poles that had been cleaned of its billet doux. Now I thought that was pretty good.

I've tried M.P.U. You've got to be slap into wind when you fly up to pick off the message, or drift throws you out and disturbs judgement to a considerable degree. You have to come down on a steady motoring glide too. Fly in at the poles as though you were flying in to a flare path for a night landing in a stiff wind. No diving at it with engine off. Or flying parallel to the ground. It's got to be a steady swoop with the bottom of your trajectory coincident with the poles, and your hook in the middle of the cord. Ruddering to fly slap over a point isn't easy. To try it with any out-of-wind drift will ruin all your chances. And when the poles disappear under the blind spot of your nose and are still a hundred feet ahead you can only wait and hope. Five times out of six your hook, that swings three feet lower than the axle, sails gaily over the cord although you could swear it's trailing in the grass. The sixth time you swear to get that flaunting bit of rag and straighten the hook out on the ground as you bash the wings through the poles and split the wing fabric. If the poles weren't made to swivel forward at a glancing blow you could say 'good-bye' to your spars, and sit on the ground for three days while the riggers repaired the dented wings. So M.P.U. has to be practised quite a lot for efficiency to be attained. But to lead a squadron down for each chap to pluck his own message off his own pole — well, I was lost in admiration. And yet, watching a couple of chaps playing shove ha'penny by a window in the ante-room after tea, I suddenly heard one of them say to the other, "Didn't go much on the M.P.U. this morning, did you?"

"No, pretty bum show, I thought." And then I realized that by the correct standards they must be right. For both of them were Army Co-operation pilots before they came on this course.

After the M.P.U. effort the three red and white Tutors did their inverted show. It really is getting impressive now. For they've been practising at three thousand feet or so, too high to really appreciate what's going on. But now they're getting it weighed off, and came down to a thousand today for the judges to see. It's far cleverer in our eyes than it probably is to the civilians who watch it at Hendon. Lower down, when you see the wings meeting the air-flow, at a curious angle, the rudder sticking *down* and the wheels sailing along on the top you really do realize that the pilot is floating along upside down. And you can appreciate the neatness and precision and effortless ease of their half rolls. Even now most of the rolls we do are adventures. We get over safely and maintain a reasonably straight course and constant height. But it's a determined, grit-your-teeth kind of affair with little things like skidding quite ignored. And as for station-keeping in threes, tight formation turns or line ahead rolls—well, we don't say much, but we do quietly raise our hats. It's not a superman's job—it's something practically all of us could do with sufficient practice. They just choose three chaps here, because three are all they want, and they fly until they can do it. But it's difficult all the same.

Since last Thursday morning we haven't done any patter. Either solo or Service type flying, with a long weekend and the King's birthday holiday chucked in. Five clear days in all, and Cowling and I very gladly went solo again in the afternoon. Sideslipping was the last thing we did, and jogging each other's failing memories, managed to reconstruct some sort of patter for the three ways of doing it—with and without drift, and off a gliding turn. Then we played at forced landings; flying off one of the fields, with the passenger of the moment cutting the throttle for the other at as inconvenient moment as possible—at height downwind on a climb usually. Then the pilot is supposed to go sweetly and calmly into his forced landing patter at once and put her neatly over the hedge of a four-by-two field at the end of it. Drifted past and through great driving curtains of rain here and there, and talked and flew on in turns until 3.30 and all the birds were homing again. You glide in with about four other chaps sliding down around you at the same time, and five or six more sitting on the aerodrome into wind waiting for you to get down before they taxy up to the filling points. Skim over the telegraph wires on the Great North Road with ten feet to spare. Then drop like a brick for the last few feet because of some curious wind current due to the ridge that you haven't experienced before with no S.W. wind, but by flattening out and landing all in one hit manage to make her kiss the turf on three points and stick there without a bounce.

At dinner tonight, Bruce, who's in this inverted flight, told me it's dead easy once you've developed a new technique for breathing. Your chest is constricted by the harness, so you have to use your tummy!

5th of June

Went to the hangars this morning really expecting a trying morning. Life in the air has been too good to be true lately. And sooner or later Mayor will say, "Now give me the patter for medium and steep turns", or something like that, and then when I've infuriated him with a hazy and inaccurate impression of those, try to shut off on a long straight glide for a landing patter on the aerodrome, and go gliding over the windward hedge a hundred feet up; cap this by miserably undershooting on a forced landing, or else dive off my back trying to roll to the left and—well, in short, come up smack against the really difficult things again. But no, our luck still holds good. I walked out with my earphone leads banging on my chest and the dangling harness buckles clinking their little tune behind me to find, on the detail board hung on the tarmac wall, our names down for the dual Bulldog.

At last! Ever since I've been a pilot I've wanted to fly a single-seater fighter and never had the chance. Single-engined bombers cruising at 110 and carrying a crew of three, similar aeroplanes on floats, and flying boats with big control wheels, two pilots, and crews up to six have been my luck hitherto. Bulldogs are old. Squadrons of them were roaring around during my Wiltshire period seven years ago; and now they're using up old stock for training purposes. They always have looked like fighting aircraft. Four of them were being warmed up by the fitters as we walked over, line abreast heading into wind, their fat short little bodies hugging the ground, their thick and stubby airscrews making the dust fly as they tore round and pulled the wheels against the chocks. Green and silver backs and yellow wheel-shields, airscrew spinners and cowling gun channels. Cockpits fairly crowded with instruments and levers and direction plates. And when they're fitted for normal squadron use, with radio telephony and wing-tip to rudder aerials, two Vickers guns sticking their feed blocks into your elbows, and a great big nine cylinder Jupiter just in front of your nose, an old R.A.F. pilot, thirsting for more speed and manoeuvrability, a trouble-free engine and guns, and a crate off which you just couldn't pull the wings, would have simply died with envy had he seen one in 1916. We clambered into the dual and did up our straps, Mayor behind. And as he explained the cocks and things in his usual way, the richest smell of all came drifting into the cockpit on warm, eddying gusts of air. Hot castor oil with a faint metally tang to it. It must be one of the seven scents of Paradise. One is never far away from it during all the flying years. Offices and even one's rooms in mess will forever now hold the faint essence of it from generations of suits of overalls worn in the air and hung up during the spells. And after a year or so away from flying on other jobs the hangar and tarmac smells, the faint keen tang of aviation petrol when they're refuelling, and the rich odour of castor and fabric dope are as keen in my nostrils as the wind off the spring meadows to the wild-eyed and heel-kicking colt, or the scent of his lofted hay to the harvest-weary farmer. Beachcomber has rated the odour of barn stored apples one of the seven scents. Give me aero-engine smells every time. Even now it is my habit, when gliding in with the motor throttled back with only the steady whine of the air over the wires left, to jack up my seat and put my head out to one side. Then you get the sharp, steady eighty mile an hour stream of air in your nostrils and a faint scent you'll get nowhere else in the world—the smell of wind a thousand feet above the earth—and it does smell. Perhaps its speed in some way affects the sensory nerves and produces the effect of smell, but there it is, indescribable and faintly sweet; and mingled with it the ghosty tang of burnt castor and hot aluminium and steel. When I'm a lean and slippered pantaloon and all the battles lost or won, those smells or their memory will set the young blood coursing again. Would I shine my pants on an office stool for the daily bread? Not I!

In the Bulldog you half lie back. The straps are tight over your shoulders, your legs straddled out to reach the rudder bar, your right fist on the spade grip and your left closed round the big throttle lever. You taxy out bumping and rocking vilely, your toes ready to stab on the foot-brakes if she won't stop swinging in the wind. Mayor does one circuit and landing to show you how it goes, and then you take off and climb up. After Tutors she fairly leaps off the ground, and climbs at a rate of knots. In level flight the airspeed needle sticks around the 130 mark, well throttled back to cruising revs. Steep turns. 4000 feet, loop and slow rolls. Rolls off top right and left. You fly them round on loops with engine. Then up to 8000 for a couple of spins. Sometimes the duals take a fair time and sane coaxing to come out, but this time she came out as sweet as a nut. Then three landings—they touch down at a fair lick and run on like old Harry. We taxy in, and a single-seater version is warming up against the chocks.

"Off you go," says Mayor.

I sign the 535, get in and do up the harness, run up and test the magnetos, wave away the chocks, and off we go. Into the air for the first time alone in what had not long ago been a first line fighter. At last my boyhood dreams are realized, and no longer am I a pupil instructor taxying out to do a few tame circuits and landings and adventurous aerobatics but a blooded ace, out after scalps up where the Archie bursts are white scratches against the pale blue of a foreign summer sky. There are two hundred rounds in each gun belt, one tracer to every twenty-five. Verey pistol and rack of lights on the right. I give the Aldis sight lens a careful rub with the palm of my gloved hand as we jockey down to the leeward aerodrome side. Into wind, look round, open up. We bump over the grass, gather speed, and up comes the tail. Then we soar off the ground, level out for a couple of seconds to gather speed, and then leave the streaming earth behind as I ease up the nose, tilt back my head, and roar up after the prey somewhere among the still banks of white cumulus cloud.

The cold at 15,000 is intense. Fur-lined boots with electrically heated socks, a sidcot with generator leads, black electrical gloves inside the gauntlets, and fine wires zig-zagging between the goggle glasses all keep one just pleasantly warm. Grease on the cheeks and of course an oxygen mask clamped to nose and mouth to defy the heights. I give the guns a few bursts to keep them warm and dividing the sky up into mental sectors, begin my search.

The ship is mine. I take a reassuring glance round the dials. Big rev. indicator needle quivering at 2000, oil and petrol gauges correct, outlet temperature all right, boost zero—for the moment!— height 18,300, airspeed 160 true. I absently pat the gun feed blocks and rock the wings, looking for a tiny bunched formation below, impatient to begin. I can swoop and rocket, poise and curve, roll over in a wide arc and come down like a plummet out of the sun with the engine roaring, the wires screaming a thousand devils' song, and the twin gun-spouts shattering spurts of flame at the target gently edged on to the hair line circles etched on my lenses. There they go! There! and the dupes think I don't know. Droning along peacefully, four of 'em, at about 8000, heading west with their own cargo of bombs. They can neither see nor hear what moves up in the blaring brightness of the sun. Two more bursts to make sure everything's all right, then down goes the nose and I close one eye to get my first bead on the prey. The speed must be 300 when I ease up under their blind spot. The controls as stiff as iron and the air blast like a solid wall. For a moment I poise the leader in the sights, then down go both thumbs and I pump a hail of lead into him. He rocks uncertainly and then goes over and down, down, down, in a long, wide, lazy curve. I ease back, and up we go in a vertical zoom, one, two, two and a half thousand feet until the speed whine becomes a gentle sigh. I flatten out and look down. Fools. Fools! They've broken up. Easy meat. I pick the next man. Load. Up with the reservoir handles. Down we go on to his tail. He turns. I batten on behind him. He turns and turns. I tighten my turn, too. Fields and woods wheel below through a mile of empty space, and the wing and strut shadows are moving bars across my goggled eyes. Somewhere to the left my subconscious knows my own aerodrome lies. He goes up into an Immelman turn. Still I'm there when his white face looks back. But not yet. Another couple left after him, and only about three hundred rounds left. We loop together. And then he plays into my hands by easing her right up and kicking her into a spin. I wait, poise, and then dive. Fix him fair and square in the sights, and then let drive! And even as I fire I feel a faint thud thud. Out of the corner of my eye I see a small row of black dots suddenly appear under the top wing and a huge silver shadow flashes past over my head. I bank vertically and nearly black out bringing her round to deal now with the remaining two scalps. They'll get me? Never on your young life. Magazine stories are written around my name...

I taxy in to render my battle report.

"All right?" says Mayor on the tarmac.

"Yes, four slow rolls not bad. Bit right wing down on the loops. Landings all right except a wheely one."

"O.K. You'd better rush now if you're to be in time for rigging lecture. Cheerio."

6th of June

We still pile up the hours. Lectures, flying, lectures, flying, all day long. A day of slumbrous warmth with the trees heaped and summer green below, the great towering cloudlands of cumulus all mixed up silver and pastel grey against the misty blue of far horizons. Rolling stuff from six to ten thousand, a summer thunder sky. Tiny yellow specks wheel here and there, turn and disappear as the others demonstrate, practise and talk. Tutor in the morning, three ways of employing the sideslip into the Stamford field. Nose into wind, nose across wind, and on a gliding turn. Try, try, and try again. In A.R.S. we begin lacing up and doping the fabric of the Atlas main-planes, getting ready to offer up and bolt home. Then in the afternoon the Bulldog again, spins and loops and rolls at 9000 feet, with bursts of engine on the glide in to keep the engine warm. My aerobatics have improved out of all recognition. I venture a swish tail landing to mark my pleasure, and by luck pull off a good smacking three-pointer at the end.

We pride ourselves on talking almost no 'shop' in mess. The hangar doors, in other words, are closed. And tonight at dinner the conversation turned to confidence tricks. Esterhazy is unconsciously in his element at dinner times, when the doors are closed and the curtains drawn, and the waiters stand only half realised in the shadows behind. Every now and then one steps forward to perform some discreet, silent service, pick up a napkin, offer a roll, or change a course, and the light shines for a moment on his set face and gleams dully on the big plated buttons of his blue nankeen coat. While down the table the lights are mirrored in the still pool of the beeswaxed top and shine on the massed silver and heaped dessert. The wine boat has been pushed from hand to hand round the mahogany and on either side one looks down a row of the instructing and instructed in boiled shirts.

The fairly intent business of eating is now over. And a hum of conversation has broken out. At the far end the President has relaxed in his chair with the arms, and lighted the cigarette that is the signal for a gentle haze of blue smoke all round. Then Esterhazy comes into his own, and you know as you watch him carefully peel a walnut with his lean fingers and his inches of white cuff with the family-crested flat links resting on the table, that when most of our ancestors were skipping around in suits of woad and mangy, imperfectly-cured bearskins, his forebears were beyond all doubt sitting up to the first dinner-table, wearing the first boiled shirt, and indulging in the first after-dinner talk.

Esterhazy began life as a merchant marine cadet. And since those days three-card tricksters have caught him no less than three times. He popped the walnut under his curved moustaches and airily waved a white aristocratic hand, adorned with a signet ring, of course, to dispose of all argument.

"And they'd have me again. Oh, there's no doubt about it. None at all. They're very crafty. Of course, the first time I was incredibly green and there was no need for any subterfuge. They know. I parted with two pounds ten that time on Spot the Lady. Had to carry my bag five miles and dine off a twopenny packet of chocolate for my pains. The second time they had me, I told myself that I really must be on my guard in future. But they had me only a few months ago. Fleeced me of every penny I had. Only a genial old countryman in the compartment when I got in. Corduroys, bandana handkerchief, gnarled hands and ruddy complexion. Real hayseed. Ay zur, man und boy, you know. We passed the time of day and mentioned the weather. Then drifted on to crops and the National Government and the Milk Board and so on. It was a treat to listen to his simple, salted wisdom on these themes.

"Then at the next station a smart Alec got in, all socks and tiepin and bowler hat; and pretty damn quick produced some cards. Would we like to Spot the Lady?

"Hayseed tipped me a ponderous wink, as much as to say 'What about seeing the boots off this nasty little townie?' I succumbed.

"Of course I lost. Hayseed was the master mind. And it struck me that when he had excused himself during our conversation to go to the heads, he'd probably waved a handkerchief from the window when he was out so that his confederate a few compartments down would know it's time to change seats at the next halt. Fly? Pouf!" He waved his white, aristocratic hand. "I'll bet they'd have all of you. And a second time too."

Loop told us a good one. A poor old half-blind, seedy fiddler was scraping away for coppers in the street. Then he packed up and wandered into a music shop across the way.

"Mister, would you mind lookin' after my violin? It's all I've got in the world. My only means of livelihood. It's a pretty good one, too. Worth about forty quid. All I've got in the world. Y'see, I've got to go down to the Labour Exchange to register. Got hopes of a job. And the crowd there's pretty — well, rough. Wouldn't like to get this damaged. Nearly did last time in the push. Mister, would you mind?"

"Certainly not. Pleasure, I'm sure."

"Thank you, very, very much. I'll be back as quick as I can."

Some time later an expensive-looking car drove up and a very elegant gentleman got out and came into the shop.

"Latest dance music scores?"

"Here we are, sir. Ten, all new, and only just out."

He turned them over, nicking the ash from his cigar as he read and here and there hummed snatches of the tunes.

"Well, I'll take this. And this. And — I say, that's a rather fine-looking fiddle! For sale?"

"Oh no, sir. Belongs to a street musician. I'm minding it for him."

"May I see it?"

"With pleasure."

"H'm. H'm. H - - m. Yes, I thought so. Cremona. Seventeen hundred and twenty — twenty-nine." He spelt out the letters as he peered into the belly of the fiddle.

"A beggar's do you say? Do you know this is worth about NINE HUNDRED POUNDS? Made by Amati himself? I thought at the first glance it might be."

"Impossible!"

"Is it? Give me twenty minutes — no, a quarter of an hour, and I'll give you five hundred in cash on the spot. That'll show you whether or not it's a spoof."

Well, of course, the music dealer wouldn't part, and the fat cigar smoker went away. But he went to get hard cash and rush back again to wait for the beggar's return. Fortunately the beggar came back before the violin expert. And the little music dealer had been thinking quickly.

"I wonder if you'd like to sell your fiddle?" he asked casually. "I can see of course that it's a genuine old piece and worth quite a bit. But actually I had a customer in just now who offered me — er, thirty pounds. Of course I said it wasn't mine. But — twenty-seven pounds? Would that do?"

"Oh no, I couldn't possibly. It's all I've —"

"Twenty-eight?"

"I couldn't."

Well, they argued and argued and eventually the deal was closed. Being a Wednesday the banks were shut, so the beggar had to have hard cash. Only just managed it — every penny in the till. And even with his twenty-eight smackers he went out sadly, faintly shaking his regretful head. Of course, neither he nor the cigar-smoker ever came back again. Clever fake. Worth at a rough estimate about five pounds.

The conversation turned to the vexed question of alleged assault in trains. You know, ladies disarranging their corsage, pulling the cord and pointing a trembling finger at your defenceless head.

"I'd assault her," said Trout. "Get my money's worth."

"I'd say," said Esterhazy, "'Now that's very interesting. If I don't give you five pounds you'll pull the cord and accuse me of — well, what you said? Pull away, dear lady, pull away. It so happens that I shall be the presiding magistrate on whose bench this case will be tried.'"

But then, not all of us look like presiding magistrates. Nor would we all be taken in at that Spot the Lady game.

Lazing in the mess after supper one sometimes hears some very good stories. Hickory always has a fund of them. He's the spring-heeled chap with the Ricardo Cortez look who can ripple syncopated stuff out of a grand piano. He's only got to go to any sort of club to be elected a life-long honorary member, and I don't believe he's ever bought a drink. And five years of Cairo and Alex. night life are about the best training there is in the world.

He brought out two new ones tonight. The first about a chap who was in wine. It was a very dark night, and in the middle of the road stood a large tree with an iron railing all round it. Clutching to this for support he carefully groped his way, all round it twice. Then he subsided slowly into a heap and mopped his brow.

"Begob, and they've locked me up."

The second story concerned four chaps, all of whom were the better for wine. Very late at night their motor-car had left the road and made mincemeat of itself and a large tree.

All four revellers, very much dishevelled, stood in the road, and Robert was taking down particulars in a big notebook.

"And which of you gentlemen was a-driving?"

"None of ush, officer. We were all in the back."

There were one or two other stories, too. But the cream of the world's wit always will be unprintable.

11th of June

We slave on from time to time in E.R.S. and A.R.S. The engines are cleaned down now, and all the inspecting for cracks, wear and flaws over. This morning we centralised the crankshafts and took enough notes on the theory of all this to qualify for an engineering B.Sc. The Atlas and Avro are gradually growing. Wings on, all jacked up with trestles and levelled with incidence boards and spirit levels ready to put the streamline wires in and true up.

The Tutors are beginning to appear now with folding green canvas hoods fastened behind the rear cockpits. Yesterday I viewed them with a growing suspicion, and today, sure enough, we weighed in on instrument flying. Most of us have done a course before—where's the log-book?—C.F.S. October-November 1933. *Avro 504N Instrument Flying*, 8 hours 10 dual, 10 hours 05 solo. Proficiency average. Quadrilateral cross-country under hood, finished two miles from aerodrome. Duration of flight one hour. Not bad.

The most gruelling of my flying life. Bumping misty weather. Not that the mist worries the pupil much. He's in a dim, rocketing existence of his own with all the world shut out by the flapping hood he pulls forward and clamps over his head; while the instructor and safety pilot in front teaches and keeps a good look-out, ready to take over if the need should arise.

But we start from the very beginning again, (a) to learn the patter, (b) to polish up. Practice is the only way to appreciate the difficulties a pupil will encounter, and to teach you've got to be able to do a thing yourself.

Mayor takes off and we climb up. First of all the patter for compass errors—Northerly Turning and Acceleration. Then a general description of the instruments used for 'blind' flying—turn indicator and Red Level. Red Level errors. Then under the hood we go.

"You've got the rudder."

"I've got the rudder."

"Keep her steady on this course." A minute passes.

"Flat turn, rate One, on to 045."

I edge round.

"Hold it... that's all right. 090. Right. Now N.W. through west... good. Now take the control column alone."

"I've got the control column alone. You've got the rudder." What a mouthful! But say 'stick' and he'll be on you like a ton of bricks.

I fly level, then climb, then throttle back and glide. It means concentrating like hell, with only the instrument board to tell you in an artificial way what the aircraft is doing. But it all comes back pretty well after infrequent squadron practice.

Lastly, ten minutes with full control, straight and level climbing, gliding, and turning on to courses. You always do 'flat' turns in instrument flying. Rudder to turn, and opposite bank to keep the wings level. In a good I.F. turn the top 'bank' needle should stick out opposite to the bottom 'turn' needle as you skid round. In an open air turn you bank as you apply rudder and go round neither slipping in nor skidding out. But the use of elevators and ailerons and rudder to keep her turning smoothly and at one height all becomes very complicated, as they act in different ways in relation to the earth. Under the hood you keep them all acting purely in their own planes to simplify things, and so skid uncomfortably but safely round. Twenty minutes for the first time is quite enough, and one is very glad when Mayor says:

"Well, that's very satisfactory. You've had enough for one day."

And you snap back the hood and emerge into the blessed broad daylight again to gulp in great draughts of the fresh slipstream air.

13th of June

Have been here for a month and a half and already done fifty hours flying. The average for the course to date is forty-six hours—

127

more flying than the last course did from beginning to end. And yet we seem to know nothing. I have practically finished all the patter now — only that for aerobatics to learn. But knowing it or being proficient at it is quite another story. There seems so much to be done, and so little time in which to do it. Until now one has learned a fresh bit of patter every other day. Which means only the afternoon in which to practise it with one's co-pupil, the next day to go over it again with one's instructor, and then on to something fresh. Although we're hard at it in the air every day, it's a fortnight since I did a patter landing, and heaven alone knows how long ago since we went over the early things. Becoming proficient to the point of infallibility on practice forced landings, sideslipping and aerobatics takes up so much time.

For a change I had the Tutor to myself for the first hour and a half this morning, and took a fitter up to practise whatever I willed. Strong wind still from the sou'-west and great piled-up layers of silver and grey cumulus cloud rolling against the blue at three to five thousand feet up. Even in mid-June we are still wearing sidcot suits in which to fly! A few days ago my aerobatics startlingly improved. Things are like that. You plug along for days and days and don't get any better, and then suddenly it comes. These days I *like* rolling to the right. Before I always faintly disliked that final inversion on to the back and the hanging on the shoulder straps. But now I do it for fun. Love it. The reason is quite obvious — the knack has suddenly come. A sweet co-ordination of stick and rudder and throttle and over and round she goes and out again as sweet as a nut, time after time, losing no height and keeping a straight course on the edge of a cloud or a distant wood. Climbed up to four thousand into a big cloud-gap, and had a good look round. With massed cloud other aeroplanes are more difficult than ever to see. But except for a couple of distant specks moving against the far curdled silver-grey of a monster vapour galleon, the sky was empty. Did three neat rolls to the right to refresh my spirit. And now for these rolls to the left. One is always meaning to come to grips with them and never does. Usually it's one fair one, one bad one, and one indifferent one, and then it's time to go home. And to reach three thousand or so to acrobat always means valuable time.

The great trouble with rolls to the left is that normally one uses the right hand on the stick, closing the throttle with the left just after passing vertical bank. Which means that unless you have a good long right arm you can't get the stick far enough over to the left hand forward side of the cockpit as you're going over. Neither Mayor or I are giants, so we compromise at first by agreeing to use our left hands on the stick and neglecting the throttle. Still, that isn't pretty. So I determined to come to grips with myself and see what could be done to the left. I tried four with the right hand. Pretty bum; nose dropping too low in the inverted position because the stick's too far back. It means hunching forward in the straps and straining your back muscles to accomplish that, too. Better with the left hand on the stick. Still, none of 'em have that sweet certainty and easy polish of the rolls to the right. There's a grim determination about them. However, we get round. Which is more than we could do three weeks ago, plunging feverishly round and hurtling out in any direction at about 120, very pleased to be topsides up again.

Rolls off the top. To the right, not bad. Left, same trouble as before. Too much straining and hasty analysing going on, and inclined to get slow before rolling off. Ah well, sufficient unto the day. Then I went down and for an hour did practice forced landings from two thousand in the Wansford field, and the sideslipping demonstrations... One has to be candid with oneself. On each forced landing I got into the field all right, but the consistency of polish is not there. Steady, sweeping gliding turns and at last a straight glide in from four hundred feet with a pretty little sideslip on the end. One gets in, and one knows how to handle the aeroplane. But vertically banked gliding turns at three hundred over the leeward hedge and a final sideslip like a runaway lift over the trees and telegraph poles wouldn't please the C.F.I. with the grass swooping up at a rate of knots into his anxious face.

I went back and landed. A final solo landing is very pleasant by way of a change. You fly round on a fairly low circuit and then shut off so that a ninety degree gliding turn brings you into wind so that you come in and sit down opposite the gap between the hangars a few yards from the petrol dump. A final piece of judgement that one soon gets weighed off after a month of this sort of flying. And the crews like it because they've hardly any way to walk out to the wingtips to taxy you to the refuelling point.

But this morning shows me I have still much to learn. And the other pupils tell you the same about their own flying, too.

129

This cricket business has started again, which can make the communal monastic life very trying at times, for by many otherwise quite decent fellows it's regarded as a grave social crime not to be interested in—nay, avid for—news of this other sport of kings. The poetry of King Willow has a sort of romantic appeal for me. The lazy, measured click of leather on bat, and so forth and so on. By association it stands for and recalls the pageant of midsummer, and one's mind becomes a pleasurable jumble of things, odd thumbnail pictures of an umpire in a white starched coat seen against a burning blue sky from the sweet grass, a Panama tilted over his sunburnt face to shield his wrinkled eyes from the glare. Of the pavilion tent in front of the burnished elms, cold and stinging cider lingering in its dark cool interior to sizzle down the parched and grateful throat. Neat white-clad figures moving leisurely in the drowsy heat stung into activity every now and then by small shocks of emergency and excitement, to relapse again into their steady regard of the duel between bowler and bat. A jumble partly of remembered reality and bits of books like *Tom Brown's Schooldays* and *Memoirs of a Fox-Hunting Man*.

But there I am very much afraid my interest in cricket ends. I salute it courteously in passing, regard it genially for a while. As a game it half terrifies and half bores me. (Exactly the same words, by the way, in which I once heard a young friend of mine who also is a pilot sum up his attitude towards flying!) At school I was coerced into playing the game, and have never quite recovered from the terror with which I used to regard the bowler thundering up the crease like a rogue elephant to hurl the very solid ball at my head. I only had one batting stroke, and that a brave slashing sweep. In this way I broke two fingers on different occasions, and was very glad eventually to be dropped from the team and left to my own quiet pursuits. Never having been blessed with a Ball Eye I could no more guarantee to bowl within ten yards of the wicket than to jump over the moon. And in the field, during the half-hour in which I concentrated on the game, the ball never came within a quarter of a mile; but a moment after I had let my mind begin to drift into a daydream a shout would suddenly go up, and I would come to with a guilty start to see the sitter of the day drop dead in the grass about two yards in front of my idle hands.

This afternoon the station team played some other team. I gently but firmly refused three separate invitations to go along to watch the game. It needs terrific resolution to do that, you know. Nice normal fellows lift an eyebrow when you say cricket leaves you cold. Unbelievers have been persecuted for far less.

At teatime the ante-room was full of both teams. Each man appeared to wear a differently-coloured blazer. Never have I seen such a galaxy of stripes. Most of them wore sweaters with stripes of different colours to those on their blazers. And some had silk mufflers with yet different colours again. At a moderate estimate, some forty different squadrons, teams and clubs represented by half as many members. They quite happily talked cricket and drank shandy from half-cans for nearly half an hour. Then trooped in to tea. Except for one of our side. Apparently coins had been spun, and by a process of elimination he had been chosen to stay in the ante-room to wait for the 4.30 Wireless Latest Score. And not to leave on the pain of death, until he got it, when he was to sprint into the mess-room to let them know, and then he could have his tea. He didn't appear to mind. In fact he seemed to think himself lucky in the knowledge that he would hear the score before the rest. He fumbled for and found a piece of notepaper and a pencil. Feverishly licking the lead, he turned on the wireless and listened intently. Pump Room music was still coming over good and strong. Then he looked at the clock and saw there were still ten minutes to go.

"Care for a game of shove ha'penny till the score comes through?"

"Rightio."

"String for start. Nearest to the line without going over."

The ha'pennies began to slide under the impulse of our dextrous mounts of Venus.

"England's not doing too well," he observed. My inner self suddenly rolled up like a hedgehog on defence. I had no idea England was playing. Nor who they were playing, nor where. And had someone told me, in half an hour I should have forgotten again.

"Ah," I observe profoundly.

"Wicket not too good either."

I agree.

"Fifty for three at lunch."

"H'm."

"Hendren ought to knock up a good score."

"Yes, he ought."

I daren't ask whether Hendren is an Australian or an Englishman. And perhaps we aren't playing the Australians at all. It may be the Gentlemen, or Nottingham, or some other team. It's all very difficult, and I am not only ignorant, but bored. I am aware that this confession will estrange me from many friends, but there you are. The truth is not always palatable in form.

We finish the game. There are still three minutes to go to the score. But I've had enough cricket as it is, and leave for tea. He is secretly very surprised, I know. Thinks I must be very, very hungry, no doubt. Five minutes later he bashes in through the swing-doors brandishing a sheet of notepaper.

"Two hundred and nine for seven!" he shouts. An excited hubbub begins and he hands the paper to our captain, a young Flight Loot who is sitting in the President's two-armed chair at the head of the feast. The two teams suddenly hush and crane their heads along the table. He stands up and reads.

"Duck six wickets for four. Spooks nine for two. Hendren fifteen not out. Jinks and Banks none. Willie seventy." And so on. The excited chatter begins again. I am reminded of a headmistress reading out messages of congratulations from old girls unavoidably absent at a reunion dinner. I masticate cake and grin heartily and hope they will think I'm agreeing what a good show it is or what a bad show it is, or whatever one should think. And covertly drinking off my tea, I quietly slide out before my neighbour can ask me what I think of Willie's seventy and Jinks' none. Nice people, my countrymen. But on occasions, queer. Very queer.

17th of June

A good day, oh a very good day. And Mondays are not always good days.

"Your turning onto courses under the hood was very good on Friday," said Mayor down the voice pipe as we taxyed out. "This morning we'll do spins."

We bumped and rocked over the ground, and turned round into wind, and stopped a moment before taking off. Two Tutors roared up at different heights ahead. A Bulldog and a Hart lurched out together to jockey for a long run-off too. I pulled myself into a tight knot of determination in the rear cockpit and lowered the seat. If you don't, when you pull the hood over it keeps drumming and flapping on the top of your helmet. Checked the wind direction on my compass and set the altimeter to nought. Summer has come. A warm sou'westerly wind smelling of clover in fragrant puffs. Big pastel-shaded cumulus clouds in a detached layer at about four thousand down the bright blue, each dazzlingly white in the hot sunshine. And something curious and yet familiar about the light. Why, yes, of course! The Tutor carrying a blind-flying pupil was doped all over with shining yellow enamel. And its reflection was casting a kind of bright, hot look over Mayor's helmet in front, and reflecting off the cockpit instruments into my eyes. I knew where I'd seen that kind of light before. In the desert, on the western side of the Persian Gulf between May and October.

As we climbed I learned what to tell the pupil about spins under the hood. How to go into them and how to recover, the things to look for, and the things to disregard. And then under the hood I went. Raised my goggles, settled down, and took the controls. In my confined world now I bumped and rocked, the engine noise toned down to the merest popping of a small motor-cycle engine as it laboured at sixteen hundred revs. while we ascended at seventy, our best climbing angle. The cockpit is in semi-darkness, lit by fingers of radiance from slits and crannies to the front cockpit, and a greenish light through the canvas of the flapping, drumming hood above. The needles of the bank-and-turn indicator sawed and flickered in the bumps; rudder and stick this way and that, as quick as thought, to bring them back every second or so. You anticipate half of the yaws and banks before they begin, or else you would never keep any sort of course. The air speed wavering from sixty-eight to eighty-five. Keep her steady at seventy. A fraction of a turn back on the tail wheel to trim off a little nose heaviness.

"I've got her a moment. Now a good way in which to turn onto courses is this. At a rate One turn she'll go through ninety degrees in forty seconds. Observe I'm flying true north now. I'll do a rate One turn to the right, and count forty. I haven't my watch. And then we'll see how near to east we come. One, two, three, four, five..." The needles stuck out opposite to each other as we skidded round... "Forty." And I glanced at my watch again. He

133

had turned for exactly thirty-nine seconds. And when the compass settled down we were three degrees off east.

"You've got her. Try that method and turn on to 190 degrees."

"Now 330. Now 172."

"All right, I've got her. Just look round to see all's clear."

By sensation it felt as though we were still flying straight on. But by the needles pointing to eight o'clock I could see we were banked over nearly vertical while he turned to look below.

"You've got her. Spin to the right."

Two years since I did a hood spin, and they're hard.

Throttle back, stick back, back, back. Rudder central. The needles stand up and down. Airspeed flickers back, forty-five, forty, off the map. Full right rudder. Woosh, round we go like a kettle dropped down a well.

"Come out."

Centralize rudder by eye. Needles saw madly all over the shop. Count two. Stick central by eye and ease it two inches forward. Immediate terrific bodily sensation of going into a spin the other way. Quite a tight, fast one too. But you disregard it entirely. Needles no good for some seconds yet, either. Airspeed begins to drop back now 100, 95, go. Stick forward a little, good solid pressure and gently open the throttle to sixteen hundred again. From four to two thousand feet in about twelve seconds. "Climb her up again." I did two more spins to the right.

"That last one wasn't so good. You came out with your right wing down and let the nose go too high. Don't suppose I could do as well myself, but you've got to reach a high standard to teach pupil pilots. Feeling all right?"

I laugh. "Why yes! Sudden silence from the rear cockpit?"

"No. But it's a good thing always to ask, particularly with a pupil, remember."

Next three spins to the left.

"All right. You've had three-quarters of an hour of it. See the Wansford field down there? Give me a forced landing in it."

I have suddenly emerged into a bright world with the cloud carpet a few hundred feet below. Sheer lovely aching blue all round, blessed light, and whole gulping gallons of fresh air after my flapping, green-lit little world.

I miraculously do him a ten times perfect patter—approach and landing. As per book to the last word. Then an equally impressive crosswind take off. Boy, I'm on top of the world. We fly back and he gets out at the aerodrome while I go off for the remaining half-hour to practise gliding and turning on my back.

In the afternoon Cowling and I share the aeroplane, landing to change cockpits for the hood. We tell each other in turn on which courses to fly and when to throttle back and turn, thus making the 'blind' pilot do the circuit and approach for the front seat pilot to take over at the last moment and land. A queer business in the back, when you see the altimeter at nought, and watch the airspeed needle falling and falling and the stick gradually moving as Cowling feels the ailerons and brings it further and further back. And then suddenly brrump, and we sit down on the ground and run to rest.

He did a take-off patter and I covertly shut off the petrol cock as he talked. Full marks though. He told the pupil to look and looked himself.

With this sudden warm weather one suddenly realizes how tawny the grass has become. It's curious to sit up at a thousand and watch another aeroplane float up off the ground, leaving behind it a pale gold, wind-blown track like a broad periscope feather in the grass. All the weekend a mechanical reaper has been at work cutting the grass under the still, rain-laden clouds. A firm cuts it free for the grass it is allowed to cultivate and reap. The tractor was at work today, creeping along warily with two big red flags flying, leaving broad, light green paths through the foot-high grass in its wake.

Did a beautiful tarmac landing parallel to the hangars and finished up twenty yards from the dump.

20th of June

The weather, as the B.B.C. Announcer said in the news, tonight, started as a joke, then became a matter for concern and has now assumed the proportions of a national calamity. Two days ago the Cranwell Garden Party and Flying Display was washed out because of rain and low cloud. An annual affair, it was to have been a minor rehearsal of the Hendon Display; aeroplanes and pilots from all over the country had flown in for it—weeks of organisation gone phut. If the Hendon show next week is to be like this, it will be pretty grim. Two years ago visibility went down to about half a mile in rain and drizzle, and the cloud came down to a few hundred feet. They put up what was beyond all doubt, to my mind, the most amazing show in the history of aviation, by carrying out a modified but still very full form of the programme without a single mishap. You will have an idea of how hair-raising it was when you know that in one event although three squadrons went over the aerodrome in formation, only the one in the middle was visible to the spectators. And two Furies doing synchronised aerobatics under a thousand feet disappeared into the cloud each time they rolled and zoomed up and yet came down from appointed opposite directions to continue weaving their pattern figures again. It was a magnificent show, but by the law of averages they couldn't get away with it a second time.

More grey weather this morning, visibility down to a couple of miles with drizzle, and grey cloud over five hundred feet, which in a Bulldog means as soon as you've left the ground. We all flew, however. That's the spirit I like to see. Pack up when it's definitely dangerous, by all means. But fly by all means when you reasonably can. A year in Iraq with 40 m.p.h. dust-storms is the medicine for qualms.

Taking off under the hood. Ever tried it? Well don't.

First of all you hoot round and do a circuit and landing to get the gyro in the turn-indicator running. Then you go under the hood and gradually assume full control. First two circuits without touching a thing, just watching the rudder, control column, turn indicator and A.S.I. to see what they do as you take off. Then you take the rudder alone for two take offs. The instructor takes over and lands each time, you stay under the hood. Then you have stick alone for two take offs. Then stick and throttle. And finally the whole bunch of tricks. He sits her into wind and you take her off. Needles sawing all over the place and nothing but a lagging airspeed needle jumping about from which to surmise roughly the attitude of the nose. Even the best 'blind' take off is a fairly erratic affair. A bad one, from the safety pilot's point of view, is startling enough to make the sweat start out. But he's too busy pulling the wing out of the grass to have time to think.

We got betterer and betterer, and then started taking off and turning on to a course, from 210 to 030 degrees, as per final cross-country under the hood. And then came in after an hour jolting about the aerodrome and roaring off again and again and again

136

with the flapping hood all round and eyes fairly popping out with anxious concentration.

Half an hour with Esterhazy afterwards *à belle étoile* doing split-ass circuits and patter landings in turn, out of sheer jubilation to be looking out of an open cockpit again.

A fair traffic jam in the Wansford field. Some sharp-eyed pilot had discovered it to be littered with new-grown mushrooms, and no less than four aeroplanes down there taxying about and ticking over while the instructors culled these dainties for savoury tonight.

Loop came in with four pounds.

Mist really settled down in the afternoon, and flying washed out. Trees at the end of the aerodrome out of sight. So settled down with a sigh to an afternoon of lectures.

21st of June

The monthly Guest Night tonight. There are three kinds of attitudes towards this ceremony. First, that of the chaps who welcome it with open arms. They invite about four officers each time from their old Squadrons, and go to an incredible amount of trouble to get them on the spot for the event. Telephone for hours, write scores of long letters full of directions, and motor hundreds of miles meeting trains. Then they incur a five-pound wine bill and a fat head apiece, and vote it the best evening they've ever had in their lives.

Next, there is the attitude of those who say after each guest night "Never again", and put on their stiff shirts with the solemn determination to drink only water, eat their dinner, stay in the ante-room for a decent interval afterwards, say an hour, and perhaps have two half cans of beer; then pay their respects to the Senior Member Present and, pleading pressure of work, disappear to their rooms to go quietly to bed. But hell being so thickly paved with good intentions, by 10.15 they're round the piano at the very top of their form, putting back the sixth drink of the evening and bellowing 'Shaibah Blues' to Jackie Hickory's inspired accompaniment. He could make 'Old Mother Hubbard' sound like the latest and best number from a Fred Astaire-Ginger Rogers film. And of course they wake up in the morning with eyeballs feeling like stone marbles and a groaning conviction that it's the worst evening they've ever had in their lives.

And lastly we have the determined ascetics who can learn a lesson and who do eat their dinner, drink water, and say "Goodnight, sir," at 10.15. But like prophets, they are few in number, wondered at on the night, much envied on the following day. We are not all fashioned of such stern stuff.

I know that after this testament old ladies may raise their hands in horror. But we're not drunkards. *In vino veritas*, you know, and not for nothing the saying "He was the better for wine". Just once in a while we become mildly convivial, indulge on an occasion the English love for an hour of unbuttoned ease, thaw out the frozen locks of polite reserve, and strive to make glad in a pleasant way the heart of man.

The servants cannot be blamed for not going into raptures over guest nights. For hours beforehand they're getting in extra tables, beeswaxing and polishing them, and shining every available bit of silver. The chef spends the whole day making trifles look like mosaic pavements and a pig's head like nothing on earth with mysterious bits of *foie gras*, galantine and sliced lemon. The place is in a general uproar. All the married officers have to desert their wives and dine in. There's a scramble for baths. All twelve people on the corridor seem to want a bath at once, and there are only two to share. One usually canters back down the passage at 7.55 like a cross between a broken-down cab-horse and a boiled lobster. Dinner at eight, and five minutes to dress. One spends those struggling into things and heartily cursing Broom. Why will he do your overall straps up to the last holes under the boots, when he knows that unless they're let out as much as possible they're too short to fit?

You get your hands black altering them. Then fool—thrice fool!—he hasn't given you a clean collar. You break two fingernails pushing studs into a fresh one, and then roar down to the anteroom doing up your vest buttons as you go. Everyone there drinking sherry and gorging prawns in aspic on biscuits. A hasty glance at the sideboard tells you that all the *bonnes bouches* have already gone. Only those damned salty biscuits left. "Sherry, please," to the head waiter as you push you way through. Bow breathlessly to the Senior Member and look covertly at the clock.

"Phew!" Just made it again. One minute to go.

Tonight I worked to plan. Half an hour's squash to whack up an appetite and a reasonable thirst. Then set about planning a bath to avoid the usual indecent haste, and get into the ante-room a quarter of an hour early, in order to sample those stuffed olives and other titbits they provide to mellow the harshness of the fact that three sherries cost two shillings dark or dry, wet or fine. I instructed Broom to put out a clean shirt (it is the longest day in the year, and broad daylight is very unkind to starched linen) and mix a bath. Repaired to this with as much stately sweeping of bathrobe and napping of slippers down the corridor as though I were a king going to his coronation, bent on relishing to the full this unwonted contrast to my usual headlong canter and clambering swerve into the water, hot, tepid or cold.

In the next bath to me was Esterhazy. To him this is the hour of the day. He shaves, he hums, he smokes a cigarette (at eight shillings a hundred) he adds Bond Street bath crystals in his bath. And he loves a *conversazione* at the same time. Were he a courtier I am sure he would receive all his visitors during the hour of the bath.

"What have you done today?" he drawls through the clouds of steam.

"Patter for rolls and rolls off the top."

"I know. Aren't they damned difficult! How I shall ever do these intricate things and talk into a mouthpiece at the same time I just don't know."

And so we go on. The ethics of instructing interest him immensely; we discuss our instructors and decide in a lofty way how the system of instructing could be improved in many ways.

Then, by the act of bathing, I am reminded of a story.

"Have you ever heard the tale about the millionaire who presented a swimming pool to the inmates of a mental home?"

"No, old boy. Tell on."

"Well, he did. And he rang up soon after the contractors had finished putting it in.

" 'And how do they like the new pool?'

" 'Oh, they think it's fine, sir. They really do. They love it. I do wish you could see them. Running along the banks and diving in. Taking headers off the top board. Plunging in... I do wish you could see them.'

" 'Wal, that's great. Guess that's mighty gratifying to an old man.'

" 'Yes, sir. What they'll do when we put some water in it I just can't tell.' "

Now that's a fairly average story, about as feeble as the rest I tell. But have you noticed how every now and then you can touch people on their humorous raw, send them off into real face-purpling hysterics with a lukewarm yarn?

I expected Esterhazy to chuckle and grope for the soap. But he waited for a moment while it sank in, and then went off into an inane roar.

"Haw haw haw haw HAW! Ha, ha ha ha ha. Hoo-hah, hah, hah, hah, hah! Oooh—that's the best I've... oooor. Ha Ha Ha Ha HA! Aha, aha, aha! Must remember that to tell to—hoo, hoo, hoo, hoo, haha!"

He was still gasping feebly when I left my bath three minutes later.

"Send Broom to help me out of my bath, will you, old boy?" he shouted weakly.

"O-hoo, ha, ha, ha!"

These nights are much different to our usual little eleven-a-side dinners at one table. Three long tables set on end, and loaded with all the mess silver, from challenge cups to sauce boats and menu stands. White waistcoats for one and all, and an inch and a half of braid (eighty per cent silver wire and twenty per cent gold) down the overall legs of every Fl.-Lieut. A brave show, my masters, a brave show. We all file out of the ante-room sedately and courteously enough to the tune of 'The Roast Beef of Old England', blared out by the Station Brass, but mercifully toned down by a couple of good thick oak doors between them and us. All seats are miraculously full in half a minute. A little quiet jostling goes on as a few poor stiffs who haven't spotted a place try to wedge themselves in at our end. We resolutely shoulder them out.

If there's a padre present he says a short grace. If not, Mr. President raps with his hammer.

"Thank God."

And we all bustlingly sit down. *A propos* of grace, of course you have heard the story of the President who said:

"Is the padre there? No? Thank God." And sat down.

Esterhazy is president. He smiles a starched, wan smile at me from a league away. I chuckle and unfold my napkin. On the table there's a 'programme of music' in a small silver stand fashioned like a four-bladed propeller.

'Presented by F. O. Turnbuckle, 1929.' Very nice. The usual intellectual treat, the good old rousing Kneller Hall stuff. 'Entry of the Gladiators', *The Mikado*, a Sousa march. Ah, an entr'acte: 'Spring has come'. Then some more bassoon-trombone pieces. Ah well. What's on the menu? Consommé Windsor. Usual beef tea, alphabet soup when there are guests. Steamed cod, not bad. Chicken, bread sauce, crisps, brussels sprouts. Now that's all right. Savoury—Scotch woodcock. The usual delusive snare—it's only scrambled egg on toast. Still, not so bad. Bring on your alphabet soup.

The band starts up with a big drum thump thump and then a muffled, brassy, obscene Teuton blare. The trombone is a blacksmith in E.R.S. in his spare time. I muse on music and eat my roll while the soup is being spirited out of the kitchen.

In small units it's rather difficult. There's not enough public money to permit every squadron to have a band of trained musicians. So a few of our fitters and riggers and clerks who are musically minded seem to get together, usually under the Orderly Room Sergeant—who always seems to be able to play six instruments and conduct—and draw those big queer brass things, a few cracked clarinets, and a brace of dusty drums from Stores. Then they practise dolefully in the gym, or far away on the corner of the aerodrome, for three nights a week until they're fit to come on Colour Hoisting Parade. Their reward is usually an extra weekend's leave a month and no guards. With this they are more than content.

When they are asked to play at a guest night this is an honour indeed. They swell their numbers with a couple of extra big brass bell-mouthed things with keys on, and bear down upon us with their collars tightly hooked up and faces scrubbed red. The more appreciated they are the louder they seem to play. Tonight's band is almost falling over itself with gratitude. There's still a thick door between us, but we're at the nearest end. Once during a lull in the conversation the music suddenly came to an end, and Loop could be heard by the Board of Directors a hundred yards away at the other end shouting into his neighbour's ear:

"If I had my way I'd sack every one of them. Diehards have always—"

Then, of course, his flow of talk suddenly evaporated and he coloured suitably at the gills.

White waistcoats are a splendid innovation. You can loosen the straps at the back as you expand. Cork's guest is a local village doctor. Every now and then Cork wanders heavily round and begs leave of absence for his guest, who rushes out to the telephone. He must be conducting a confinement over the line. How awkward. Then the telephone outside rings with a muffled and insistent note. A glazed look comes into Esterhazy's eyes. He drops his napkin and half rises. Then sits again and looks round anxiously for the duty waiter. In a moment that worthy returns. Yes—no. Yes, it is! He whispers in Esterhazy's ear. Esterhazy scrambles hastily to his feet. Signals with upraised brows to the President-in-Waiting, who comes up to take his chair. Then Esterhazy apologises to the C.O. and leaves the room. Love lends wings to his feet. Another trunk call.

Broom has been impounded for the evening to be a waiter too. He breathes heavily down my neck as he gives me another roll. The P.M.C. sighs and quietly puts away the pipe that, like me, he has been longing to light up. In one of my squadrons we had a Flight Lieutenant who was never seen without a pipe. A little, wiry, sandy-haired man, he had been flying since 1915. Flown thousands and thousands and thousands of hours. Aeroplanes haven't always been reliable, and he'd had fifty-two crashes. That was his third tour of duty with that squadron, and it was slap in the middle of the desert. But Sandy just doted on the place. We believed he slept with a pipe in his mouth. He certainly always flew with one there—filled up and ready to light when he landed. And another one, filled up, too, stuck in the belt of his shorts to light when the first one was smoked down. By this cunning he always kept a cool pipe. In the dry summer most of us either feebly smoked dry, chaff-tasting cigarettes or else entirely gave it up. But he kept going serenely at his pipe through all the long, hot months. He smoked quite a dark, heavy flake, too, costing in England only eightpence the ounce.

"Cool. Coolest tobacco you can buy. I've smoked it for eighteen years."

Two pipes before breakfast. And yet on his annual medical exam he always went through with flying colours, and kept the mercury up for longer than any other man in the command.

The dinner murmurs and clinks and laughs its way on.

The officer's hardest trial is not always campaigning. Peace too, besides her victories, can have her trials. And once a month, unbeknown to civilian life, our mettle may be grimly put to the test. We have to be breakfasted by eight and into the air by eight-thirty, guest night or not. And there can only be one tougher trial than spinning under the hood after a really late night, and that's putting out into a Channel lop on a grey dawn in a torpedo-boat destroyer. Which Kipling, you will remember (although I'll bet you don't), once described as 'half switch-back, half water-chute, and hell continuous'.

(One of our most successful diplomats, by the way, used to greet foreign big shots with this growl:

"How are you? Not that I give a damn how you are." And they loved it. He went across big.)

We foregathered for the usual navigation lecture at 8.15, and mustered at full strength. I was lost in admiration for the way we all did it. A logical night for any guest night is a Friday, with Saturday morning holiday to follow. But the Englishman is, and always will be, mad. Therein lies half the secret of his greatness. He has his guest night on a mid-week day and turns to at the usual time the next morning.

At 8.10 Trout was in his bath. At 8.15 his six foot four of youthful bulk bent to enter the lecture-room door. Scrubbed, rosy, breakfastless, but there. Garrick, more like Sydney Howard than ever, roamed up the road, more left wing low than ever, and beamed expansively on us as he swerved into the doorway. Cap tilted on the back of his head, pile of books and instruments haphazardly swept up under his arm, he looked as though he didn't give a damn if it snowed.

Trout roared with mirth.

"Look at Garrick coming along," he said. "Look at his eyes!"

"His eyes?" said Cork in the thickest of thick Irish brogues. "I can hardly see him."

Another real midsummer day. One straight out of the pages of Dan Chaucer or *A Midsummer Night's Dream*, and the thermometer still sizzling up in the eighties although the shadows are already beginning to lengthen on the sun-steeped lawns and all my casements are open to the golden light of seven o'clock and the linnet's song.

Orderly Officer again today, a necessary evil. But I have been in squadrons where it is far, far worse. Here they temper discipline, and provided that one obtains the Adj's formal consent and informs the telephone exchange and guardroom of one's deputy's name, there is no objection whatever to another officer standing by whilst one flies oneself. Mayor always arranges himself to stand by for me without my even asking, so I always fly my full whack even on duty days.

At 8.30 this morning our shirts were already sticking to our backs, and it was like heaven to bounce and surge off the aerodrome in an old, bright yellow-enamelled 1914 vintage Avro into the heat haze and up to the cooler layers of 4000 feet. A Bulldog and a Hart followed us up on the same errand, to leave behind that quivering, burdening heat below and cool their bodies in the steady upper winds. They both slid past us and were at their aerobatic height half a mile above, while we still laboured slowly up at our pancake-climbing angle and the fields and roads and lanes were still close below our shell-cambered wings at a thousand feet. But we got to a height, Cowling and I, and I was determined to vindicate my honour and do some decent aerobatics in a Crab for a change. It was too easy. Five slow rolls and four loops off the top, and I had it really wrapped up. Once you've learned and mastered the tricks you can't go wrong. Try to roll in the ordinary way, and the nose skids thirty degrees coming out and drops as many below the horizon, which was what I was doing the other day. But centralise your ailerons when you've half rolled off your back again and put on the engine to help you, and she rolls off as neatly as you like. And to roll off the top, dive her to 130 with the tail wheel wound hard back, then ease full back and make her rip over and off the loop, and you do a regular copy-book stunt. Cowling had several pretty bum attempts, skidding and yawing all over the show and blowing our goggles off with side draughts. I suspect it to be much easier from the rear cockpit—

I just couldn't crawl under the centre section into the front in my heavy boots and horse bandages. So having mastered them from the rear, I must see next time how we get on with only the cross-bracing wires and engine in front of our nose. Did one beautiful practice spin off a tight engine turn. They fascinate me. Go into a normal steep turn with engine on. Gradually tighten the turn and increase the angle until you're going round vertically banked with the engine roaring away at seventeen hundred revs., the loading nearly forcing you through the bottom of the fuselage, and the horizon a maze of things whistling round like a top. Ease the stick hard back, and eventually she stalls. There's no flopping or gradually sighing and dying out of speed as in a straight stall, and the needle still shows a healthy 90 m.p.h. The nose just quivers and drops a fraction. But then you deliberately imitate the pupil's error and stick on top rudder to bring the nose up again; and there's a beautiful and original stall with yawing couple applied. She gives one terrifying woof and rips over the top straight into a spin with engine on, about five hundred turns to the minute. Recover in the usual way... I could go on doing those all day!

Cold gooseberry tart and cream for lunch, and whacked Cork at shove-ha'penny. Am getting regular shove-ha'penny player's clothes these days, faint white chalk patches rubbed into my tunic and breeches that even hard brushing won't wholly eradicate. Then off in the old Avro again with Cowling, to try out more patter and demonstration for two hours. What a life—cruising round above this summer earth in a flying machine all the afternoon for a living! While the poor termites toil in shop and factory and on dust-weary roads for their daily bread. I wouldn't join them for all the Crown jewels with the Crown land chucked in.

25th of June

Instrument Flying cross-country test this morning. First of all you go up solo and find by the reciprocal course method the wind velocity at the height you propose to fly. Next you work out your courses and E.T.A.s for the turning points in the flight office. It's a quadrilateral course taking about an hour to fly. Then you and the instructor clamber in, he with a map to plot in your actual track over the ground, you with a stop-watch hung round your neck on a loop of kite-cord, and a piece of paper, marked with the courses to steer and minutes and seconds to be flown on each leg printed large and clear, to pin to your dashboard. In the queer, cooped, drumming, flapping world under the hood the instruments tend to become hypnotic after a while, and after about three-quarters of an hour your ability to concentrate diminishes by a fair amount. You find your flying becoming more ragged, and curse yourself for carelessness whereas it's really fatigue. Sometimes after a long spell with your eyes riveted on the instruments, moving altimeter — compass — turn indicator — airspeed — to and fro, to and fro the whole time, it all suddenly means nothing at all to you. Nothing whatsoever. Your brain simply refuses to interpret the messages the instruments send, and muscles refuse to obey, checking and correcting with rudder and stick this way, that way, this, that, small, ceaseless movements all the time to keep the course flown straight and the height constant within fifty feet. Then you relax, shut your eyes tightly, vigorously shake your head, and for a few seconds let the aeroplane take charge. When you open your eyes again with a sigh and concentrate once more, the dashboard messages assume significance again and your arms and legs respond without conscious thought.

The instructor does one circuit and landing to get the gyro in the turn indicator running, and then heads the aeroplane into wind with a long clear run ahead.

"Righto, lower the hood."

You snap the hood over and secure the clip.

"Hood over."

"You've got her. It's all clear. Off we go when you're ready."

"I've got her."

Altimeter at zero. Petrol and oil O.K. Set the heading on the compass verge ring, grids parallel to the north-seeking needle, to help keep a straight climb. Tail wheel wound forward to help her attain flying position. Then centralising rudder and control column by eye, you slowly open up the throttle and begin to move along the ground. No eyes for anything but that bottom, rudder needle. The slightest swing to be checked at once, coarsely at first, and more gently as she gathers way. The engine is turning over at full throttle, the wheels rumble and bounce on the ground. Dimly you take in the top needle and know she's level. Then the bouncing and wheel noise dies away, and you know you've left the ground by a foot or so. Where it is you haven't the faintest idea. The airspeed indicator still lags and is of no use. Imperceptibly flatten her out to gain flying speed. Too much, and the wheels hit the ground again. Now you have plenty of speed. Ease her gently back, and climb up. Curse that bottom needle. Keep still. About five degrees out of wind by compass. Rudder gently back. Hell, airspeed sixty-five; climbing too steeply. Ease her forward. That's it, seventy-five. Damn, too much. Eighty. Back to seventy-five. Hullo, eight hundred feet already. Throttle back a bit. Steady. Gentle, Rate One flat turn to the right. Count—one, two, three, four... a predetermined number of seconds. As you climb you are making a wide circuit of the aerodrome. Two thousand feet. Level out, throttle back to cruising revs. and get your airspeed steady. Warily set the first course on your compass and clamp up the verge ring. Steady. Stop turning. Now settle down.

"Now!" comes a faint voice down your earphones. And that's the first and last word he'll say until your calculated time is up.

It means you're passing the aerodrome landing circle. You set the stopwatch going and settle down to concentrate on your first course.

Just on an hour later you sigh the biggest sigh of relief in your life.

"Finish."

"I've got her. Come out."

Back goes the hood with a rush and you sway gratefully in your seat and, pushing back your goggles, pass a hand wearily over your eyes. Blue sky and rolling white clouds dazzling in the sun above and around.

"You've got her. Throttle back and land. You're into wind and the aerodrome's just in front of the port wing."

You take over and tilt the wing to peer incredulously. Why, so it is! Damned good. Hit it off within a mile and a half. You go down in triumphant, sweeping, gliding turns, and whether he likes it or not, give him a swishtail landing. No comment. Then he's quite pleased, too.

"Quite good courses. I'll show you the plot and my remarks before I hand them in."

And he waddles off with his maps to the clink-of-the-buckles tune, to trace out your tracks on cartridge paper and fill in the pro forma for the C.F.I.

Well, well, well. Thank heavens that's done. Tea and a pipe as it's break-time, and then off for a rip-roaring half-hour of aerobatics in the Bulldog, cheerfully watching the compass needle career all round the bowl as you swoop and turn and dive. Red on Red can go hang!

Afternoon, practise forced landings in a hired farm field with Cowling. Then after tea in the Doc's old Morris to catch the last hours of lovely weather and swim from the river bank down by The Haycock. Lots of daddy-longlegs skittering noiselessly about our rooms, and a plague of earwigs is upon the land.

28th of June

Revision now, back to the dim and rusty Effect of Controls and Stalling, Climbing and Gliding. In a Crab, too. A grim, sweaty hour of concentration with Mayor, and then forty minutes spot landings in the Atlas with Cowling again, to sweeten our souls.

Each of us has to give a lecture during the term on any subject we care to choose. The C.F.I. draws names out of a hat and then gives the next for duty ten days in which to prepare his stuff. We've had four lectures already, 'Beer', 'Submarines', 'The Atomic Theory', and 'A Long Distance Flight from Iraq to Singapore'.

The beer one drew a large crowd. All the ruddy-faced beer lovers in the front row, and people jostling for room in the back seats. Were we bored? It was Capstain's lecture. His guv'nor is a brewer, and he simply wrote to the head foreman for a bunch of notes. It *was* dull. The chemistry of the thing, all about yeast and ferments and nitrogenous warts. The look of pained and patient concentration on the faces of the front row after half an hour was a study to behold. I'll bet their beer hasn't tasted the same since. Submarines was damned good. Doe was a flying-boat pilot and keen on the game. They do plenty of sub. and anti-sub. work, and shadowing and position reporting by W.-T. take up a lot of their time.

"Submarine commanders hate shallows. They won't dive in under ten fathoms if they can possibly help it, so if you can drive them inshore they're yours. The best time to catch 'em is at dawn. They have to surface to recharge their batteries; they can't use the oil motors underneath, so have to run on the electric ones, which they can only feed for a limited space of time. Patrol the sectors where they're hidden on exercises and you'll catch a half-dozen at dawn as sure as eggs, stretching their limbs, getting fresh air, and charging up..."

We really listened to old Doc.

One of the airmen pilots, Slot, gave the Atomic Theory talk. Immensely keen on his subject and he'd obviously been at great pains to read it up. He rattled away at breakneck speed for his forty minutes and it was all completely above our heads. By the end he had completed a drawing on the board that looked like a giant puffball exploding in all directions. In some remote way it had atomic significance, that we did know.

Pilot Sergeant Kingpost addressed us on the three-Wapiti flight with long-distance wing tanks. He spent most of the time saying how he'd have done it had he been the C.O. They got there and back without mishap, which seems to be all that matters as far as I can see. Now the bounders have pulled my name from the hat. I submit 'T. E. Lawrence, or Aircraftsman Shaw' for my subject, and draw from the school library every book I can find on the man, his life, and his work. A good chance to make myself read up his amazing exploits. And we're not conscious enough of the honour of having had him serving in our ranks.

After tea, a lot more earwigs in my room, and another river bathe with Flaps, Nacelle and the Doc. This evening we hired a punt. Swamped it with water diving in, and of course fell in twice and drenched our heap of clothes. Had to smoke the whole time to keep the gnats away.

A lot of local poppets are swimming and sunbathing by the river these days. Lots of fellows from C.F.S. are suddenly becoming very keen on this swimming game.

Nacelle and the Doc were both in merchant service ships before they came into the R.A.F., so they have great times swapping shellback yarns. Burma, Kobi, the Seychelles, and all sorts of queer names keep cropping up in their talk, and E.B.P. is mentioned more than once. This means Every Bloody Penny — the wages due to you that you elect to draw before going ashore in a decent foreign port.

During the summer months we only have compulsory dining nights twice a week. Dinner-jacket supper on Monday, plain clothes supper on Wednesday and the weekend days. Supper's grand—you wander in when you like and comfortably dressed. Soup and fish always hot. And then two whacking great sideboards stacked with stuff, pickles, salad, cold meat, and then the bowls of fruit, pineapple, blackberries, pears, strawberries and a thumping great dish of stiff cream. And swimming does give an appetite, even in June.

Wherever you find Joule, our Air Navigation instructor, there you'll find amusing talk too. He is a Flight Lieut., rising thirty-six. Iron-grey hair, firm and by Dame Nature waved. Cheerful bulldog face, always a cracked old pipe, and always a grin. He's been teaching Air Nav. at flying schools for the past ten years, and what he doesn't know about it isn't worth knowing. He teedles around on an ancient bicycle with a reduced-to-clear look about it and a pile of books stacked in the basket in front. And every now and then he huddles up into the back cockpit of a Hart and makes pupils fly cross-countries, so that he can complete the last section of his terminal reports. We've each done one with him, treating him as a pupil for purposes of examination and giving him wrinkles and tips on how to steer, correct, keep a log, and map-read. He always takes over the duplicate control at the end and does a couple of very polished and accurately-judged circuits and landings to amuse himself before taxying in.

Joule can do amazing things with a C.D.C. The Course and Distance Calculator is the airman's best friend, two flat discs clamped together, one of ivorine and the other of celluloid. Squares and numbers and compass points stamped all over them, and two metal pointers that rotate and carry sliding cursors. We work out courses, winds, simple slide rule problems and so forth on them. Joule can also reel off betting odds and comparative rates of exchange and things like that when he has a C.D.C. in his hands. Says they just fit into the crown of a grey top-hat at race meetings. He also illustrates his lecture points by telling appropriate funny stories; regretfully remarking afterwards that pupils almost invariably remember the stories long after they've forgotten the facts they were intended to underline.

Joule set the ball rolling in the ante-room after supper by discussing Service Clubs. First of all there's the Caterpillar Club, of which you all know. If you bale out then you automatically become a member of the club. Irvin's, the parachute manufacturers, send you a little gold caterpillar mounted on a pin. Some chaps wear them on their coat lapels when in plain clothes, others have them fixed to their cigarette cases.

Then of course there followed reminiscences of the Deck Landing Club — each mess has at least one member who for his sins has served with the Fleet Air Arm. Their old school tie is like the Royal Artillery's, only it's a light blue zigzag on a dark blue ground. You can attribute the far-away look in their eyes either (a) to gazing at misty horizons or (b) to gin at tuppence per tot. I forget how many deck landings you have to do to qualify for membership. But, at any rate, when you're a real old salted seagull, have filled up about two flying log-books, and your 'wet litany' has been heard ('from running into palisades, Good Lord deliver us'), then you may be elected to the élite.

Young bachelors who have served in a carrier Mediterranean way seem to have liked it. But the doddering Fathers of Three (some of them as old as thirty-five) are not so keen. To them the height of human felicity is to potter in the garden pruning rose bushes, and ploughing the grey Atlantic waters in a steel-hull does not quite fill their book.

To one such I once said:

"But it can't be so bad. You don't spend much time at sea. And quite often go ashore."

"My dear fellow, it's nice enough going ashore. But an awful thought is lurking at the back of your mind the whole time — it is as though instead of going home to bed afterwards you are to return to sleep in the boiler-house."

Joule's stories were by far the best. "Some paragraphs in K.R.s have curious origins," he observed. There is a paragraph which reads, 'Dogs and Hounds will not be carried in a Service Aircraft'. It used to read simply, 'Dogs'. One day an officer, interpreting the regulations to the letter rather than in the spirit, chose to take his Alsatian by air. Well, he piled up, whether or not because of the presence of his pet history does not record. But when he woke up in his little white bed and gingerly began to feel his bent jaw, he observed, as through a haze, a lot of Gold Braid around his bedside. And to a man they were all gesticulating wildly and pushing under his nose open copies of K.R.s.

"Look! Look!" they raved. "No Dogs to be carried in Aircraft."

"Wasn't a Dog," replied the pilot with the best he could do in the way of a bright smile, "was a Hound."

Of course no trained lawyer would advise prosecution in face of that, and he got away scot free. And in due course an A.L. List to K.R.s and A.C.s came out, stating amongst others things that forthwith all copy-holders should amend 'Dogs' to read 'Dogs and Hounds'.

Our heat wave continues. Four moths gyrating madly round my table-lamp, two earwigs in the folds of the bath towel, and three in the comb.

1st of July

Of course, we all pushed off to London (or 'the Smoke', as the troops call it) for the weekend and the R.A.F. Display at Hendon. Knowing the ropes we go at 10 a.m. to avoid the rush, stick our cars in the front row to use as grandstands, and if we don't use the R.A.F. Club enclosure, dig out a friend in the City of London (Auxiliary) Squadron and have whole lashings of strawberries and cream to our tea in theirs.

Hendon is a grand place for meeting chaps you haven't seen for years. They all seem to be there. There's not so much of the "women swooning into the arms of pseudo-blasé males", as the Press puts it these days. The show gets higher and safer every year. Soon the wing formations will be droning over, mere specks, at 10,000 feet. If you want to thrill a crowd, in our junior and humble opinions, you've got to come low and make a healthy noise. The niceties of the thing, precision of timing and interception, are quite lost on the city man and his wife. The Bulldogs doing not-too-hard diving and bombing thrilled them to the core. Our inverted flight peacefully droning round left them almost unmoved. That show comes on at the end too, which is a great pity, because people are beginning to drift off to avoid the crush.

Flight Commanders' tests are beginning. Each flight has one Flight Lieut. in command. Two junior officers to help him — usually one younger Flight Lieut. and a Flying Officer. And a couple of sergeant pilots. All five instruct. Towards the end of term the Flight Commander tests all pupils to confirm, enlarge on, and generally check up the instructors' reports. In like manner, one of the officers tests the Flight Commander's pupils.

Test on Instrument flying this morning. Did that fairly well, patter for explanation of flat turns and compass errors, then hood work, taking off general flying, turning onto courses and changing altitude. We are getting apprehensive now though. Open-air flying tests are soon to come, first by the Flight Commanders, and then the supreme test, that of the C.F.I. Soon we'll all have the jitters good and proper. Already we have heated arguments about categories.

A1 means 'an exceptionally good instructor who has demonstrated by practical work his suitability for the highest category.'

A2 'a very good instructor.'

B 'a capable instructor.'

C 'has the makings of an instructor with practice.'

Of course, you are never made A1 directly after a C.F.S. course. Once in a while they make an A2. We all say we wouldn't be A2s if they offered it to us, knowing we are quite safe in assuming that they won't. "No instructor can be said to be very good until he's proved that he can teach pupils to fly," we argue. "He may be the most brilliant pilot in the world. His patter may be faultless. But has he patience? Can he let a pupil bounce for his own good and yet not let him bounce too hard? Only time can show."

Periodically, a batch of C.F.S. instructors tours the flying training schools, and it may be recognized that the trip to Egypt is much sought after. On these visits they test odd pupils, a sort of percentage check to ensure that they are being taught to fly in the correct way, and they also test the instructors who have been on the job for some time. Then, if they're good enough, they are re-categorised a step up. The need to demote anyone never seems to arise. In the rare event of an instructor not being up to scratch, his Flight Commander soon spots as much in his general flying and conduct, and in the way his pupils fly. Then action is taken at once—either he goes to C.F.S. for a refresher, or back to Squadron life.

After the instrument flying, three quarters of an hour doing sideslipping patter—nose held into wind, across wind, and on a gliding turn. All very difficult, talking and at the same time trying to judge an approach into a small field. Afternoon, an hour of aerobatics in a Bulldog again at the bright blue, dazzling and freezing heights of 8000 feet. A good landing in Bulldogs sounds just as though you've dropped a bagful of old tin cans when the tailskid gets down, and you run like a dingbat for about a mile after touching down, on a windless day.

I keep noticing this disturbing chit pinned up on my dressing-table mirror:

From: Chief Flying Instructor.
Date: 27.6.35.
Subject: Pupils' Lectures.
Your lecture on Lawrence of Arabia will be required to be given at an early date. Your notes should be prepared accordingly.

Beyond a little desultory reading, I've done nothing to come to grips with the monster yet. I find that I fit very neatly into one of the psychologist's pigeon holes. "Numbers 1 and 8," says Herr Flugel, "may be found together and manifest themselves in a important type." That at least is something! "Such person, will, for instance, delay action in important matters until the last possible moment, and may then become feverishly energetic and perform prodigies of work in a short time." So now we know.

This making up of flying logbooks is a great game at the beginning of each month, when they have to be totalled up, stamped, and rendered to the C.F.I., for checking and signature. Total dual and solo for each type flown, (a) during month, (b) at unit. Then instrument flying totals and grand totals, passenger, dual and solo. During the month some of us try to cope with this by jotting down each trip on grubby scraps of paper. These either get screwed up in our pockets until they are too smudged to read, or else end up as pipe-spills. If we do hoard them we find ourselves trying to decipher something like this when it comes to entering up:

"26.0815 B3219 self 25 1500 6798.34 not too bad."

It's no use whatever one does, so there's a mad rush about now to get at the hundreds and hundreds of sheets — Form 79s — giving the details of every flight etc. carried out. A regular traffic jam in the little flight office, everyone smoking or falling over each other as they grope about in sidcots, flying boots and parachutes going to or returning from aircraft, all waiting for a turn at the 79s.

We always produce totals different from those of the flight clerk, who keeps a check tally of all we do. If ours don't agree with his he alters them. His never agree with those of the C.F.I.'s clerk, so they're altered again. In fact, whatever you do, you're bound to be wrong.

The hay is coming in now, the loaded wains leaving their wisps stuck in the high bushes of the country lanes. Of course, we go bathing again in the river. Warm as milk, and two damsels on the bank we haven't seen before.

4th of July

Great towering cloud countries of cumulus rolling up from one to five thousand feet with enormous chasms of steep blue in between, the earth just a faintly coloured patchwork beneath, only half guessed at and seen. I amaze myself with aerobatics these days, they're so good. I have learned to roll to the left by starting off with barrel rolls. You get a good upward and outward swing on her before you turn her over. It's a tip worth remembering if ever you get stuck on your own. Fairly quick, over-we-go barrel rolls. And then progress gently up to the 'rolling round a pin-point' stage. To do a decent roll off the top you have to crane your head well back and begin applying the ailerons to roll off directly you see the horizon coming up. This is rather difficult when you've got to keep your head down telling the pupil down the voice pipe what you are doing and why.

"A few scattered words should suffice," says Mayor in his typewritten patter. "Put in just enough to maintain your prestige."

Inverted turns suddenly come easy after about four practices. One's chances to try them are so few. The ordinary Tutor engines won't run continuously upside down, so you have to clamber up to about 8000, turn over on your back, and then glide down. You need opposite bank and rudder this time—an explanation on paper would be too involved, but a model with working control surfaces will soon convince you why. The bank looks much steeper than it is. Down you come, your head arched hard back, trying to turn forty-five or ninety or a hundred and eighty degrees by objects on the ground. And before you know where you are you're down at 3000 again and have to come out, to find that your time's already up and somebody else is waiting for the aeroplane.

About sixty chairs against the sunny mess porch at lunch time. If you please, a photograph of the Course. We collect with the Staff Officers and Sergeant Pilot instructors and group ourselves tastefully in four rows. Then Mr. Emulsion, the school photographer, disappears into his dark cloth, fiddles and turns knobs and clicks things. 'Pop' and it's over.

Next one with caps off, please. We wrinkle up our faces to keep off the sun and he presses the bulb again. And next week one more 'group' will be hung on the line in the billiard room; and with all our names printed underneath, we'll be able to buy copies to hang with the School XV and F.T.S. pictures and tasselled caps in our rooms. *Vive l'esprit des écoles publiques.*

Today the C.F.I. began his tests. Trout was the first lamb to the slaughter. We are haunted with the dread of boobing on our forced landing. Obviously he can't test one on the patter for everything, so he chooses only one or so of the easy things, stalling, climbing, gliding, one type of turn—either medium, climbing, gliding, or steep, effect of controls, and so on. But taking off, landing, spinning, aerobatics, and a forced landing are absolute certs. You can boob to a minor degree on all of them except forced landings, and get away with it. But overshoot, or worse still undershoot, your little field and you're done. We sweat a little when we think about it, and dig our nails into the palms of our hands. Trout is another man now. This morning he was tetchy and inclined to roll his eyes—a nervous habit—and twitch at any loud and unaccustomed noise. *Te moriturus saluto,* his manner seemed to say. But now he is all broad smiles, quips and youthful jollity. He got in all right each time with both Fl.-Comdr. and C.F.I. In other words, he did 'sideslip off the surplus height and land well up the field.'

"What was he like?"

"What did he give you?"

"Did you get a cross-wind take off?"

"Does he curse if you boob?"

156

"Did you give him any scares?"

"Did you have to roll to the left?"

We pepper him with questions over the rock cakes and China tea.

Forced landing patter with Cowling this afternoon, and he got me stone cold. When the wind's from the S.W., just after you take off from one of our practice fields, you cross over a large wood at a low altitude if you climb up into wind. One gets so used to keeping straight into wind after getting off; but at three hundred feet he gently closed the throttle.

"Now do something."

Of course I was wimpoled. I managed to slam her round into a vertically banked gliding turn and might have just skated back over the trees into the field I'd just left, but going downwind. And it would have taken at least three dividing hedges and a mile of pasture to arrest my progress then. And you can't expect a pupil to act like that. We opened up again, and when Cowling had his go and took off again, he did what I had forgotten to do, banked and turned about forty degrees to the left, apologising formally down the telephones as he did so.

"Normally, of course, one climbs up straight into wind after leaving the ground. But in this case you will observe that there is a large wood directly ahead of us, on which we could only effect a landing by pancaking onto the tops of the trees. So we turn a little to one side in order that should the engine fail"—and here he closes the throttle and glides to demonstrate—"we could make a slightly cross-wind landing in this large open field straight ahead."

After doing practice forced landings so often in a Crab lately, the Tutor is too easy for words. With a Crab you have to sit up at 2000 nearly over the leeward hedge and fairly dive down in your gliding turns. Any hesitation about the patter and you're lost—you have to rip through it very clearly and decisively to get it all in. Then turn in feeling you're going to overshoot to hell to get in at all. Watching like a hawk for drift. Going back to a Tutor one finds that one has gone clean through all the patter and there's still a thousand feet in height to lose! Say what you may, I think the old 504N is a splendid training aircraft, archaic and draughty and slow though it may be.

The heat wave continues, and I slew sixty-five earwigs by the count in my corridor and room tonight. All the prophylactic measures of the mess committee seem incapable of stemming the tide.

9th of July

C.F.S. soon moves back to its spiritual home, Upavon on the broad-backed Wiltshire downs. The Avon flows sweet through the chalk from above Marlborough, and passes Upavon a mile away on the crest of its left bank. Three miles further down, the old low black hangars of Netheravon drift past against the soft white cumulus over the high ground. And as the river winds on towards Salisbury, dimpling and blue through its osier beds, trout-ring-flecked and pure clear, Larkhill passes on the Western Downs. Within a five-mile circle lie all these old, still active aerodromes. Over Larkhill still poise great silver, shining, motionless balloons, anchored to their winches by two, three, four thousand foot cables. A stone's throw from it stands a solitary inn on what was once the Salisbury to Devizes coaching road, the Bustard, with its low-raftered rooms and sagging floors, sunny south wall, and cobwebby highwayman's cellar. Sheep stealers, poachers, travellers, drank and lodged there two hundred years ago. In 1911 it became the first R.F.C. mess, when the 1st Aeroplane Company formed at Larkhill.

This small ring on the Salisbury Plain holds the very roots of the traditions of the R.A.F., and if you serve there, then you serve in the spirit of its past. Upavon, too, has been in continuous use since the early flying days when "Boom" Trenchard (he's always "Boom" to the Service), was the first Commandant of its Flying School.

Two fighter Squadrons replaced C.F.S. when it moved to Wittering in 1927. And now, with a turn of the wheel, the old order is restored again.

Netheravon saw a concentration camp of four military aeroplane squadrons in June of 1914, Nos. 3 and 4 Squadrons then being well established at the place. It has been Squadron base, reserve pool for overseas squadrons, home for 11 and 13 Squadrons, No. 1 F.T.S., Fleet Air Arm, and now for the newly formed No. 6 F.T.S., all in turn, with the changes of European policy and our shrinkages and expansions to meet the current case. Some old buildings have disappeared and new ones taken their place, but many of the old 1914 manoeuvre wooden huts and the original wooden hangars still stand, redolent for ever now of rotary engine castor oil. And I for one shall grieve in silence when at last they do have to come down to make way for yet more high, concreted affairs with smooth stone floors, adjustable floodlights, and observation gangways high up on the roof.

Here were our Johannsteil days. Cody flew his biplane—was it really in 1908?—off the long slopes above Salisbury, and the wind still sings gently through that wiry downland grass. From Eastchurch, our first scientific centre, and Brooklands, the happy-go-lucky and carefree, the early army and naval officers came to Wiltshire to teach subalterns and sub-lieutenants to fly. And do you know, by the way, that before the War Mrs. Hewlett qualified for one of the first Aero Club certificates at Brooklands, and then taught her husband Maurice, the novelist, to fly?

Until the end of 1911 the army merely dabbled in aviation and trained its pilots in the Air Battalion, an offspring of the Balloon Company of the R.E. The Navy did its first training at Eastchurch. They flew Box Kites chiefly, a 50 h.p. rotary air-cooled Gnome mounted in the framework behind the pilot to push him along. 35 m.p.h. was his top speed, and the ceiling with two up only 1500 feet. No air-speed indicators, turn indicators, or the like. Indeed, to turn at all with bank was then unknown. The only instruments were an oil gauge and a rev. indicator, and the pilot brought his own dry card compass and flew with it strapped to his wrist.

In 1912 all the air activities of both services were combined in the Royal Flying Corps, with a naval and a military wing. Flying was taught at Upavon and research and building done at the 'Factory', Farnborough. Some army officers bitterly opposed this; the Sappers, they said, were a scientific corps which should have full control, and it was quite mad to suppose that any other branch of the Service could ever acquire sufficient scientific knowledge to cope with aeroplanes. The brass-bound chiefs, however, wisely differed. Treat aircraft as you treat bridges, huts and trenches, they argued, and research will only be a branch off the main trunk. But put it on its own and then, and then only, will the full tactical possibilities be explored.

In 1912 also, aircraft were employed at Larkhill in military trials on the September army manoeuvres. The trials were open to all nations, and the designers had to produce something that would stay in the air for 4½ hours at 55 m.p.h. and climb to 1000 feet in five minutes.

Those were hazardous days. Four officers were killed flying to the manoeuvres and most of the prize-winners cracked up in the air later on with fatal results. But aviation got the fillip it deserved, and its value in reconnaissance was established for good and all.

In 1913 and 1914 they worked on gun spotting and air photography, bomb dropping and gun mounting, and even night flying experiments on Salisbury Plain... but dammit, what started all this? And you can read it presented much better in the official histories.

C.F.S. goes to Upavon very soon. Oh, yes. And our young marrieds have been getting short leave to skate down to Wiltshire to find thatched cottages near to the aerodrome, in which to shelter their wives and their own weary frames after the day's toil in the months to come.

This C.F.I.'s test looms closer and closer. The reaper clicks faintly on the broad aerodrome in the summer evening, and against the still silver and grey cumulus of warm summer the roses are now blowing in the gardens, where the tulips so lately stood. Fortified after a walk for oxygen and then a half-can at The George, I get down to this serious business of my Arabian notes. How often has that old writing-room oak panelling heard talk of flying since the Stamford 1914 days?

14th of July

This course isn't too long after all. I am weary of patter the nonce, and the authorities are right once more. Found three earwigs in my tie this morning, and had my Flight Commander's and my C.F.I.'s test. In a sudden unexpected rush suspense has reached its climax and then vanished clean away.

Cowling would have gone, too, but over the weekend he got himself engaged. And the excitement was still a little evident when he came up to the hangar this morning, so Mayor congratulated him and then gently urged him to drift away and sit in a quiet corner to dream over his notes until this cold, hard business-like world returned in full reality again.

The F.-Comdr. gave me effect of controls, medium turns, and a roll to the right with patter. Then a roll to the left and a simple loop without patter. Action in the event of fire. And then the forced landing. I boobed, chaps. I boobed. The smallest field of all and not a breath of wind. I know I should not on this occasion have tried to land well over the leeward hedge, or come in at the usual gliding speed. But I did. Beautiful approach; faultless patter. Then "turn in tending to overshoot. And when you are certain that you can get in, sideslip off the surplus height and land well up the field."

But she wouldn't stall and sit down. Instead the far hedge came skating at us at an incredible speed.

"Open up," said a quiet voice behind me.

I did so, and sank with shame and mortification into the seat.

"Go round and just do an ordinary landing in the field."

I sweated with concentration and managed this all right. Not a word.

"Fly back to the aerodrome and land. Do one climbing turn at 500 feet going up, and one gliding turn at 500 going in."

I saw him in the little mirror peering at the instruments, turn indicator, height and speed, as I flew round and glided in. I nearly sobbed on Mayor's neck.

"That's all right. You've been consistently quite good with me, and we all boob once in a while. Don't worry. Like to go with the C.F.I. this afternoon? Right, report at A Flight at 1420 and get his aeroplane started up for him."

C.F.I. — grand. Good take-off. He chose a nice large field for my forced landing and I put down a peach. Then patter for Climbing, Further Effect of Controls, Climbing and Gliding Turns, and a roll to the right and a loop. Finishing up with an aerodrome cross-wind landing, wing down to correct for drift in the approved way.

"Rumble in," he said calmly, "we're a little too close to that harrow for my liking." And that's all he said.

An honestly earned eighty per cent marks, I should say. Wings not quite level when the horizon came up on the loop. Still — why worry?

Phew — what a relief! And then a slack, golden hour after tea, dead beat with three hours of concentration in the air. These late afternoon hours in the mess during the summer all have a curious quality about them. Everyone sagging in chairs, half-asleep over newspapers. Their shoes dusty and top tunic buttons undone. The lazy click of the ha'pennies on the board going on in the corner where the sun streams in and turns the dust notes to bars of hovering gold specks. Joule and I competing each with a copy of *The Times* crossword. We always find Monday's dead easy, the mid-week ones pretty stiff, and the weekend ones slacking off again. The compositor is a psychologist in his way! Joule is a past master at these things. The *Telegraph* and *Morning Post* ones he can rip off in twenty minutes apiece. And he even makes some show of *The Observer* Torquemada every Sunday afternoon. Since I discovered this, I have treated him with great respect.

Indeed, I feel altogether like Atlas with the globe removed, for last night I finished my lecture notes with *Revolt in the Desert* on my knees and a map spread on the seat in the last King's Cross-Peterborough Sunday train. Compared with note taking, the ordeal of speech delivery will be as naught. And in any case I can rely on half of the audience to draw pictures on the tops of the desks or go to sleep.

Listen to some of my notes, and see if they aren't charged with the spirit of romance:

Born 1888, five brothers no sisters. Mother missionary, father sportsman. Age of 13 bicycle tour sketching armour and rubbing brasses. Eight tours of France on nix, studying cathedrals. At Oxford only read medieval stuff, midnight to 4 a.m. Played no games. For Honours thesis *walked* across Palestine and Syrian desert in summer doing research work, two fevers, and nearly murdered. Lived with Arabs and learned dialect, 1st class Honours.

...1910 controlling Arab gangs at Carchemish excavations for 15s. a day.

...1914 unfit for Army, so ran entire map room at Whitehall after 3 weeks. Intelligence Staff Captain, Cairo Map Section—got under Staff's skin by knowing job better than they did!

...Lawrence a real *romantic*. Nose in Scott and Tennyson, head in Morris and Malory and French-Latin romances. Then plunged into epic with Feisal and Auda as first two chapters. Saintly and knightly himself, but to keep scepticism alive and prevent from becoming another Don Quixote, carried on Arabian Campaign, Malory's *Morte D'Arthur*, Comedies of Aristophanes, and Oxford Book of English Verse. Accepted Auda as fellow medievalist.

...Rode 50 miles a day for a month—only few dates, dirty bread and polluted water. 1400 miles, weak and ill with dysentery, boils, and saddle-sores. Little sleep, great anxiety, and hottest country in world at hottest time of year. Weight dropped 11—7 stone.

...Ghazala (his white camel) twice did 143 miles in 24 hours—acted as unwilling C.O. to tribe and in 6 days settled 12 cases battery, 4 camel thefts, 1 marriage, 14 blood feuds, 2 thefts, 1 divorce, 2 evil eye, 1 bewitchment... 17 Turkish trains blown up in 4 months. Turks scared... Lived on camel for two days. Blue with cold and fever. Blew up train and collected 5 bullet wounds and broken toe... Turks now had £20,000 on his head. Asked to be made Colonel—told 'em it would get him better berth on train through Italy! Called it his 'Taranto Rank'.

...Allenby wanted to smash Turks. Lawrence worn out. In 1½ years had ridden 1000 miles a month and 1000s more in crazy aircraft and cars. Dreaded pain and badly wounded in 5 fights. Still suffering from hunger, heat, frost, poisoned wounds, and guilt of fraud to Arabs and massacre of Turks. Allenby made him go on... Jaafar given Iron Cross in 1915 and C.M.G. in 1918... DAMASCUS TAKEN. Terrific reorganising work necessary, hospitals, prisons, water, light, food supply, railway. Finance—an Australian gave £500 to an Arab to hold horse's head for 5 minutes. Lawrence set about it. Akaba gold to restore currency—newspaper to restore confidence. Found forage for Chauvel's 40,000 horses.

Left 3 days later, and left a govt. that endured for 2 years in a war-wasted country without foreign advice. And Feisal and Allenby saw and approved. 'Feisal large-eyed, colourless and worn, like a fine dagger. Allenby gigantic and red and merry, fit representative of the Power which had thrown a girdle of humour and strong dealing round the world.'

...*a foreigner and unbeliever* had led greatest Arab revolt since Mohammed.

Fought in vain for Arabs at Versailles... fed up and took seven years' research fellowship, All Souls, Oxford.

Wrote *Seven Pillars*, seven out of ten books in Paris Feb-June 1919. Eight books stolen in a train—re-wrote 250,000 words—twice size of *The Good Companions*—in under three months. World's record for Book VI—written sunset to sunrise of one night, 34,000 words. 1-2,000 is usual literary man's output.

How did book get name? Some say seven great cities of East—Cairo, Damas., Baghdad, Mecca, Constantinople. Others from *Book of Proverbs*, a key perhaps to Lawrence's whole life.

"Wisdom hath builded a house: she hath hewn out her seven pillars. She crieth upon the highest places of the city 'Whoso is simple let him turn in hither... if thou be wise, thou shalt be wise for thyself'."

16th of July

A most amusing game now that the serious stuff is over—Mayor has elected to be a real greenhorn of a pupil and I am to teach him how to fly.

First of all he keeps me waiting in the cockpit for hours with the engine ticking over (pupils take an incredible time to get dressed), and then comes charging out red in the face, treads all over the wings getting in, and knocks off the duplicate switches and stops the engine.

"Oo, sir, I *am* sorry, sir."

He's a born comedian. Having strapped himself in wrongly, he finds he's forgotten his goggles and has to roar back to the hangar again for them. By now the fitter and rigger are in convulsions. When we get into the air I can see him behind me, reflected in the little mirror on the centre section strut, doing all the things I am supposed to notice, allow for, and possibly correct. Wildly clutching the sides of the cockpit when we bank with any degree of steepness, looking round the wrong way, to the outside, during turns, and flying along with his head in the office, eyes riveted to the airspeed indicator because I told him to keep the speed at about 95. He treated me to a swinging take off, and a vicious pump-handle landing at the end. Then told me my faults for a change.

Today we were asked to state where we would like to go on leaving C.F.S. First and second choice. Abu Sueir in Egypt, Digby and Cranwell in Lincolnshire, Sealand near Chester, Grantham just north of here, Leuchars in Scotland, and the new schools soon to be opened at Peterborough and Wittering — these are the places where pupils are taught or to be taught to fly. This causes much speculation. Doe asks for Leuchars where they train naval pilots. Trout and Flaps ask for Cranwell, their old alma mater. The rest of us dither in suspense. Six of us plump for Netheravon as our first choice. Of course they'll only want about two. But it seems to be by far the best of the bunch — good country, if out of the way. No fenland or factory smoke, and the sweet south within easy reach. And next week the C.F.I. takes his list up to the Air Ministry to confer with the C.F.I.s of all the other schools.

More bathing in the river, six of us piling into Nacelle's old Lancia to go. Then we fell to talking and reading old copies of *Punch* and *Razzle* in The Mermaid, another old hostelry we have discovered in Wansford, until we saw that it was too late to get back for supper. So we had bread and cheese and more strong ale, a merry, table-thumping party, and came home under a big yellow harvest moon with a black monster of a night bomber droning across the stars on some exercise at four thousand feet, its wing tip navigation lights burning ruby and emerald clear.

Only ten earwigs in my room tonight, but a new plague is upon the land. About fifty maybugs, hovering around the eaves, and lying on their backs in the window-sill, buzzing and kicking like silly things. They hoot around like panic-stricken armour-plated bullets if you do tip them over with a ruler, so it's best to shovel them straight back into the night. Still, better a cycle of maybugs than one day of tarantulas and scorpions, England, my England, my own!

17th of July

We have finished assembling the Lynx and Jaguar. Sarge has bench-tested them, and now into the airframes they go. The Atlas and Avro are fully rigged, and as the engines go in we are busy doping and varnishing the planes. Sergeant Stagger, the rubicund little Cornishman, who looks as though he has always lived on schnapps, and watches over our desperate rigging efforts with a twinkling blue eye, has just got his Long Service and Good Conduct, his "Rooty" Medal—as he says—"for eighteen years of undetected crime."

We suitably congratulate him. He, too, wears wings, having been a sergeant pilot soon after the war. He, incidentally, was among the first five members of the Caterpillar Club, elected when Monos were our training aircraft and Foxes our fastest line.

We like him for his sense of humour; he says he tries to imagine which Dickens character every newcomer represents, he interprets life in terms of Dickens, and for him the world is populated entirely with Squeers, Dombeys, Micawbers, Olivers and Davids, Bob Cratchits and Fagins and Bumbles. I'm not sure he isn't right. There's still an uncommonly large number of Bumbles about. He runs over, too, what questions we might get in the rigging exam. "Intelligent anticipation" he calls it, with the faintest suspicion of a wink.

The exams begin next Monday, in five days' time. Far too remote yet to bother about. Remember Flugel's types 1 and 8. And of course we'll do no work over the weekend as on Friday we have a Grand Farewell Dance; it is to be thrown not only to the departing course, but to all the good friends of C.F.S., all who have given tennis parties and taken interest and been kind during the past umpteen years.

Great preparations are in hand, and we are having our meals anywhere, in the ante-room or card-room while they prepare the long dining-room, fixing streamers and coloured lights, importing palms and erecting a staircase up to our minstrels' gallery for sitters-out. I've often looked sadly at that gallery during guest nights and thought how pleasant it would be if we could import the Dolmetsch family to discourse soft music to us during dinner, *Eine Kleine Nachtmusik* and the like, the violins singing, the heights brave with serpent and hautboy and lute. But, alas, the echo is too bad and the reverberation off the roof too deafening to permit any sort of music up there at all. And so it stands, an empty and neatly garnished Folly.

Esterhazy is beginning to swot, which alarms me considerably. So I drag him out for a walk over the aerodrome after supper, then back for a pint of lemon squash apiece with ice tinkling in it, three games of shove ha'penny, then to bed to read drowsily and to sleep. So we pass our days.

21st of July

The dance in all its splendour has come and gone, and the Stamford hotel keepers have made whole packets out of sheltering our lady loves. The old people enjoyed it tremendously, and Hickory, after much persuasion, did so well getting dance music out of the deserted grand piano, while the band was having its supper, that nobody wanted the band to come back at all. Anode[1], the Signals Officer, did a sterling job of work; sunk coloured lights into the cool depths of the goldfish pool, lighted up the fountain, and tricked out strings of lanterns among the trees and rose bushes. Then, at 10 p.m. pressed a button and the whole show leapt into twinkling life. All we wanted after that was the Queen of All the Fairies to come tripping on.

Carriages were for 2.30, but at 3.30 we were putting away bacon and eggs in the card-room and vowing the night yet young. Most of us saw the dawn break, and got to bed at 6.30 a.m. The mess servants finished their squaring up and reeled off to bed at 10 a.m.

And now, after using fifteen gallons of petrol, getting in only ten hours' sleep in two nights, and spending some seven pounds, hey ho for the exams, tomorrow.

I reluctantly commit myself to an inky three hours with books and notes and the strong smell of midnight oil. While a white moon outside shines serenely over the glow of my small study lamp within.

At five p.m., all revelling at last sternly put aside, Holt-fflair and Hickory, Flaps and Nacelle and Cork armed themselves with books and set out in the old Lancia to find a quiet field in which they could swot. A roof over the head was altogether too much to bear.

---

[1] As Squadron Leader J. W. Gillan, CO of No. 111, the first Hurricane squadron, 'Anode' made the historic downwind dash from Edinburgh to Northolt, 327 miles, at an average speed of 408 mph on the afternoon of February 10 1938.

Whether or not they intended to dispose themselves at silent ten-pace intervals along the leeward hedge the better to aid fierce concentration I do not know, but it seems that long before they discovered a suitable field they fell upon and into a tavern called Ram Jam further along the Great North Road. Where, local lore tells, Jem Belcher used to fight bare-fisted, and fighting cocks were set to one another with hackles up.

I turned over when the earth turns and breathes in its sleep at about 3 a.m., to hear a blundering and soft cursing along the flower beds below. Nacelle, having convinced himself that the proper way in which to enter a room was through the window, was finding his way to bed.

25th of July

Most of a week of glorious sunshine has passed while we stewed over three-hour examination papers day after day. We were let loose today, and armed with bath towels rushed off to the river in the afternoon heat to swim. Esterhazy and I flew the Avro and Atlas in turn, and pronounced our handiwork good. The others were too keen on the cold plunge to wait, so they will fly before they leave on Friday.

All six of us who asked to go are Netheravon bound. And all of us have got 'B' categories except one, who roped in an 'A2'. This is very satisfying, and, I believe, a record for good uniformity. Most courses produce a few 'Cs' and some even the old 'D' category, now obsolete, which meant that the pilot was to be an instructor on no account!

Tomorrow we start on Clearance Chits — each armed with a buff form to wander round each department, Library, Stores, Flight, Parachutes, P.M.C. and so forth, obtaining signatures to certify that we are 'cleared' by them and hold no goods or chattels on our charge. The chap you are seeking is never in, so you always spend a day and walk about ten miles to get your chit completed.

And for the last evening we see the setting sun shining in the white-framed rectory windows and hear the lazy click of the batted cricket ball on the green; go for our last wander over the aerodrome meadows where the sheep munch by the hedge, past the willows where the horses and stray cattle whisk off the flies and drink, and the rabbits burrow and build. Through the grasses to startle thrushes and larks into flight, along the village street where the labourers stand at their wicket gates talking in the slow Rutland burr, under the elms where the rooks are settling in for the night and the first owl is beginning to hoot; and so past the low gurgling doves on the lawn and home.

In this book you, too, have flown. And perhaps you will not wonder now why in our secret moments, having tasted different draughts, we sometimes feel as men apart; and that now and then aircraft and the cloud heights are mixed in our dreams.

You have been with me through Central Flying School and seen some cross-sections of the R.A.F. at work and at play as well. Good citizen taxpayer, your money isn't wasted. On the whole we're a fairly useful and a very happy crowd! And finally, if ever you're learning to fly, or how to teach others to fly; or, at the Mecca of all pilots, teaching those who are to teach others to fly—a pilot cubed, as it were—remember this cheering motto that has helped me over so many a stile: "What one fool can do, another can as well."

Frank Tredrey

A BIOGRAPHY BY THE AUTHOR'S DAUGHTER, LOUISE ELLIOTT

Frank Darker Tredrey, my father, was a Cornishman. Born in 1908 he joined the RAF when he was sixteen. When he left in 1953 I was still a child, so for the full details of his service career I am indebted to Peter Hearne.

He entered Halton in January 1925. Towards the end of his apprenticeship he won a scholarship to RAF Cranwell for a permanent commission cadetship, one of four or five awarded to the top apprentices of the year. But he failed the medical due to temporary eye strain brought on by so much studying.

My father graduated from Halton as a Corporal in April 1928 and went to No. 1 Flying Training School at Netheravon as an Aero Engine Fitter Group 1. In October 1929, he was posted to 30(B) Squadron in Iraq in the same position on Wapitis. In July 1930 he was selected for training as a Sergeant Pilot.

After nine months at No. 4 Flying Training School at Abu Suier near Ismalia, he was posted to Egypt and then back to Iraq to Nos 55 and 84 Squadrons, flying the ubiquitous Wapiti.

He returned to England in 1933 and joined 207(B) Squadron at Bircham Newton (Norfolk) as an Acting Pilot Officer flying Fairey Gordons and by 1934 he was flying Seaplanes and Flying Boats, first at Calshot and then at Lee on Solent. In later years he frequently expressed his regret that the use of seaplanes and flying boats by the RAF was discontinued. He had been particularly fond of them and it was something that he always believed to have been a big mistake.

In April 1935 he went to Central Flying School at Wittering and it is his training and experiences during those months that are the subject of this book which was published in 1939, shortly before the outbreak of war.

My father left CFS in July 1935 with the top exam marks of 94.8% and started his instructor's career back at Netheravon, now the home of No. 6 FTS. He was instructing on Tutors and Harts and as often as he could he flew one or other of the Hawker Furies which were on the school's establishment. He was upgraded to an A2 Cat flying instructor.

In October 1936 he was appointed Chief Ground Instructor of No. 6 FTS with the rank of Flight Lieutenant. Although he continued to fly the Fury, Hart and Tutor as time allowed, his flying hours per month were halved as he took on this new role.

In April 1939, with war obviously approaching, he was selected to command 185(B) Squadron a bomber squadron with a training role. Initially based at Thornaby, flying Fairey Battles, 185 moved to Cottesmore in the summer of '39 and converted to Handley Page Hampdens and Avro Ansons.

As CO he was fully involved in all the aspects of the ground and flying instruction which were essential if the rapidly expanding numbers of graduates of the Flying Training Schools were to achieve the level of experience and skill needed to become 'operational' in Bomber Command. This Operational Training Unit role was formalised when 185 Squadron became No. 14 OTU in April 1940.

However in December 1940 his group Commander, Air Commodore Ralph Cochrane, as he then was, became Director of Flying Training at the Air Ministry. It was at the start of the build up of the highly ambitious world wide Empire Air Training Scheme which had been envisaged before the start of war.

Cochrane, one of the most intellectual of RAF senior officers, recognised that he was going to need people of similar calibre if the quality and uniformity of air crew training standards in this very diverse organisation was to be achieved. So my father was moved from 14 OTU and posted to the Directorate of Flying Training as Wing Commander. He stayed there until August 1945, by which time he had been promoted to Group Captain and was Deputy Director Flying Training of the RAF.

During these five years my father held a number of positions, one being as head of the Training Publications group which had the task of producing a wide variety of effective training literature which could be easily understood by the extraordinarily diverse range of individuals, of all backgrounds and nationalities, who were beginning to make up the aircrews of the war time service. He was sometimes assisted in this task by Anthony Armstrong, a well known pre-war humorist, who became closely associated with the unforgettable Tee Emm (i.e. Training Memoranda) service periodical which was a staple diet for good practice by aircrews throughout the war.

He also worked with Smith Barry, the 'founding father' of the CFS method of flying training in WWI, on the up-to-date revision of the original flying instructional 'patter' notes, as related in the section on CFS history.

At the end of hostilities in 1945 he was posted to command a number of RAF stations in SE Asia Command during the Demobilisation period. In 1947 he came back to the UK as a member of the Directing Staff at the RAF Staff College at Bracknell. From there he returned to the Air Ministry as Deputy Director of Personnel Services and in 1953 he learned that he was to be promoted to Air Commodore and posted to the Imperial Defence College (The Royal College for Defence Studies).

My father had joined the RAF as a boy because he wanted to fly. Flying had been his great love and he had enjoyed training pilots. But, despite being very gifted and capable in its execution, administration had always been for him a duty rather than a vocation. He knew that inevitably the higher he rose through the service the more desk-bound he would become. So before his promotion was gazetted he decided to take voluntary retirement. He had received the OBE in wartime and on his retirement was awarded the CBE.

During the war years he had come to know Wing Commander Douglas Blackwood, heir to the family firm Blackwood and Son. The Scottish publishing house William Blackwood was founded in 1804 and published many of Britain's most illustrious authors including Sir Walter Scott, George Eliot and John Buchan. In 1817 *Blackwood's Magazine*, 'Maga' as it was affectionately known, was founded; published monthly it contained literary criticism and political comment, but its life blood was the contributions from professional and often acclaimed writers, members of the services and civilians in all parts of Britain and the Empire. It was in every officers' mess and, like *The Illustrated London News*, was an institution.

Learning of my father's passion for literature Douglas Blackwood invited him to join them should he ever think of leaving the RAF. So in 1953 he changed to the civilian uniform of the day, bowler hat, briefcase and furled umbrella, and took command of Blackwood's London office. There he shared in the selection and editing both of books to be published and articles for the magazine, to which he himself was a frequent contributor.

When he joined Blackwood's, of which he later became a director, it was about to celebrate its one hundred and fiftieth birthday. He was commissioned to write a history of the firm and *The House of Blackwood* was published in 1954 to excellent critical reviews.

My father stayed with Blackwood's until 1973 and then continued his association with them on a consultancy basis for many more years. In 1976 he published *Pioneer Pilot*, the biography of Robert Smith Barry whom Lord Trenchard considered to be 'The man who taught the air forces of the world how to fly'. He also edited Maurice Baring's *Flying Corps Headquarters 1914-1918*.

In his retirement years my father was able to give full rein to another passion—sailing. He and my mother were keen small boat racers, they also cruised the English coast and those of France and Holland and Belgium. However, she chose to remain in port, supplier of victuals and comforts, when he went ocean racing and on the Fastnet.

He sailed up until his late seventies and wrote until the last few days of his life, diaries, journals, memoirs of his time in the RAF, day books, scrap books, a huge and detailed collection. Shortly before his death my father assembled all the Blackwood papers and records still in his possession, the firm having sadly closed down, and donated them to the Blackwood archive at the National Library of Scotland. All the rest of his papers, excluding his personal diaries that were kept by the family, he donated to the RAF Museum at Hendon.

Frank Darker Tredrey died, after a short illness, in 1988, aged eighty.

Louise Elliott
Brisbane, Australia
January 2000

Appendix I

THE ROYAL AIR FORCE CENTRAL FLYING SCHOOL

ORIGINS

The Central Flying School, almost always referred to as CFS, is one of the oldest units of the Royal Air Force. It was established at Upavon in Wiltshire jointly by the War Office and the Royal Navy as a flying unit in 1912. Initially its role was to turn existing qualified pilots into operational military pilots, the pupil intake being officers who had first to have obtained their basic Royal Aero Club pilot's certificate privately. This arrangement soon changed with the events of 1914 when ab-initio pupils started basic instruction at one of the Reserve Squadrons and then passed to the Central Flying School or to a service Squadron for their operational training.

The first entry at CFS included no fewer than two future Chiefs of Air Staff, namely Trenchard and Salmond, as well as many destined for the higher ranks of the Royal Air Force. It also contained a certain Lieutenant Robert Smith Barry, an Irishman with an unusual mix of far-sightedness and drive together with a great deal of unorthodoxy which sometimes, in later life, bordered on eccentricity.

In another of his books entitled *Pioneer Pilot*, Frank Tredrey describes how when Smith Barry was the CO of No. 60 Squadron in France in 1916 he became appalled at the inadequate standard of pilot training which was being produced by the existing flying instruction system. Making use of his earlier contacts he badgered his old No. 1 Course colleague, Trenchard, now the GOC of the Royal Flying Corps in France, to get permission to introduce a much more thorough form of flying instructor training.

The result was to change the face of flying training across the world for ever and to establish the well defined procedures which have been employed universally since that time for safe and effective pilot training,

Before Smith Barry flying instruction was a very unstructured affair in which the pupils, and often the instructors, had little idea of the basic facts underlying the control of an aircraft in flight. Training methods were based on the pupil imitating the actions of the instructor, sometimes in non dual control machines in which the pupil laid his hand over the instructor's on the single set of controls. Equally worrying from the point of view of failing to produce aggressiveness and initiative in the face of the enemy, the emphasis seemed to lie in being told what *not* to do so as to avoid accidents, rather than demonstrating the limits to which the aircraft could be flown safely.

Smith Barry's appointment as CO of one of the Flying Schools at Gosport in January 1917, later to become the School of Special Flying, changed the whole scene for the better and forever. Training aircraft were all standardised as dual control Avro 504Ks and after an abortive attempt at electrical intercom, the effective 'Gosport' speaking tube system finally allowed instructor and pupil to communicate with each other intelligibly throughout the flight rather than only at snatched quiet moments near the stall.

Most importantly Smith Barry and his staff, particularly Sidney Parker, analysed in some depth the basic elements of piloting and theory of flight with the object of producing a logical sequence of demonstrations and flying lessons by which a pupil could obtain a full and thorough understanding of what could safely be done to exploit the capabilities of his aircraft.

Lastly Gosport produced the so called 'patter book' which set down on paper the basis of a standard phraseology for instruction in the air. This enabled the instructor to impart a standardised and thorough form of instruction in the air. The object of the 'patter' was to ensure that all of the content of the training exercise was put across to the pupil in a readily comprehensible manner, which was synchronised with the demonstration of a particular movement of the controls and the corresponding response of the aircraft; not always easy when, as at the start of a spin demonstration, you are being buffeted by the slipstream in an open cockpit and the world is rotating round you faster than you can talk!

Later known as *Air Publication 1732*, the Gosport patter book and flying training syllabus has formed in its evolving forms the foundation for ab-initio flying instruction in the Royal Air Force and all UK flying training since that time.

TREDREY AND SMITH BARRY

When Frank Tredrey came to CFS in 1935 it was a world-renowned organisation and many overseas airforces were sending the pick of their future instructors to the three-month courses. Little had changed in the concepts since 1917, which was not a sign of inertia but an indication of the rightness of Smith Barry's original ideas.

One change that had taken place, however, was not for the better. The Gosport patter had been turned into 'Whitehall speak' with the result that instructors were having to write up their own notes in a style that could be 'got over' in the air to the pupil in the essential synchronisation with the aircraft's manoeuvres.

This had an interesting outcome during Tredrey's time in the Air Ministry in WWII when he was given the task of rejuvenating the Gosport patter book, during which period Smith Barry, now a newly re-engaged Pilot Officer, was posted into his branch. As Tredrey's later book reveals, a friendship struck up between them. (Perhaps I might add that as one of very many users of the revised 1732 I found it an admirable document, little knowing from whose pen it had flowed.)

CFS AT WITTERING

After the end of World War I and the temporary destruction of the German 'threat' a situation developed in which British Home Defence Forces were deployed to counter any hostile action by France, who remained the other most powerful nation in Europe. In consequence the front line units were deployed near the South coast and displaced second line units moved to more Northern stations.

Wittering had been designated as a permanent station to house the Central Flying School and a number of new buildings including married quarters, messes, workshops and Station offices were erected. Of these, the Mess, which is one of Sir Edwin Lutyens' earlier designs of 'standard' RAF officers' messes, still remains in AD 2000 very much the same as when it was first built in 1925. Although the front entrance is now covered in creeper, little else has changed in what is now a listed building, and the mess gardens of which Tredrey wrote approvingly are still lovingly tended by the gardeners as the 1999 photo shows. The decorative pond remains as peaceful as ever, and even the stone table referred to on page 69 keeps its place, although the current occupants do not know the story of its origin.

CFS arrived at Wittering in the summer of 1926 and left 9 years later in summer 1935 when it was realised that the German threat had returned. CFS went back to Upavon from which it had come and after a short interlude Wittering became a full time front line operational station, a role it has retained virtually ever since. During WWII it was a very active night fighter station and for a number of years afterwards was the base of various V Force nuclear bomber squadrons.

Today RAF Wittering has been the main UK operating base and centre of RAF Harrier operations since 1970. In 2000 it is equipped with the GR7 night attack version which is capable of flying and fighting at night with the same effectiveness as in daylight conditions, a British development that Tredrey could not even have imagined in 1935.

But, as any visitor to Wittering will learn, the pilots of the year 2000 possess the same skill, verve and enthusiasm as that earlier generation. Meeting up by chance with some of them in 'The George' in Stamford it felt as though time had rolled back to those earlier days and that one was sitting around with Esterhazy, Nacelle and Cork, the only differences being the airspeeds quoted in the 'lines' and the price of the beer!

CFS AND AIRCRAFT DEVELOPMENTS

Although CFS had started off at Upavon as an advanced flying school, it also acted up till the end of 1916 as a Service flight test centre, at which time the test effort became so great that the Aeroplane and Armament Experimental Establishment was formed at Martlesham Heath, later moving to Boscombe Down at the outbreak of WWII in September 1939.

This was not, however, the end of CFS's contribution to the development scene. Two of its better-known efforts concern Flt. Lt. W. E. P. Johnson, a CFS staff instructor who surprisingly had been a Patent Agent before he joined the RAF. Flying Officer Frank Whittle had been, like Tredrey, an apprentice entrant, who had also won a scholarship to Cranwell. Whittle can truly be described as a genius whose vision, hard work and determination, technical understanding and all round engineering skill gave the world practical, safe and reliable jet engines. When Whittle was a member of No. 30 Course at CFS in 1929 he expanded his original ideas which he had formulated at Cranwell for new types of power plants for high speed, high altitude flight. His further thoughts led to the fundamental seminal idea of using a jet from an aircraft gas turbine as the propulsion prime mover so as to avoid the limitations of ever decreasing propeller efficiency at high speeds. Johnson strongly encouraged him and ensured he got a hearing with the Commandant and later the Air Ministry in London. The latter, in the classic British tradition, turned him down initially, partly because Whittle's ideas conflicted with some of their scientists' own personal projects.

It is impossible to overestimate the importance of Whittle's personal contribution to the creation of the practical aircraft gas turbine, which he achieved with little outside assistance and, in the early days, only grudging acceptance and sometimes direct hostility. Johnson's role and the ambience of CFS were a vital catalyst in this story and without them the world would have been a very different place.

On another matter of great importance to the future security of Britain, Johnson was responsible at CFS in the early 1930s for the initial development of Instrument Flying techniques and training in the RAF, which became a vital requirement for WWII airforces. Plate 13 shows Johnson making a solo I/F take off in an Avro 504N in 1931.

Stemming from this work was the development of the Standard British Blind Flying Panel, which in contrast to the random, haphazard instrument layouts on almost all other nations' military aircraft, was an optimised and orderly standard layout of blind flying instruments. The design layout of this panel was fitted to virtually all British military aircraft, except basic trainers, from 1937 onwards. Even today, as with the Gosport 'system', the fundamentals of this work lives on in the so-called 'Basic Tee', which is a standard instrument layout, based on the RAF panel, and which is found on most civil aircraft and even, in an electronic form, in the new Electronic Flight Instrument Systems.

At the sharper end of the business CFS instructors such as D'Arcy Greig, Atcherley, Stainforth and Waghorn had played a major part as pilots in the RAF High Speed Flight in the 1929 and 1931 Schneider Trophy races with the Supermarine S6 series floatplanes. Their efforts resulted in Britain winning the Trophy outright plus a world air speed record by Stainforth of 407 mph. This type of involvement with what is now called the 'leading edge of technology' played a major part in enabling CFS staff to develop the new operating skills and methods required to cope with the 1936 generation of monoplanes equipped with such devices as variable pitch propellers, automatic boost controls, flaps and the like. A major element of this was the development of Pilot's Notes which set out in a comprehensible fashion what a pilot needed to know to operate one of the many, relatively much more complicated aircraft then coming into RAF service in the years immediately prior to WWII.

This work was carried out by Handling Squadron, which became a vital part of CFS at that time. As well as evolving the necessary piloting techniques which could be easily absorbed by both new and existing service pilots, CFS made a major contribution in the form of the first developments and universal use of the concept of 'Vital Actions' or 'Cockpit Drills' with their odd mnemonics such as BUMPFF (Brakes, Undercarriage, Mixture, Pitch, Fuel, Flaps), that were to save the skin of many an unwary or tired or wounded pilot.

Interestingly Tredrey in his post in the Air Ministry appreciated that with multi-crew aircraft, such as Wellingtons and Lancasters, it was equally essential to develop 'Whole Crew' vital actions drills. His papers record that this concept was adopted as a standard procedure in the RAF and in other airforces for aircraft with multiple crew members and crew positions, something which continues to the present day.

CFS TODAY

Royal Air Force Central Flying School has gone through many metamorphoses since 1936, perhaps the most major being its temporary elevation during the war to being the Empire Central Flying School at a time when the standardisation of quality and experience of the many thousands of aircrew being trained throughout the Commonwealth and the USA was one paramount issue.

Today, 2000 AD, CFS is based at RAF Cranwell with outstations for training fast jet and helicopter instructors at RAF Valley and Shawbury, together with Tucano instructors at Linton. It still maintains that level of achievement in aviation which has characterised its activities over the 88 years of its existence and has won it the respect of all of the world's airforces as the standard bearer of excellence.

Its legacy includes the extraordinary achievements of WWII, when the implementation of the CFS flying training methods in the many Flying Training Schools spread across the Commonwealth countries gave the British air forces that vital supply of well trained aircrew essential for victory.

Then, as now, CFS training as always lay behind the high standard of RAF operational capabilities, something we see today regularly on our TV screens in the world wide variety of RAF operations ranging from hazardous helicopter rescues through famine relief drops and, when events demand, air combat and bombing operations,.

And perhaps the most visible manifestation of CFS is seen every summer in the flying displays of its Red Arrows formation aerobatic team. Their world famous performances reflect the original ideals of Smith Barry in their demonstrations of the ultimate in aircraft handling and manoeuvre achieved by a combination of knowledge and understanding, flying skills and judgement, the embodiment of Airmanship in its highest form.

GEOGRAPHIC GUIDE

GOSPORT 50 50′ N 01 10 W′ 33ft amsl. An early Royal Flying Corps aerodrome on the SW side of Portsmouth Harbour naval base. In 2000 no longer an active airfield but home to a major naval aircraft repair depot.

UPAVON 51 17′ N 01 47′ W 575ft amsl. The original airfield and location of CFS on its formation in 1912. In recent years it served as the principal RAF Group HQ for offensive attack operations but is now occupied by a British Army formation. Located on the top of the escarpment on the North of Salisbury Plain its grass airfield is still used as a Service gliding site.

WITTERING 52 37′ N 00 28′ W 273ft amsl. Also an early RFC airfield with a long operational history continuing to the present day as the centre for UK Harrier force operations. Located between the cathedral city of Peterborough and the Norman town of Stamford., it lies on western edge of the USAF 8th AF airfields.

Appendix II

TRAINING AIRCRAFT AT CFS, 1935

The aircraft that Frank Tredrey flew at CFS in 1935 were typical of the intermediate stage of development between the wooden biplanes of WWI and the monoplanes of WWII. In 1924 the Air Ministry, aware of the potential problems of shortages of high grade timber and the disadvantages of wooden structures in the operating conditions of the RAF's new overseas role, made the decision to move to metal structures for their future airframes. Despite the existing experience of light alloy airship structures most manufacturers, taking into account the embryonic state of aluminium alloy metallurgy, chose to use a combination of High Tensile steel for the highly stressed components and light alloys for the secondary elements. It was not until the development of stressed skin construction for which steel was excessively heavy that light alloy usage began to predominate.

The aircraft depicted, apart from the Lynx engined Avro 504N, which was derived from the basic 1913 Avro 504 design, used this basic technology and were essentially evolved versions of the World War I aeroplane with improved powerplants and better flying characteristics. But with the exception of the Hawker Hart they would not have looked too much out of place on an RFC aerodrome in 1918.

The principal aero engines, the 14 cylinder Armstrong Siddeley Jaguar and its smaller brother the 7 cylinder Lynx (which was widely used in contemporary small aircraft) had their origin in a WWI design; a later variant, the Cheetah, remained in full production for RAF training and communications aircraft up to the end of WWII. Only the Rolls Royce Kestrel, a monobloc V12 design, in the Hart Trainer represented the 'new' design thinking starting to emerge in the mid 1920s.

However, aero engine reliability was much improved and consequently the incidence of forced landings much reduced. But as Frank Tredrey suggests in his foreword the aircraft of the early thirties were of limited effectiveness. It was Frank Whittle, whose time at CFS helped him to realise his extraordinary vision, who ultimately provided the propulsive power which made the modern military and civil aircraft so effective in their different roles.

Except for one outstanding exception, the De Havilland Tiger Moth, which began to supplement and then replace the Avro Tutor and Avro 504N in the RAF flying schools from the mid thirties onwards, *Pilot's Summer* marks the final high point of the biplane era. The Magisters,

Masters, Harvards and Oxfords which came into service in 1938/9 may have been better suited to the pilot training needs of the new generation of monoplane fighters and bombers, but somehow the charm of that earlier period began to fade.

Frank Tredrey's account captures what is truly a lost 'Golden Age'.

COLOUR SCHEMES

A key date in the colour schemes of RAF Trainers was the delivery to CFS at the end of 1933 of a Tutor in a trials Trainer Yellow scheme. By the time of this book, as the diary suggests, it is certain that all of the Tutors in regular use as school aircraft were painted in this scheme, essentially polished metal cowl and nose panels, with other fabric surfaces yellow overall. Wing and tail struts were black and undercarriage struts were the airframe yellow. Contemporary pictures also show that a number of CFS aircraft of this era had the CFS 'Pelican Crest' painted on the fin. The entry for the 3rd May relates that 'A' Flight had vertical red bands about the fuselage and 'B' flight blue bands. Unhelpfully Tredrey's log book shows that he was in 'C' Flight! Among the individual aircraft he flew were K3294, K3292, K3238 and K3241. These latter two aircraft had previously formed part of the CFS aerobatic team in 1933.

In those years, as today, CFS provided the RAF aerobatic team which then specialised in inverted formation flying. When flown in this team the upper surfaces of both top and bottom wings and tailplane and elevators of the Tutors were painted in a red and white sunburst with no wing roundel markings. David Howley's drawing depicts one of the formation, K3238, in the earlier 1933 colour scheme. The team aircraft (incidentally including K3241 and K3238, see above) are shown in Plate 10 which was taken in Summer 1933. It should be noted that all photos of these 'team' Tutors show them with the front windscreen removed and cockpit faired over.

In 1933, prior to the introduction of Trainer Yellow, such of the basic colour scheme that still remained on the team aircraft was of the earlier silver with green anti glare decking; this is confirmed by an excellent 1/24th model in the CFS museum at Cranwell. Taking into account the financial exigencies of the pre-war RAF it would seem likely that the sunburst colours were in roundel white and red as shown on the CFS model.

After the Trainer Yellow scheme was introduced a later team which flew, among others K3263 and K3265, featured aircraft with the existing yellow fabric covering with a bright orange sun ray pattern on upper surface wings and tail again with no roundels so as to help spectators readily to identify inverted aircraft. Black and white photographs show a short 'green'? anti-glare panel on the top decking of the fuselage extending to the position of the rear windscreen whilst the rear top decking behind the rear cockpit appears to be of the same colour as the sun rays. Wing struts are black and the remainder of the metallic front fuselage panels and the complete circumference of the Townend ring are in natural aluminium. The undercarriage struts are yellow. This was the scheme in being at the time of Tredrey's time at CFS, the Orange sun ray pattern probably being a special colour dope supplied by Cellon.

By contrast many of the Avro 504Ns had retained their silver scheme, as indicated by the mention of 'staring yellow struts' at one point in the narrative. This is not surprising given that they were shortly to be withdrawn and the cost of re-doping was probably unjustified. Similar remarks apply to the Armstrong Whitworth Atlases (K1472 and K1479) which Tredrey flew and which were also coming to the end of their Service life, being replaced by the Hart variants in both operational and training roles.

However some 80 or so 504Ns had been rebuilt from old stored 504K airframes. Tredrey's logbook records flying one of these, E3318, which had originally been built in 1918, in a bright yellow scheme on 24th June.

Lastly the two CFS Hawker Hart Trainers, K3155 and K3156, shown in Tredrey's log books, though from the first 1933 Hawker production batch are most likely in May 1935 to have been in Trainer Yellow with polished natural metal nose panels.

OTHER TYPES FLOWN

Whilst Frank Tredrey was at CFS, two flights in Bulldogs, 2-seater K3170 and single-seater K2946, were his first in a single-seater fighter type, the realisation of a dream. Details of the Bulldog trainer version are given in the Osprey Aerospace publication *On Silver Wings*, which gives an excellent account of inter-war RAF biplane fighters.

After he left CFS he went to No. 6 FTS Netheravon, where, as well as Tutors and Harts, whenever he could he flew that most beautiful of all biplanes, the Hawker Fury, which unfortunately he had 'missed' at Wittering; Serials K3738 and K3739 (ex-43 Squadron aircraft) appear in his log book. The CFS Fury II K8238 shown in 'Fighter Silver' on Plate 11 was one of the later batch built by General Aircraft Limited Hanworth and delivered directly to CFS in 1936. The early Furies which were relegated from the frontline squadrons to the flying training schools adopted Trainer Yellow fabric colouring with polished metal nose panels and yellow struts, something which is confirmed by a photograph of K3737 at 6 FTS in 1936.

Furies were eventually replaced in FTSs by Harvards and Masters from 1939 onwards.

Later, as CO of No. 185 Squadron at Thornaby and Cottesmore, Frank Tredrey flew Handley Page Hampdens (2x 1000hp Pegasus radials), specimen serials P1273, P1276, P1281, which would have been in standard pre-war camouflage, probably with Type B red/blue roundels. Initially the squadron code letter in grey was ZM changing to GL when they amalgamated to form 14 OTU in April 1940. He also flew Avro Anson I Trainers, (2x350hp Cheetah radials) specimen serials N5211, R9832 and R9833. These aircraft, used for navigation and crew training, whilst silver for some time before the outbreak of war, would have adopted the standard upper surface Green/Dark Earth camouflage with black undersurfaces.

A final oddity is that No. 185 was unfortunate enough to receive a flight of Herefords which were Hampdens fitted with Napier Dagger 1000hp air cooled 24 cylinder H engines. These engines proved markedly deficient with serious overheating problems caused by their cylinder layout and a very high noise level stemming from their high rpm. Frank Tredrey flew these aircraft only 5 times including aircraft serials L6000, L6008, and L6016. They never entered full scale operational service and the hundred or so that were built mainly remained in the training role; a number were re-converted to Hampdens.

It would have been interesting to hear his views on them!

OUTLINE TECHNICAL DETAILS
(REFER TO PLATES 17-20, FOLLOWING PAGE 188)

AVRO 504N
(ARMSTRONG SIDDELEY LYNX 7 CYL. RADIAL)
PLATE 17

Span 36 ft 0 in; Length 28ft 6 in; Wing Area 320 sq. ft.;
Max Weight 2240 lb; Empty Weight 1584 lb;
Max Speed 100 mph; Cruise 85 mph; Rate of Climb (sl) 770 ft/min.

The original Avro 504 had flown before WWI and indeed in the hands of the Royal Naval Air Service it carried out one of the first raids of the war on the Zeppelin sheds on Lake Konstanz. However it is as a trainer it became best known and was favoured by Smith Barry as the standard RFC ab-initio trainer in 1917. By the end of the war some 7000 or so had been built of which over 2000 were in RAF Flying Training Schools.

Thus in the mid-1920s, when the Air Ministry was looking for a new trainer, the idea of an upgraded 504 had some appeal. Development work had already taken place to replace the old rotaries with modern fixed cylinder engines with conventional throttle controls, and a new undercarriage with oleos and a distinctive form of articulated struts had been produced.

Starting in 1927 something over 500 new airframes were built and a further 80 refurbished from old 504Ks.

The new version designated the 504N was fitted with the Armstrong Siddeley Lynx IV C of 215 hp, the same that as used in the Tutor, and the weight and speed all went up somewhat compared with the earlier versions. Later aircraft, such as those used at CFS, had Frise ailerons to reduce adverse aileron drag in turns and square wing tips. Some of these also incorporated welded steel tube fuselages which greatly reduced the difficult iterative process of truing up the wooden fuselage and all of its individual bays by adjustments of the internal wire bracing, something which presented a real challenge to the uninitiated. Those used in the Instrument Training Flight had their dihedral reduced by 1 degree to reduce stability and make things harder for the pupil!

With a 215 hp Lynx the 504N had a reasonable performance for a 1913 design and the resultant aircraft was properly 'aerobattable'.

Readers will see that Tredrey had a good opinion of the 504N as a training aircraft as they required some skill to fly well and could be demanding in difficult conditions such as cross winds. After the end of WWI 504 models of many different versions found themselves being exported and operated in different parts of the world. The later 504N was among these and was also built in under licence Belgium.

AVRO 621 TUTOR
(ARMSTRONG SIDDELEY LYNX 7 CYL. RADIAL)
PLATE 18

Span 34 ft 0in; Length 26 ft 6in; Wing Area 301 sq. ft;
Max Weight 2458 lb.; Empty Weight 1850 lb. approx. (with in-service mods e.g. tailwheel, etc.);
Max speed 120 mph; Cruise 105 mph; Rate of Climb (sl) 930ft/min.

Despite the success of the 504N upgrade it was recognised that it was an interim solution and that a later design with more modern handling characteristics would be needed which incorporated the metal aircraft technology then favoured by the Air Ministry. Originally flown as a private venture aircraft known as the Avro Trainer with a 150 hp Armstrong Siddeley Mongoose radial it was finally selected in 1932 as the winner in a fly off with a similarly powered Hawker Tomtit.

The Tutor introduced a degree of class and comfort which had previously been absent from ab-initio trainers with adjustable seats and pedals, brakes, comfortable draft proof cockpits together with improvements in speed and climb, which enabled the instructor to position the aircraft more readily in the particular part of the sky he wished to use for his exercise. A sizeable aircraft, it is not too different in dimensions and weight to the Boeing Stearman, though most think its appearance and handling qualities to be more attractive than the beefy US machine.

David Ogilvy, who was General Manager of the Shuttleworth Trust for many years comments that the controls are pleasantly light but also low geared which leads to fairly large stick movements in more vigorous manoeuvres. Whilst the controls are 'not outstanding' at the lower speeds they become progressively crisper as airspeed increases, a good point for a training aircraft.

It was perhaps Frank Tredrey's felicitous description of the Tutors as 'gentlemanly little things' that has stuck and has led many subsequent commentators to refer to it as a gentleman's aircraft or suchlike term. And in that phrase lay the clue to its rather early demise during WWII.

Although very pleasant to handle with good aerobatic qualities it was forgiving of pupils' mistakes and its soft, long stroke undercarriage soaked up bad landings. Moreover the fuel consumption of the 215 hp Lynx IV C in the production aircraft was more than was needed to enable a smaller two seat aircraft to carry out ab-initio training to the same level. Consequently, as war approached and the need for greatly increased numbers of training aircraft became apparent, the Tiger Moth with its more demanding flying qualities and lower purchase price and operating costs was selected to replace it as the RAF's basic trainer. This was a rather bizarre outcome considering that the Tutor had replaced the Tiger at an RAF Flying Training School in 1933 and that a further reason for the Tiger Moth purchase was the need to utilise wood-working productive capacity for wooden aircraft so as to free up the industry's metal capacity for operational aircraft.

Nevertheless something like 800 Tutor airframes were built and some 400 served as a principal RAF trainer up to the beginning of WWII. It spawned a whole series of variants, many of which along with the original version, were exported in respectable numbers, ranging from a 175 mph armed fighter trainer to the lighter Club Cadet civilian club trainer.

HAWKER HART TRAINER
(ROLLS ROYCE KESTREL V 12 LIQUID COOLED)
PLATE 19

Span 37 ft 4in; Length 29 ft 4in; Wing Area 349 sq. ft;
Max Weight 4150 lb.; Empty Weight 3020 lb.;
Maximum Speed 165 mph; Cruise 145 mph; Rate of Climb (sl) 1500 ft/min
(Trainer variant with Rolls Royce Kestrel I B 525 hp or V de-rated 510 hp).

The Hawker Hart was an early example of one of those types of fast light/medium bombers which could outpace the contemporary opposing fighters, something which Britain has often been so good at producing, witness the Mosquito, Canberra and Buccaneer. Some 30 miles faster than the RAF's standard Siskin fighter when introduced in 1930, some Harts were even given the role as a defending fighter in the 1931 Air Exercises presaging the Mosquito.

The performance 'jump' of the Hart stemmed from the 75 hp increase in the power of the Rolls Royce Kestrel 525hp liquid cooled V12 engine over the 'standard' radials then in service together with some very determined attempts at aerodynamic drag reduction in a very well balanced design by the Hawker team led by Sidney Camm. The elegant designs which emerged were undoubtedly inspired or spurred on by the earlier Fairey Fox and its American Curtis D12 engine, which had also shocked the fighter community with its performance when it first flew in 1925.

But as with the later aircraft the much higher performance revealed a need for a more representative trainer as a result of which two Hart Trainer prototypes were flown in 1932. When the first production deliveries began in 1933 the wing sweepback had been reduced from 5 degrees to 2.5 to correct for the cg shift caused by the deletion of the rear gun mounting.

Some 500 Hart Trainers were produced and together with the later issue of some 170 or so trainer conversions of the somewhat more powerful Hind, they formed the basis of advanced single engine training in the RAF from 1934 until the arrival of the Master and Harvard in mid 1939.

The Hart series represented an almost magical craft after such 'Spanish galleons' as the Wapiti and Fairey III F. Duncan Simpson, who as the Chief Test Pilot at BAe Kingston ('Hawkers' in many people's language) flew their preserved Hart for some 18 years, has written:

'Open up to 2 psi (boost) — the tail comes up after about twenty yards. The Hart literally 'floats off the ground and climbs away at 70-80 mph, the propeller thrashing away, the loud crackle from the exhausts, the vibration of the flying wires and lower wings--the super abundance of fresh air'. 'Handling is straightforward with well harmonised controls, light on elevator and rudder...' However he comments that the ailerons were the heavier control at higher speeds and that the control system mechanical design and the lack of ailerons on the lower wings restricted the rate of roll. Nevertheless both he and Tredrey speak very favourably of its aerobatic qualities as well as the need for a well-judged hold-off in a three-point landing if a 'stratospheric bounce 'was to be avoided.

The Hart and its multitude of variants proved so successful that at one time most of the major aircraft firms in England were building them under Air Ministry contract. They were extensively used by the RAF in a wide variety of roles ranging from the Demon two-seater fighter, later fitted with a power operated turret, to Army Co-operation with the Audax, the Hind bomber derivative upgrade and later the Dagger powered Hector as well as the naval deck landing Osprey.

From the start of Hart production through to the end of the Hector line a remarkable total of over 2500 aircraft were delivered plus further small batches from overseas licensed production.

Substantial numbers of various members of the Hart family were exported to a number of Commonwealth and foreign airforces, justifying the phrase that 'what looks right, flies right'.

The Hart's single seater lookalike was the wonderfully elegant Fury, with which it shared many common constructional features which could also could be found in the early Hurricanes, a link between the old and the new technologies.

Sydney Camm, who was the Chief Designer of all Hawker aircraft following the Horsley up to the Harrier, was well known as not being a sentimental man. Nevertheless he rightly regarded the Hart as his masterpiece and favourite design and would often 'drop by' to look in on Hawker's preserved aircraft.

Perhaps the last word on the Hart should come from Duncan Simpson: 'After shut down a post flight inspection is difficult to resist--it is a pleasure just to look at it!'

ARMSTRONG WHITWORTH ATLAS MARK I
(ARMSTRONG SIDDELEY JAGUAR 14 CYL. 2 ROW RADIAL)
PLATE 20

Span 39ft 7in; Length 28ft 7in; Wing Area 390 sq ft;
Max Weight 4020 lb; Empty Weight 2560 lb;
Max Speed 142 mph; Cruising 108 mph; Rate of Climb (sl) 980 ft/min.

The Trainer version of the Armstrong Whitworth Atlas was ordered by the Air Ministry as a Service advanced trainer and general communication aircraft for use by individual stations.

The original Atlas flew as a Private Venture aircraft and was intended to meet the specification for a pantechnicon type of aircraft which was emerging. This was aimed at a dedicated army co-operation aircraft to replace the war time Bristol Fighter design still in service in this role. Required to be capable of carrying 3 valve type radio sets, to try to overcome the eternal difficulties of air to ground communications between air force and army, together with reconnaissance cameras, message pick up hook, rear gun mounting and 4x120lb bombs it is not surprising that the aircraft could politely be called 'workmanlike' or 'rugged'. Its competitors from Bristol, De Havilland and Vickers were equally or more deserving of the description!

Although the Atlas first flew in 1925 and had been virtually selected the Air Ministry by August 1926 it underwent a lengthy development period which included a change of wing construction to metal, a different wing section and continuing criticism of its handling qualities. The introduction of slats improved the stall and the aircraft entered service in 1927 but the continuing dissatisfaction with its directional response resulted in the drastic action of replacing the fixed fin/rudder combination with an all moving rudder on later aircraft AFTER the aircraft had entered service. The lozenge shaped surface is shown in David Howley's diagram (Plate 20) and in Plate 8.

As late as 1932 Flt. Lts. W. E. P. Johnson and Fletcher were carrying out spinning tests on the Atlas at CFS, presumably to clear the revised configuration for instructional purposes.

Nevertheless it gave good service as an advanced trainer in Flying Training Schools up to 1935/36. Frank Tredrey did his advanced course on Atlases at No. 4 FTS Abu Sueir near Ismalia, Egypt in 1930, so it obviously was considered acceptable, if not ideal, by that time. At CFS where he flew K1472 and K1479 the diary shows him carrying out dual aerobatics on 20th May when he describes the big Jaguar 14 cylinder two row radial as smooth running and the controls as very sensitive, so it cannot have been all bad. The Atlas's bulk was drawn or 'pushed' through the air by the Armstrong Siddeley Jaguar IV C of 400hp, which along with the 9 cylinder Bristol Jupiter was, in its various forms, one of the staple British 400/450 hp radial engines of the late 20s early 30s.

Something like 40% of the 440 odd Atlases delivered to the RAF were of the two seater advanced trainer/communications aircraft variant, a highish percentage.. Only some 30 additional aircraft were exported of which just under 50% were of a later Atlas Mk II version with an uprated 535 hp engine which went to China. This version was not adopted by the RAF.

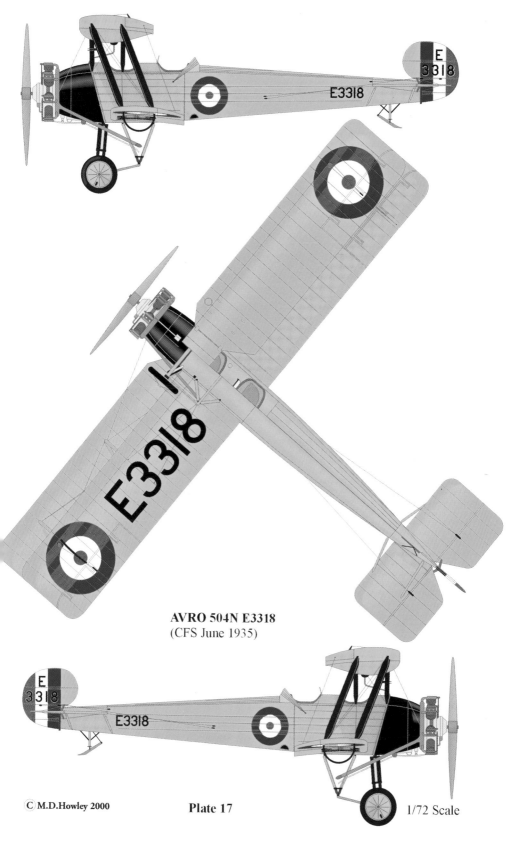

AVRO 504N E3318
(CFS June 1935)

Plate 17

1/72 Scale

AVRO 621 TUTOR K3238
(CFS Display Team June 1933)

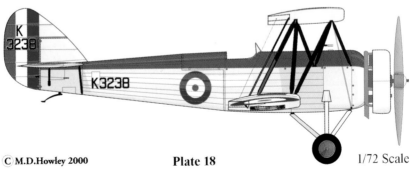

Plate 18   1/72 Scale

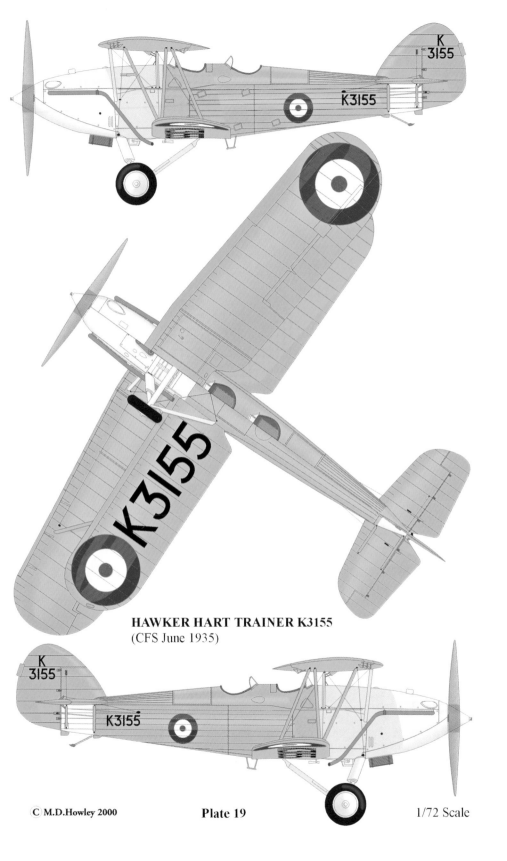

HAWKER HART TRAINER K3155
(CFS June 1935)

Plate 19

1/72 Scale

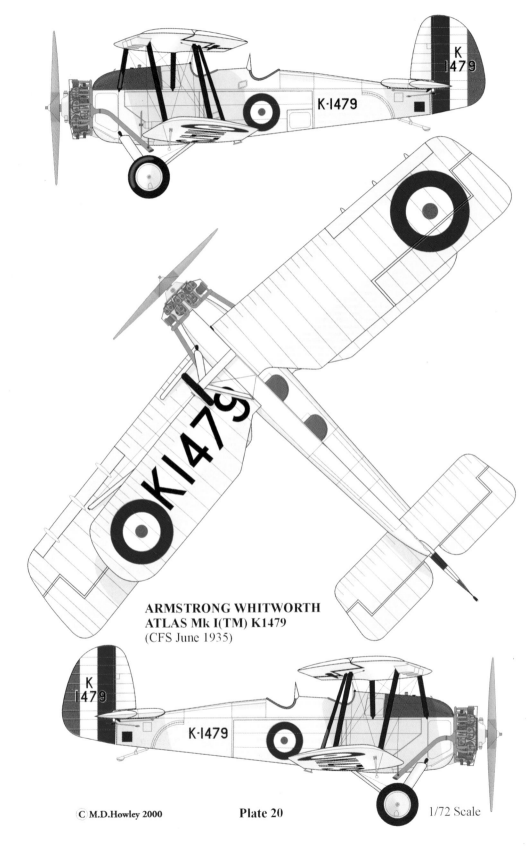

**ARMSTRONG WHITWORTH
ATLAS Mk I(TM) K1479**
(CFS June 1935)

K-1479

K 1479

K 1479

K·1479

K·1479

Plate 20

1/72 Scale

Acknowledgements

In August 1939 as an 11-year-old-boy lying in bed with measles I was given *Pilot's Summer* to read. It literally changed the course of my life, since from then on all thoughts of becoming a doctor vanished and aviation became my chosen career.

41 years later in 1980 I was able to acknowledge my debt to its author, Frank Darker Tredrey, in an article in *Aerospace*, the Royal Aeronautical Society news magazine.

Although the original edition of *Pilot's Summer* had received very favourable reviews from such diverse quarters as *Flight*, *The Times Literary Supplement* and the *Yorkshire Post* the uncertainties and shortages at the outbreak of war in 1939 limited sales of the book to some 1500 copies.

As will be seen from the Foreword, there was talk of a new edition in 1973. Unfortunately this did not appear and there was a danger that the book might fade into the archives.

In retirement I felt that I had to make an effort to save what the lucky few who had read it regarded as one of the classics of flying literature. Sadly Frank Darker Tredrey had died in 1988 but after a number of false starts I finally made contact with his daughter, Mrs Louise Elliott, herself a professional writer now living in Australia. To my great pleasure and delight she agreed to my idea for a new edition with additional background material to place the diary in historical context for future readers and her contribution of ideas, information and enthusiasm in equal measures has been invaluable.

I am also indebted to the many members of the Royal Air Force who have so willingly assisted me in helping to gather the additional data for the new edition, amongst them Air Chief Marshal Sir John Allison, in 1999 recently retired as C-in-C Strike Command, Air Commodore Malcolm Prissick, Commandant Central Flying School, Group Captain 'Dez' Dezonie, Station Commander RAF Wittering, Squadron Leader Peter Singleton of the Air Historical Branch, Ministry of Defence and not forgetting Air Commodore Reggie Spiers whose shared enthusiasm for the project has spurred me on.

Duncan Simpson, former CTP of 'Hawkers', and David Ogilvy have very kindly allowed me to enhance the descriptions of the Hart and Tutor with their own first hand experiences and David Howley has provided some excellent colour plates as well as introducing me to a network of aero-historians who have patiently tried to answer my inquiries regarding 1935 training aircraft colour schemes, something of a byway in aviation history! Ian Huntley's encyclopaedic files were particularly helpful.

Most importantly Peter Elliott (no relation), Senior Archivist at the RAF Museum provided the vital link with Mrs Louise Elliott, which was crucial in enabling this new edition to proceed and both Brian Riddle of the RAeS

Library and Paul Gladman of Quadrant Picture Library ('Flight' Library to the older readers) have given freely of their time and advice.

I am eternally grateful to Robin Saikia of Tiger & Tyger for all of his encouragement and help in what has been a labour of love.

I hope previous readers will be gratified to reacquaint themselves with an old forgotten friend and that new readers coming for the first time to the Frank Tredrey's account of his 'golden summer' will share the enormous pleasure that it has already given to aviators of all generations.

Envoi

After we had started collaborating on this new edition Louise Elliott sent me a copy of a note which she had found tucked into her father's own copy of the original edition.

It started 'At the age of 11 I read a book which changed the course of my life' and concluded 'It is certainly the best book I know about flying'; it was Frank Tredrey's hand-written transcript of my published comments in 1980.

The Fates of the Ancients that purpose our ends seem still to dwell with us in our modern world — something which I hope would have pleased him as much as it has me!

Peter Hearne
Wateringbury
Kent UK
Summer 2000

Peter Hearne, who together with Louise Elliott (née Tredrey) has prepared this new edition of *Pilot's Summer*, has been involved in aviation matters since joining the Air Defence Cadet Corps (greatly under age!) at the beginning of WWII. He is a professional aeronautical engineer and served as President of the Royal Aeronautical Society 1980-81. A pilot and one-time flying instructor with over 4000 flying hours on a variety of aircraft, he also holds a Diamond C gliding badge and is currently a vice president of the British Gliding Association.

Bibliography

A Short History of the Central Flying School. Unpublished CFS, 1975

Bowyer, Michael J. F. *Bombing Colours.* Cambridge: Patrick Stephens

Donald, David (ed.) *The Encyclopaedia of World Aircraft.* Leicester: Blitz Editions, 1997

Janes All The World's Aircraft, 1931-1935. London: Sampson Low

Ogilvy, David *Shuttleworth, The Historic Aeroplanes.* Shrewsbury: Airlife Publishing, 1989

Robertson, Bruce *Aircraft Camouflage and Markings 1907-1954.* Letchworth: Garden City Press, 1961

Royal Air Force Wittering 1916-1995. 80th Anniversary Brochure

Taylor, John W. R. *CFS, Birthplace of Airpower.* London: Jane's Publishing Co., 1987.

Tredrey, Frank D. *Pioneer Pilot, The Great Smith Barry Who Taught The World To Fly.* London: Peter Davies, 1976

Putnam Aeronautical Books Series:

        Jackson, A. J. *Avro.* (revised edition) London: 1990

        Mason, Francis K. *Hawker Aircraft.* London: 1971

        Tapper, Oliver, *Armstrong Whitworth.* London: 1973